W9-CSX-044

The Films of

Clark Gable

BY GABE ESSOE

FOREWORD BY CHARLES CHAMPLIN

For Mom, to be shared with Nana, Lib, Mimi, and any other girls who see a little C.G. in their man.

MERRY CHRISTMAS 1973

from Beav

P.S. Feel free to loan this to my future wife someday (whoever that may be) After all, I do a great "Frankly, Scarlett..."

THE CITADEL PRESS, SECAUCUS, N.J.

TO MY WONDERFUL PARENTS

Grateful acknowledgment is made to
the many individuals and organizations
who gave of their time, their knowledge
and/or helped gather stills in the
preparation of this book:

Metro-Goldwyn-Mayer Studios: Bill
Golden, Dore Freeman, Barbara Jampel,
Nick Noxon. Academy of Motion Pic-
ture Arts and Sciences: DeWitt Bodeen
and the library staff. Paramount Pictures
Corporation: Mike Berman. Twentieth
Century-Fox: Frank Rodriguez. Warner
Brothers-7 Arts: Jack Kingsley. Disney
Studios: Dave Spencer, Earl Colgrove,
Eddie Jones, Kay Mulvey, Tom Jones.
Joan Crawford, Betty Barker, Rosalind
Russell, Louise Griswold, Edward
Dmytryk, Mike Druxman, Lana Turner,
Frank McFadden, Jimmy Sarno, Joan
Blondell, Bob Raison, Paul Fix, Larry
Barbier, Emily Torchia, Eddie Lawrence,
Greer Garson, Clarence Brown, Mary
Astor, Bill Boyd, Howard Strickling,
Cesar Romero, Clarence Bull, Richard
Thorpe, Tony Thomas, George Joelson,
John Lebold, Gunnard Nelson, Bresse
Van Hecke, Raymond Lee, Bosley
Crowther, Bob King, the UCLA Theatre
Arts and Research library staff, and
especially Franz Dorfler and Meredith
Brucker.

Special thanks to Charles Champlin
for his Foreword (Copyright © 1969
by Charles Champlin).

Gratitude is also expressed to Miss Joan
Crawford for granting permission to
reprint an excerpt from: *A Portrait of Joan:*
An Autobiography by Joan Crawford
with Jane Ardmore.
Copyright 1962 by Joan Crawford
Steele. Doubleday & Co., Inc. Reprinted
by permission of Joan Crawford.

Second paperbound printing, 1973
Copyright © 1970 by Gabe Essoe
All rights reserved
Published by Citadel Press, Inc.
A subsidiary of Lyle Stuart, Inc.
120 Enterprise Ave., Secaucus, N. J. 07094
In Canada: George J. McLeod Limited
73 Bathurst St., Toronto 2B, Ontario
Designed by David November
Manufactured in the United States of America
ISBN 0-8065-0273-8

CONTENTS

FOREWORD BY CHARLES CHAMPLIN

The tales they were spinning might be—often were—the silliest kind of cotton candy nonsense. But whatever they were saying, the movies from the beginning could not help telling a good deal about all of us as well.

Their heroes and heroines reflected the real if improbable aspirations of vast numbers of movie-goers, dreams of courage, wit, wealth, security, adventure, desirability and love. And even though Hollywood's heroes and heroines might be large magnifications of reality, they also at some basic level reflected the audience's vision of itself. The stars' priorities as displayed on the screen were the audience's priorities. And this rough parallel was, as indeed it still is, a prerequisite for stardom.

Clark Gable was the greatest heroic male star of his time, and to think about him now, at the beginning of the 1970's, is to realize with sorrow and a double sense of loss how much we and the world have changed and how distant and uncomplicated his time already seems.

He was unabashed virility, but the world moves toward unisex. He was an outdoorsman, but the outdoors is being macadamized in our day. He portrayed men of action and instinct, and we survivors feel paralyzed by numbers, rules, costs and awareness. To think about Gable now is to experience an almost unutterable nostalgia, not only for the gruff and dashing figure he was but for the unsubtle and straightforward period in which he moved.

No small part of Gable's great charm and attractiveness was that he always seemed to view Gable the Film Star with a kind of half-amused, half-chagrined detachment, as if parading before cameras was not quite the sort of thing a grown man ought to be doing. In fact he worked very hard at his craft, but our impression of his bemusement made the roles somehow seem all the more virile and credible. No one after him has played the raffish, roguish male nearly so well; it is a lost art, as it is a lost breed.

Although they were contemporaries, Gable and Humphrey Bogart, for example, already seem to have arisen in different eras: Bogart anticipated the later day of the faintly or heavily neurotic sophisticate who was likely to be anti-heroic if not actively villainous. Bogie was heroic, but he tended to be the abashed or reluctant hero. Gable, the unabashed hero was reluctant to be drawn into the very modern world (witness the rebellious adman in *The Hucksters* or, far more tellingly and impressively, the cowboy born out of his time in *The Misfits*).

It is not quite right, for once, to say that an era died with Clark Gable. The truth is that an era had predeceased him. The kingdom of film over which he reigned for so long had begun to crumble and change a decade at least before his death. But more than that, the kind of hero-figure Gable was has come to seem an impossible dream in our days—not undesirable but unachievable. And this, of course, is a commentary not on Gable but on all of us, tethered by the paper chains of circumstance and vibrating to the hum of computers.

Gable the King—impudent, free, rascally, courageous, resourceful, direct, uncomplicated, charming, all-male but without need to over-assert it, sane and self-reliant, gallant and natural— remains what we would wish to be, but what we sense we can now fully be only in spirit.

We make do with lesser and more brittle gods.

Preceding page:
Columnist Ed Sullivan presents King and
Queen of Hollywood crowns to Gable
and Myrna Loy over NBC Radio in 1938.

*Signing autographs on the set of MGM's
"Dancing Lady," 1931*

One morning early in 1938, Spencer Tracy drove to work at Metro-Goldwyn-Mayer Studios and was unable to get on the lot. The entrance was blocked by a crowd of autograph hounds and star-struck fans who had surrounded Clark Gable's car. No one in the throng seemed to notice Tracy. Somewhat annoyed, yet trying to be good-humored, he stood up in his convertible, bowed to Gable and shouted, "Long live the King! And now for Christ's sake, let's get inside and go to work."

Word of the incident spread around the studio. And a few days later somebody with a sense of humor got a brass crown out of the Props Department and had it covered with white rabbit's fur. Tracy was appointed to officiate at the ceremonies and that afternoon Gable was crowned King in the MGM commissary. The crown was too small and the pictures taken were ridiculous. The matter was dropped.

Ed Sullivan, who was writing his syndicated column from Hollywood at the time, heard of the stunt and had an idea. He invited the entertainment editors to poll their readers across the country to select a King and Queen of the Movies. The idea was preposterous because Hollywood, then in its Golden Age, was rich in hundreds of truly big names like the Barrymores, Douglas Fairbanks, Jr., Garbo, Tracy, Joan Crawford, Gary Cooper, Bogart, Edward G. Robinson, Cagney, Bette Davis, John Wayne, Errol Flynn, Fred Astaire, Claudette Colbert, Katharine Hepburn, Mae West, Dietrich, Wallace Beery. The list goes on and on. To select a King and Queen from these ranks would be almost impossible.

Yet the very absurdity of the idea caught the imagination of the American public and they rallied to the challenge. With an overwhelming majority, Clark Gable was elected King and Myrna Loy Queen. Ed Sullivan held an official coronation ceremony and formally proclaimed the pair.

Although Gable was secretly pleased about the honor at first, he grew to scorn it. Late in life, he snorted: "You know, this 'King' stuff is pure bullshit. I eat and sleep and go to the bathroom just like everybody else. There's no special light that shines inside me and makes me a star. I'm just a lucky slob from Ohio. I happened to be in the right place at the right time and I had a lot of smart guys helping me—that's all."

Thirty years later, the Queen is all but forgotten, but the King lives on in a new posthumous triumph aided by the recent reissue of *Gone With the Wind*. Besides reaffirming its position as the most popular and successful film ever made, this sixth

Shortly after having been crowned, "The King" waits on the set of "Idiot's Delight," 1939

theatrical showing of the four-hour-long 1939 screen classic fanned the campfires of a national "Gable cult." The Gable revival—similar to the Humphrey Bogart boom a few years ago—has swept college campuses, inspiring many film festivals in his honor. Wall posters and Gable buttons abound. Stills and other memorabilia from Gable films have suddenly multiplied in value. And the King's movies on TV, which were instrumental in initiating the cult, have taken the form of week-long cycles in many areas.

To take advantage of the growing interest in Gable, MGM, Clark's home studio for a quarter of a century, produced an hour-long TV documentary on his life. It racked up such top-notch ratings that MGM planned, without success, to do a whole series of documentaries based on their once great roster of talent.

The image of Gable that MGM so expertly set forth in their documentary was, for the most part, the image that they had created of him in the thirties, which was largely responsible for his winning the King of Hollywood title in 1938. In the same way that MGM invented a star *persona* for Garbo by surrounding her always with snow, furs and palace guards in white breeches, in the same way that Dietrich's identity was fashioned from sequins, cigarette smoke and men's trousers, a star equation had been constructed for Gable by surrounding him with Hollywood's women.

Jean Harlow, Joan Crawford, Norma Shearer, Claudette Colbert, Greta Garbo, Myrna Loy, the most desirable, witty, elegantly emancipated women in America bantered with him and fell in love with him on the screen. As often as not, he could resist them, walk out on them and go back to his work. And if they protested, he would manhandle them. For the feminine audience to whom the female stars represented all the possibilities of their sex's liberation, Gable was the ultimate reassurance. Even if women became equal with men, they need lose nothing by surrendering their traditional femininity to a super-male. MGM made Gable the symbol of just that super-male. Muscular, bare-chested and brutal, he was able to see through female pretentions and restore the historical relation of the sexes.

While living up to the image that Metro had created for him, Gable, whose self-confidence began to assert itself strongly after his second marriage, found that he was projecting increasingly more of his own personality from the screen. People began to see that he was more than a boudoir brute who got

With Marion Davies

With Joan Crawford

With Madge Evans

With Dorothy Mackail

With Carole Lombard

With Helen Hayes

With Constance Bennett

what he wanted from women. For example, his affinity with the rugged outdoors became evident. A more complete Gable emerged.

He soon built up a reputation as the most total male that ever brawled or loved his way across the screen. He was instant desire to all women because they saw in his lusty manner the personification of romantic fantasy. And while hoping somehow, some day, to be confronted with his overpowering earthiness, they dreaded any actual contact for fear that they would be unable to match his fire.

Yet, unlike the great lovers who had preceded him, Gable established immediate camaraderie with all men. He was a big sportsman. He drove fast cars. He ate like a tiger and drank prodigiously, but kept both the food and booze under control until late in life. He doted on women and they on him, but he was not self-indulgent like Errol Flynn and some other contemporaries. Men admired his direct approach to life and imitated his pursuit of sensual pleasures.

Gable was a roguish, down-to-earth, adventurous man's man; a sort of vagabond whose only roots were in himself. He was at home everywhere—in oil fields, in city streets and penthouses, astride a horse, in stifling jungles, in any historical era. He nearly always played a self-made man and the role carried with it a built-in contempt for the man who inherited his wealth or was not driven by the same lust for life that motivated him.

There was something exhilarating about his sheer brawn, whether he was swashing the decks of the *Bounty,* or boxing with Spencer Tracy in *San Francisco;* pouring a carafe of ice water over the Big Boss' head in *The Hucksters,* or facing a charge of bull gorillas in *Mogambo.* In *It Happened One Night,* when he took off his shirt and revealed a bare chest, he changed a basic habit of American men, who overnight stopped wearing undershirts. In *Gone With the Wind* when he snarled, "Frankly, my dear, I don't give a damn," he introduced swearing to the screen.

With *Gone With the Wind* Gable hit his peak. He had been designated as the only actor in Hollywood who could play the role of Rhett Butler by the same American public who had voted him "The King" and was now caught up in Margaret Mitchell's panoramic novel of the Civil War. As Rhett, Gable gave the most memorable performance of his life; it seemed as if he and the character he portrayed were interchangeable. He admitted that "I was practically playing myself."

With Mary Astor

With Jean Harlow

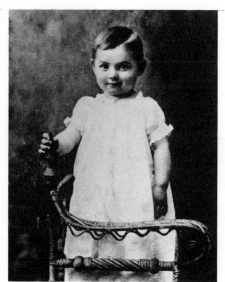

Gable at eighteen months old in Cadiz, Ohio (1903)

Adeline Hershelman Gable, Billy's mother, who died of epilepsy when he was seven months old

Little Billy Gable (third from left, holding baseball bat) at Hopedale Grade School (1909)

William Clark Gable (his first given name was dropped in 1925) was born in Cadiz, Ohio, on February 1, 1901. He was the only child of William H. Gable, an oil driller and farmer, and Adeline Hershelman Gable, both of German ancestry.

The fiction that Gable's parents were of Dutch-Irish descendency was created by the MGM publicity department. His mother's family, the Hershelmans, were part of the migration to Pennsylvania to escape the persecutions in Germany following the revolution of 1848. His father's family name was Goebel before it was anglicized. His family, too, had come from Germany, but somewhat earlier. Since Clark hit his peak about the same time as the Nazis, it would have been poor publicity to admit that there might be a link between Gable's ancestors and the family line of Joseph Goebbels. Consequently, the actor became Dutch. And to help the box office, a little Irish luck was thrown in.

Clark's mother, who was fragile and had difficulty bearing him, died from epilepsy when he was seven months old. His grandparents took care of him until he was two, at which time his father remarried and gave little Billy his first real home, in Hopedale, Ohio. His stepmother was Jennie Dunlap, a milliner. She was a gentle, cultured person who raised the boy as her own. Clark later described her as one of the tenderest human beings he had ever known. "She was a wonderful woman," he said, "although I didn't realize it then. She was always looking out for what I needed. She must have loved me very much, because I was certainly not what you'd call well-behaved. I was rather spoiled."

His education was hardly noteworthy: Hopedale Grade School and two years at Edinburg High School. At fourteen he was already six feet tall and weighed 150 pounds. He was on the baseball team and he also played French horn in the school band. An aimless, troubled sort of youth, he liked to hang around with the older boys. One such boy was Andy Means, the athletic hero of nearby Cadiz.

One day Andy told Clark that he was going to Akron, sixty miles away, to work in a tire factory. Although he still had two years of high school to finish, Gable decided to go with him. He had a terrible fight about it with his father, but after Jennie talked to him, he was allowed to go. That was the end of his schooling.

Shortly after his arrival in Akron, he wandered down to the Music Hall and saw a play called *The Bird of Paradise*. He was so fascinated by the wonderful scenery and costumes that while continuing in his job at the tire factory he took an unsalaried position as a backstage call boy with the stock company.

A year later a telegram came from home that Jennie was dying. Clark rushed back and a few days later she was dead. After the funeral, there was another row with his father, who refused to let him return to the stock company. He never approved of acting as a livelihood for a grown man with a strong back and good mind. He took his son with him to the Oklahoma oil fields, determined to make an oilman out of him.

Clark hated the violent, dirty world of his father. He wanted to go back to the theatre. He had already gotten to play bit parts, and although he was an extremely inept actor, he knew that acting was what he wanted to do. In the oil fields they worked twelve hours on and twelve off, seven days a week. He kept saying to himself that he was going back to the stage as soon as he could save up enough money to try it again.

On his twenty-first birthday, he inherited $300 from his grandfather and with that left his father, causing such hard feelings that they would not speak again for ten years. He went to Kansas City, where he joined a traveling troupe, the Jewell Players. After he had been with them for two months, they folded, leaving Clark stranded in Butte, Montana, with three dollars in his pocket.

He hitched a ride to Bend, Oregon, and worked in the lumberyards there for a month or so until he had eaten a few meals and had enough money to get to Portland, where he got a job selling men's ties in a department store. By coincidence, one of his fellow salesmen, Earle Larrimore, was about to join a little theatre group going to Astoria, and he invited Gable along. Also in the troupe was a young aspiring actress named Franz Dorfler, with whom Gable fell hopelessly in love. Although an awkward youth, he soon wooed her, and by the time their stock company went bankrupt, they were engaged. Fearing for his health, Franz invited Billy, as he was known then, to her parents' farm to regain his strength. Several years of insufficient food had left him thin, his teeth bad, and his skin a sickly hue. Although she was in love with Billy, she could not marry him because he was penniless, and she had her career to think about.

When Franz joined another traveling troupe, Gable returned to Portland, doing odd jobs for a newspaper and later for the telephone company, while taking singing lessons. Upon learning that a new little theatre group was being formed, he made an

Billy Gable (fourth from left) at ten years old played the French horn in the Hopedale Town Band, Ohio (1911)

Eleven years old (1912)

At sixteen, Billy Gable left his parents and struck out on his own for Akron, Ohio, with a friend, Andy Means (1917)

appointment for an interview. This group was organized and headed by a well-educated, well-traveled ex-actress who was to become the greatest single influence in Billy Gable's life.

She was Miss Josephine Dillon from New York, where she had been leading lady to Edward Everett Horton on Broadway. She was both brilliant and patient, a most remarkable combination in an actress. Now she was a gifted coach and director.

Although fourteen years older than Billy, she took an immediate and strong liking to the awkward but charming young man who wanted so desperately to be an actor. When she began to show an interest in him, Gable broke his engagement to Franz, telling her that he was finally going to get somewhere, that he too had ambition! This statement about ambition was to become one of the truest things he was ever to say.

In 1924, when Josephine moved to Hollywood, Billy followed her, and on December 13, they were married. Josephine was not old enough to be a mother replacement for Billy, but almost. Their marriage was not a happy one, partly because they had no money and lived from day to day, but mostly because their relationshp was more pupil and teacher than husband and wife.

The only drama coach Billy Gable ever had, Josephine Dillon taught him the fundamentals of acting. This remarkable woman took the raw amateur and smoothed his rough diction; she lowered the boyish whine of his voice to the hoarse masculine tone for which he became famous; she taught him how to handle himself in front of people and what to do with his clumsy hands and feet.

She fed him properly, made him rest, and had his teeth fixed. (They were later to be replaced with false teeth at MGM's expense.) In short, she worked a fantastic transformation on him. It was she, in fact, who suggested that Billy was too young a name for him, so he dropped it in favor of his middle name. Cynics were later to charge that "Clark Gable was the creation of his first wife."

In addition to her coaching, Josephine got Clark jobs as an extra in many silent films, among which were *The Merry Widow* (1925) starring John Gilbert and Mae Murray, *The Plastic Age* (1925), starring Clara Bow and Gilbert Roland, and *North Star* (1926), featuring Virginia Lee Corbin and Stuart Holmes.

These were the days of Rudolph Valentino and John Gilbert, when Hollywood's leading male stars were all of the aesthetic,

Franz Dorfler, Gable's sweetheart while he was playing with the Astoria Stock Company in Oregon.

At seventeen. At this time he was working in a tire factory in Akron, Ohio, and also as an unpaid backstage boy at the Akron Music Hall.

Two extras and Gable, with Strongheart, Virginia Lee Corbin and Stuart Holmes in "North Star."

Extra Gable watches director Paul Powell (center) and actor Stuart Holmes (right) on set of "North Star," 1926.

As an extra in "The Merry Widow."

narrow-shouldered, nostril-twitching variety. No matter how handsome, which Gable really wasn't in his early twenties, anyone of his size or ruggedness was automatically overlooked for the good parts. Unsuccessful in getting anything worthwhile, Gable decided, "Definitely, there was no future for me in Hollywood. I was no Valentino or Gilbert. I was somewhat of a roughneck."

Separating from his wife, Gable shifted back to the stage.

Through Louis O. MacLoon, a West Coast impresario, he landed a part in the touring production of *Romeo and Juliet,* in which Jane Cowl was featured. Then he played the juvenile lead in Lionel Barrymore's production of *The Copperhead.* This was the beginning of a long friendship.

"Barrymore petrified me," Clark admitted years later. "He was none too keen on me because he considered me an unskilled amateur. He bawled me out during rehearsals like I'd never been bawled out before or since. On opening night, I had an accident on stage and dropped my straw hat into what was supposed to be a deep well. Instead of leaving it there, I reached in and plucked it out. And the audience howled—right in the middle of a serious scene. I was surprised he didn't fire me right then and there. I learned very much from him."

A number of plays later, he felt he was ready to crack Broadway. When he arrived in New York, an agent sent him to see Arthur Hopkins, who was casting *Machinal* (1928), Sophie Treadwell's play about the inhumanity of the big city. With a recommendation from Louis MacLoon, Clark was given the part of Zita Johann's lover and created quite a stir. Of the four New York productions in which he appeared, this was the only one that was successful.

But it was a difficult time on Broadway. The theatre, its plays and actors were all abruptly changing. The disillusionment that followed the World War I Armistice had ended the dominance of unabashed sentimentality and blood-and-thunder dramas. And out with them went the black-caped, mustachioed villains and pure-as-snow heroines. The playgoers of the mid- and late twenties were becoming increasingly more sophisticated and wanted to see reasonable facsimiles of real life on the stage. And the new playwrights, Eugene O'Neill, Philip Barry, Sidney Howard, and George Kelly, among others, supplied realistic situations that made for a different type of play.

The actors working their way up were also a whole new crowd. They were neither beautiful, epicene types, nor did they

Gable in 1925.

Gable's first wife, Josephine Dillon, at the time of their divorce in 1930. She gave him his early stage training and got him extra parts in the silents.

With Ria Langham, his second wife. Taken in 1930, shortly after their marriage.

resemble the bigger-than-life performers, like Otis Skinner, whose great day was just then fading.

These newcomers were like the characters they played. They were sweaty, hard-muscled, tough-minded, bold, volatile. They were prone to error, but also to moments of great perception. Many of them were destined to become the cream of the film stars of the next decade. Among them were James Cagney, Humphrey Bogart, Spencer Tracy, Paul Muni, Edward G. Robinson, Robert Montgomery and Fredric March.

This was the sort of competition that Gable had in getting good parts. Perhaps that is why he was so often without work, always wondering whether or not he should give it up and get a steady job. His fears of once again going hungry haunted him. Between plays he would sometimes go on tour with a stock company. On one such tour through Houston, he caught the eye of a thrice-married, wealthy Texan socialite, Mrs. Ria Langham, who reportedly followed him to New York. She had money, charm, and poise, and soon became his constant companion, but one that he did not show off to his actor friends. Although he had always been clothes-conscious, she now taught him to dress like a suave New Yorker and he began to sport a derby, spats, and cane for ordinary street wear. She improved his manners, introduced him to Social Register families, and kept renewing his wardrobe.

This training from Ria had a lasting influence on him. George Joelson, a veteran of the MGM police force remembered, "The thing that impressed me most about Clark Gable was the fact that he was always dressed to the teeth. He always looked like a million bucks. You knew he was a movie star the minute you laid eyes on him. He wasn't ostentatious or pretentious. But he always looked like the King he was."

Together, Ria and Clark saw Spencer Tracy in the role of Killer Mears in *The Last Mile,* a sensational melodrama built around a prison break, greatly impressing Gable. Soon after that, Ria, the second woman to influence Clark's career, gave him his biggest break. She allegedly arranged the Los Angeles opening of *The Last Mile,* in June, 1930, with Gable in the part that had made a star of Tracy on Broadway.

Memorable as the desperate criminal, Gable was applauded by the critics and the film studio casting directors took notice. At the time, Hollywood was looking for talent for the new "talkies" that were turning the silent screen hierarchies upside down. Former matinee idols found themselves out of work

overnight. Most notable was the tragic decline of John Gilbert, whose squeaky voice was greeted by derisive laughter instead of swoons. Stage experience became a "must" as the sound pictures began to draw on the theatre for fresh faces with strong voices to replace the discards of a bygone era.

Lionel Barrymore went to see Clark in *The Last Mile* and was so gratified at his improvement that he set up a screen test at MGM for which Clark was put in a sarong with a hibiscus behind one ear. Barrymore hoped to get Clark a part in *Never the Twain Shall Meet,* a picture he was supposed to direct. The test was a failure; and Barrymore's film never came off either.

However, Clark's fame in the play won him other tests, one of which has become a favorite Hollywood legend. At Warner Brothers, Darryl F. Zanuck, who tested him for the lead in *Little Caesar,* a part that eventually went to Edward G. Robinson, turned him out with the words: "His ears are too big. He looks like an ape."

To Gable's rescue came, naturally, a woman. Agent Minna Wallis (producer Hal Wallis' sister) saw the abortive MGM test and was sufficiently impressed to take Gable to Pathé Studios, where a medium budget Bill Boyd Western, *The Painted Desert* (1931), was being cast. Because Miss Wallis had promised that Gable was an excellent horseman, he was given the role of the villain at $750 a week. Very pleased, but at the same time a bit nervous because he didn't know the first thing about horsemanship, he began intensive riding lessons immediately. The only notable thing about this film was Clark as the leering heavy. The Gable mannerisms that were to become famous within a year could all be seen in this picture.

From Pathé he went to Warners to play the brutish chauffeur in William Wellman's *Night Nurse,* starring Barbara Stanwyck and Ben Lyon. Strangely, this mediocre film was not released until after Clark had become a sensation at MGM later that year.

The attention given to this unknown caused MGM to give him a bit part in *The Easiest Way,* a Constance Bennett vehicle in which he was the laundryman husband of Anita Page. (Another beginning actor who had an equally small role of a cigar store clerk was Jimmy Stewart.) Clark's name was buried in the credits and the studio was flooded with inquiries about "that handsome laundryman."

Shortly after *The Easiest Way* was finished, in late 1930, the company whose boast was having "more stars than there are in heaven" signed Clark to a two-year contract with six-month

Assisting with the lights on the set of "The Easiest Way," his first MGM film.

contract-renewal options. His starting pay was $350 weekly. For the first time in his life Gable could count on having a regular salary for at least half a year.

Oddly enough, the first person, Clark told about his Metro breakthrough was his old flame, Franz Dorfler, who was working in a Hollywood dress shop. He celebrated by taking her to Christmas dinner at the Brown Derby. He bought her no Christmas present, however, explaining that he was saving every penny in case MGM didn't renew his contract. In his insecurity and his recollection of past poverty, Clark was driven to extravagant thriftiness, socking everything away for a rainy day. This developed into a lifelong practice of not giving tips or presents, an idiosyncrasy he often interpreted as "not wanting to buy anyone's friendship."

Uncertainty about how long his success would continue also presented itself in Clark's occasional insistence that he would soon retire from the movies. He said he intended "to make hay while it lasts," and then quit before his luck soured. While his good fortune continued, he was not forced to that decision.

The cruel irony of his MGM contract was that Josephine Dillon, the wife without whose help he might never have achieved it, had eight months earlier agreed to divorce him and was waiting for the final decrees. Miss Dillon later made one of her rare public statements, telling reporters, "Clark told me frankly that he wished to marry Ria Langham because she could do more for him financially. He is hard to live with because his career and ambition always come first."

Miss Dillon asked no alimony and was given none, although years later Clark did make the final payments on her acting studio so she could continue to fend for herself. On March 30, 1930, one day before the divorce was final, Clark turned his back on her completely and married Ria in New York. They later remarried in California on June 19, 1931, for legal purposes. Josephine had feared that she would lose her husband to a younger woman; ironically, it turned out to be an older woman. Ria was seventeen years Clark's senior.

On the "Hell Divers" set. 1931.

MGM in the meanwhile had loaned him to First National Studios for *The Finger Points* (1931), starring Richard Barthelmess. It was another gangster role for Clark. Barthelmess played the film counterpart of the hoodlum reporter Jack Lingle, who was rubbed out by the Capone mob in Chicago.

Right from the start the press saw what Gable had to offer and the *Hollywood Reporter* announced that "A star is in the

Getting sprayed with mud makeup for "Susan Lennox," 1931

Showing a group of youngsters how to hold a baseball bat on the set of "Laughing Sinners," 1931.

making." But MGM seemed oblivious to it and put Clark in a moral melodrama, *Laughing Sinners,* in which he, as a Salvation Army worker, redeems Joan Crawford from a life of sin. In this, his first romantic part, he seemed improperly cast. He didn't project the proper subtle type of love the script called for, but rather the opposite, an aggressive, animal kind.

The grooming and spotlighting of Clark's amazing physical quality came about in his next picture *A Free Soul* (1931), with Norma Shearer, the then queen of the Metro lot, and Lionel Barrymore. Through the cumulative effort of many, though all seemed to be working independently of each other, Clark developed the first of his devil-may-care, sexy super-male roles.

Here's how it happened. Sensing Clark's unusual force and wanting to exploit it, Clarence Brown, one of Hollywood's shrewdest early directors, had him manhandle Miss Shearer in some of *A Free Soul's* initial scenes. From the beginning, Clark dominated the picture.

Between scenes on the location of "Hell Divers," 1931

When Irving Thalberg, the youthful genius in charge of MGM production, who was married to Norma Shearer, saw what was happening, he altered the script and had Clark throw Miss Shearer around even more. He wanted to make Clark more villainous in order to direct sympathy away from him. However, upon seeing the rushes of the daily shooting, the brilliant publicity director, Howard Strickling, got the idea of featuring a new kind of hero in the publicity for the film. Louis B. Mayer agreed with him. They figured that the era of the poetic matinee idol was over. With the violence and unrest of the Depression, the public was ready for a new type of leading man: one who wooed his women with his fists and cynicism rather than with the once-popular hand-kissing elegance. A new breed of movie hero was born when Gable assaulted his leading lady and won her.

Norma Shearer later said, "It was Clark who made villains popular. Instead of the audience wanting the good guy to get the girl, they wanted the heavy to win her." The main thing was that Gable took no nonsense from women, and the public loved it. He opened the doors for other Depression heroes like Cagney, Bogart, Garfield, and Raft. Lionel Barrymore may have won an Oscar for his portrayal of the father in *A Free Soul,* but it is Gable's performance that everyone remembers.

In an even dozen films his first year Gable went from an unknown extra to a star. The circumstances that led to his skyrocketing to fame, affecting a reversal in motion picture heroes,

making him the most sought-after leading man in Hollywood, were created by a chain reaction of events that can be termed nothing but sheer luck. Clark happened to be in the right place at the right time. And a good publicity man made the most of it.

That publicity man, Howard Strickling, was to play an important role in Gable's entire life. The two became extremely close friends and Strickling, who later became a Metro vice president in charge of publicity and advertising, personally handled all of Clark's private affairs. Although always remaining in the background, Strickling was there at all of Clark's weddings and divorces, on personal appearance tours and other trips. Everything there was to know about Clark, Strickling knew and kept from the press or released as he saw fit. Whenever Clark needed something done, Strickling arranged it.

One example of Strickling's effectiveness in his job was the night in 1945 when Clark, drunk and driving home alone on Sunset Boulevard, lost control of his car, hit a lamp post and ended up on the lawn of a private residence. Somehow Strickling learned of the accident, and before the police arrived on the scene he was able to whisk the slightly injured actor off to a nearby hospital and prepare a statement for the press. The following day the papers reported how Gable had heroically avoided a head-on collision with a drunk who was driving on the wrong side of the street by swerving his car off the road, thereby incurring a small head injury.

Strickling was also the confidant to most of the other Metro stars. It is said that he kept more news out of papers than he released to them. If anyone could write a truly stinging and accurate exposé of Hollywood, Howard Strickling could. But he never will. In fact, when solicited to write about or to be interviewed about his relationship with Gable (or any other personality he knew intimately), he replies that he will not exploit his friendships or betray any confidences.

With no small thanks to Strickling, Clark Gable was acclaimed the most sensational new personality of Hollywood in 1931. Even among the MGM lion's roster of talent, which included Greta Garbo, Ramon Novarro, Joan Crawford, Lewis Stone, Marie Dressler, Wallace Beery, Leslie Howard, Marion Davies, Mary Astor, Helen Hayes, Franchot Tone, Robert Montgomery, the Barrymores, Lupe Velez, and dozen of others, he stood unique with his magnificently suave brute force. A new catch phrase swept the country: "Who do you think you are? Clark Gable?"

With his second wife, Ria Langham, a wealthy Texas divorcée.

Gable and Mary Astor watch Victor
Fleming direct Jean Harlow in scene for
"Red Dust," 1932

Cleaning his gun on the set of "Red Dust,"
1932.

Now a part of the MGM stable, he was kept constantly before the public with one picture after another. His big hit of the following year was *Red Dust* (1932), in which he teamed a second time with Jean Harlow, the fast-rising platinum-blonde sex symbol who had become famous for not wearing a brassiere and was slowly convincing everyone that she could also act. She and Gable sizzled in their love scenes because she was just as earthy as he. They shocked everyone in a scene where he discovers her bathing nude in a rain barrel. This great duo was to make five films together; Harlow died of uremic poisoning before production was completed on their last film, *Saratoga,* in 1937. Final scenes had to be shot with Harlow's stand-in, Mary Dees, and the picture fell very short of its initial promise.

Shortly after *Red Dust* Paramount borrowed Clark for a minor comedy called *No Man of Her Own.* His co-star was Carole Lombard, a blonde cutup who began her career as a Mack Sennett bathing beauty and was then married to William Powell. She and Clark developed an immediate rapport. He liked her screwball antics, like inviting some of the industry's top brass to a formal party in a straw-filled room. On one occasion she attended a ball at which all the women were asked to wear white: she arrived in an ambulance wearing a white hospital gown and was carried in on a stretcher by two white-clad orderlies. She swore constantly, and "Kiss my ass!" was her favorite retort to producers who tried to tell her what to do. There was nothing phony or hypocritical about her, no fussiness about unimportant things. But most of all, she delighted Clark with her enthusiasm for his favorite hobbies, hunting and fishing. Following her divorce from Powell, Clark saw increasingly more of her, setting the stage for the most magical of filmdom's love stories.

Within two years of his start in pictures, Clark was a major star and had a new contract with Metro for seven years at $2500 weekly, which by 1935 jumped to a record $4000 per week. He splurged on custom-tailored suits and ordered a roadster which he specified was to be a foot longer than Gary Cooper's. Although his status and salary improved, his pictures did not. MGM kept assigning him more of the "treat 'em rough" roles. Arguing for a change, Gable asserted, "People are bored to death when I rough up disagreeable women. And I'm getting pretty sick of it myself." When he refused to play another "gigolo role," as he called them, his MGM fathers decided to discipline him by farming him out to Columbia for a Frank Capra comedy called *It Happened One Night.* His co-star was to be

Claudette Colbert, who was being loaned to Columbia by Paramount Studios, also in a disciplinary action.

Although neither star approached the picture with much enthusiasm, it proved to be the biggest milestone in each of their careers, winning Academy Awards not only for Gable and Colbert, as Best Actor and Actress, but also for Capra as Best Director, and Robert Riskin for Best Adaptation. The film itself was voted Best Picture.

Gable, astonished at his own success, established himself as a fine comedian. Relaxed and casual, he completely entered the spirit of the story—a comedy about a runaway heiress and a newspaperman traveling from Miami to New York by bus and hitch-hiking—which tried to say, "Let's laugh ourselves out of the Depression." This picture, incidentally, prompted a great many young ladies to travel by bus in search of romance and adventure.

After *It Happened One Night,* Clark was finally given a wider range of parts. But it is ironic that he should win his only Oscar in a film not produced by his home studio. Later, his greatest achievement was also to be produced away from Metro.

The following year Gable turned in another outstanding performance, as Fletcher Christian in *Mutiny on the Bounty* (1935), a superb film which won the Oscar for Best Picture and opened new horizons for Clark as a dramatic actor. He shared billing with Charles Laughton and Franchot Tone and earned a nomination for Best Actor. Clark had originally refused to do the part, thinking that he could not handle an English accent and would look silly in knee breeches and a pigtail. He was talked into it by the perceptive Irving Thalberg, who was to die a year later at thirty-seven, leaving an unfillable void in the Metro creative force.

Once *Mutiny on the Bounty* was finished, Gable referred to it as one of his favorite films: "I was wrong. It *was* something you could get your teeth into, for it was history, a story about the struggle of real men, without the usual load of cinema romance." An unusual, but revealing reference to cinema romance by the world's leading heartthrob.

Just prior to the release of *Mutiny on the Bounty,* Clark and his wife went on a cross-country personal appearance tour. Women rioted in every city in which he appeared. In Kansas City, nearly three thousand female fans met him at the railroad station in a screaming frenzy. The more agile ones jumped the railroad tracks and climbed over the coal cars to get to him. In one hotel, Clark woke up to find the chambermaid stroking his cheek. In

With Mickey Rooney, Metro child star who portrays Gable as a kid in "Manhattan Melodrama," (1934)

With Robert Montgomery on the set of "Forsaking All Others," 1935.

Skeet shooting with John Barrymore, 1935.

Ria Gable lunches with Columnist Hedda Hopper at the Brown Derby, 1935.

Clark Gable and Wife Separate

Clark Gable, ranking screen lover, and his second wife have agreed on an "amicable separation." Mrs. Gable announced in Hollywood. "Just a case of temperament," she said. Gable is vacationing in New York.

November 13, 1935 newspaper clipping

Reunited with his father, William Gable, who finally came to Hollywood in 1935.

Baltimore, a love-stricken teenager jumped him in an elevator and covered him with kisses. In New York City, women of all ages blocked traffic outside the theater where he appeared, and even tried to break down his dressing room door. Police had to smuggle him in and out. In every town there were women who begged to have a baby by him, promising never to bother him with the child afterwards. Several girls removed their bras for him to autograph. Clark lost dozens of handkerchiefs, ties, cuff links, even his watch, when they mobbed him.

Gable was at a loss to explain this phenomenon, even astounded by it. "This power over women that I'm supposed to have," he declared, "was never noticed when I was on Broadway. I don't know when I got it. And by God, I can't explain it."

About this time it became evident that Clark and Ria Gable were miscast as husband and wife. He had outgrown his need of her and became weary of proclaiming that he preferred older women because they were more worldly. Hollywood gossip linked him in affairs with at least half a dozen women, including Carole Lombard, Joan Crawford, and Loretta Young, his co-star in *Call of the Wild* (1935).

In late 1935, Ria and Clark separated. She told reporters that there would be no immediate divorce and that no other woman was involved. "Clark has been working very hard in recent months and has been quite temperamental. Little differences, ordinarily of minor consequence, arose between us, which under stress assumed grave proportions." She was not going to release Clark until he was ready to pay for his freedom.

Beyond his estranged wife, Clark's only living relative was his father, who finally consented to come to Hollywood. Clark put him up in a bungalow, and although they were back on speaking terms, Mr. Gable loftily ignored his son's activities. He never visited the studio, and never approved or understood "those queer, wild, acting folk." In fact, old Will Gable used to needle his son: "Why don't you quit this foolish business, kid? We'll go back to the oil fields and hit it rich, working together like we used to. And you'll feel like a man again, kid, once you start doing man's work."

Perhaps because of this heckling Clark wasn't as sympathetic toward the old man as he made out to be. His business manager reported confidentially that some months it was extremely difficult to get Clark to send his father the $500 support check, even though Clark was making many times that per week. Will Gable died in the late forties without ever uttering the

...able and Carole Lombard relax in the
...orway of a Paramount sound stage during
...e filming of "No Man of Her Own."

words of praise his son was hungry to hear.

Clark's professional activities at the time were highlighted by *San Francisco* (1936), which featured another screen heavyweight, Spencer Tracy, and the angelic first lady of the movie musical, Jeanette MacDonald. Some of the most magnificent special effects were created for the 1906 San Francisco earthquake scenes.

Critics wrote that Tracy stole the show. And Gable thought so too. Clark, who felt himself a captive of his own screen image, envied Tracy's ability to play any role with conviction. He respected Tracy's prowess as an actor. By the same token, Tracy admired Gable and envied his popularity. Oddly enough, although these giants made another two of the standout films in their respective careers together—*Test Pilot* (1938) and *Boom Town* (1940)—they never became close friends.

Perhaps motivated by feelings of inferiority as an actor, Gable tried to break the mold with *Parnell* (1937), in which he stepped completely out of character, playing a sensitive, poetic Irish patriot. He looked sorely out of place. This performance was the one real disaster of his career, prompting many indignant letters from admirers. In her own wacky way, Carole Lombard never let Clark forget his pretentious characterization in *Parnell.* After this picture, whenever Gable felt chesty about any part he was doing, Carole would hire a plane to drop leaflets on the Culver City studio saying things like:

"If you think Gable is the world's greatest actor, see him
in *Parnell,* You'll never forget it. If Parnell was as
woozy a goof as Gable portrayed him in that picture,
Ireland still wouldn't be free."

All this clowning delighted Clark—especially because Carole knew when to stop. She was able to read him like a book and understood him.

Clark was later to contend, "I'm not really an actor. I was just lucky. If it hadn't been for people like Howard Strickling, I'd probably ended up a truck driver."

A few months after Gable put his footprints in the sidewalk of the world-famous Grauman's Chinese Theatre in 1937, an Englishwoman seized the headlines by charging that Clark Gable was the father of her thirteen-year-old daughter, Gwendolyn. Mrs. Violet Wells Norton declared that Gable had gone to England in 1922-23, masqueraded as a tutor under the name of Frank Billings, and seduced her. The allegation was, of course, false, but it had to be refuted in a Federal Court. In her testimony,

In his most disastrous role, that of Parnell, a sensitive Irsih patriot (1937)

Carole braves a cold night on the set of "Too Hot to Handle" to be with Gable.

Sid Grauman, far left, watches as Gable puts his hand prints into a fresh block of cement in front of the world-famous Grauman's Chinese Theatre on Hollywood Boulevard, 1937.

Gable visits New York in 1935, just before the release of "Mutiny on the Bounty."

Gable and George Arliss as caricatured in a 1936 Walt Disney short called "Mother Goose Goes Hollywood."

"Dear Mr. Gable—You Made Me Love You"—a musical love letter from Judy Garland in "Broadway Melody of 1938."

Mrs. Norton, a rather large and ordinary looking woman, naively insisted: "Hit's 'im all right. Hit's the syme big ears. Hit's the syme un'appy face what used to light up so tenderly when 'e'eld me in 'is arms back in Billericay."

Clark proved he was not in England at the time by calling on Franz Dorfler, his first sweetheart, whom he had not seen since the time they celebrated his MGM contract seven years earlier. She testified that Clark had spent the time in question with her in Oregon. Mrs. Norton was then charged with using the mails to defraud. (Franz Dorfler's own story of her romance with Gable appears elsewhere in this book.)

In return for her help, Clark arranged for Franz to be hired by Metro for their small stock company. She remained there until the start of World War II, when she was laid off and went to work for UCLA. While at MGM, she rarely saw Clark because he did not like to be reminded of his past. Once Clark became famous, he turned his back on his struggling days and the people associated with them. He never returned to his hometown in Ohio or to Portland, Oregon. Possibly Clark's attitude can be explained in terms of his fears of a return to the poverty he once knew should his bubble of success suddenly burst.

The years from 1935 to 1940 were Gable's peak years, which included a long series of unforgettable films—*Call of the Wild, China Seas, Mutiny on the Bounty, San Francisco, Test Pilot, Too Hot to Handle, Idiot's Delight, Strange Cargo, Boom Town, Comrade X*—topped off with *Gone With the Wind*, the monumental Civil War epic and the ultimate screen classic. Released in 1939, it was Clark's greatest picture, even though Vivien Leigh as Scarlett O'Hara was the central character and, in comparison to the other key stars, Leslie Howard and Olivia de Havilland, Gable spent little actual time on the screen. But the strength of his personality gave lasting effect to his performance as Rhett Butler.

Curiously, it was not MGM but an independent producer, David O. Selznick, who masterminded "GWTW." With Clark under exclusive contract to Metro, Selznick, whose family and past business activities had put a strain on his relationship with the major studio, had to bargain with great delicacy for the use of Gable in the role of Rhett.

Selznick had to agree to release "GWTW" through MGM and to surrender half the gross. When the dealing was over, it had cost Selznick $25 million for the loan of Gable, not one cent of which was passed on by MGM to the star. Gable drew only

his weekly salary of $4500. It was the most profitable transaction in MGM's history. Louis B. Mayer, the iron boss of the Metro lot and Selznick's father-in-law, later bought all rights to the picture when Selznick liquidated his company during the war. MGM has since reissued the film every seven or eight years. This last time, in 1967, it played in an exclusive engagement for almost a year. All in all, the film has probably grossed over $130 million worldwide.

Appraising the price he had to pay for Gable, Selznick insisted, "It was worth every penny. I don't know of any actor who could have played Rhett Butler as well as he did. Clark made you believe whatever he was playing. He had that God-given thing: a theatrical personality, the ability to communicate with the audience, something all the training in the world cannot give you. It is only enhanced by experience. Without this quality, there is no such thing as a star. It is not just being photogenic. It is an indefinable thing which I like to think I can spot immediately in a person. The public caught it in Clark Gable the first time he walked across the screen."

Gable, who was not known for being a particularly good judge of his own work or for selecting parts for himself, did not want to play Rhett Butler anymore than he had wanted to wear knee breeches and a pigtail in *Mutiny on the Bounty.* "I never asked for the part," Clark admitted freely while "GWTW" was being filmed. "I was one of the last to read Margaret Mitchell's novel and did so only at the urging of friends who insisted that Rhett was so obviously written for me. To them I replied that when the book was being written I was a four-dollar-a-day laborer in Oklahoma and not in anybody's mind for anything, much less the hero in a Civil War novel. My reaction to Rhett was immediate and enthusiastic. 'What a part for Ronald Colman,' I said.

"I cannot say that I did not want to play Rhett. I did. But he was too popular. Miss Mitchell had etched him into the minds of millions, each of whom knew exactly how Rhett would look and act. It would be impossible to satisfy them all, or even a majority. I knew that. So when Dave Selznick offered me the part, I told him with some pleasure that I was sewed up by my MGM contract. And added that I didn't want the part for money, marbles or chalk. He said that he'd try to make a deal with the studio. And since my contract states that I have no choice in roles, I said nothing. I could see myself being sold down the river."

When the picture, which followed Miss Mitchell's novel

August 25, 1938. Gable, Selznick and L. B. Mayer sign the contracts for "Gone With the Wind."

Gable, Vivien Leigh, and director Fleming chat on the set.

Rehearsing dialogue with Vivien Leigh.

Director Victor Fleming discussing script changes before going into a take.

Gable meets Margaret Mitchell, author of "Gone With the Wind."

With producer David O. Selznick on the set of "GWTW"

quite closely, was finished, Gable was not altogether reluctant to agree with Selznick's insistence that "Rhett will probably remain among the most memorable roles Clark's ever created on the screen. It was a difficult and frightening role for him to tackle only because of the unprecedented public interest in the character."

Amid claims that it was the greatest picture ever made, "GWTW" took the country by storm. It was the longest picture to date, with the most elaborate publicity campaign directed by the now legendary publicist, Russell Birdwell. He had concocted a fantastic two-year-long search for the actress to play Scarlett O'Hara, giving Selznick time to meet other commitments before filming could begin.

Many troubles plagued the production, mostly stemming from the attempt itself of condensing the longest novel (1037 pages) within memory into slightly less than four hours of film. Five directors, including Victor Fleming, Gable's favorite director, worked on the picture intermittently. At times several directors worked simultaneously. It was too much for one man alone. So was the script which, although credited solely to Pultizer Prize-winner Sidney Howard, was molded by many, including Selznick, F. Scott Fitzgerald, Ben Hecht, and a dozen others. Rewriting continued almost to the last meticulous day of shooting.

The Oscars that year were no surprise. *Gone With the Wind* swept the boards to set a new record with ten Academy Awards: Best Picture, Vivien Leigh for Best Actress, Victor Fleming for Best Director, Sidney Howard for Best Screenplay, Hattie McDaniel for Best Supporting Actress, and five others. But Gable, who was nominated a third time for Best Actor, was bypassed by the Academy, which in its idiosyncratic inadequacy failed to bestow the honors on the King for the performance of his career. The Oscar went instead to Britisher Robert Donat for *Goodbye, Mr. Chips.* Possibly taken into account was the fact that Gable had already received an Oscar five years earlier for *It Happened One Night,* which, although a charming movie and a delightful role, couldn't compare with the excellence he achieved in "GWTW." The casting had been too perfect, and Gable had made it look too easy.

If he was disappointed, Gable didn't show it. He was absorbed with something far more important. During the filming of "GWTW," Ria had agreed to a divorce settlement of $286,000, which was a prohibitive amount even for him. However, with the help of MGM, he paid it off and was a

Arriving in Atlanta for the premiere. Publicity man Howard Strickling is at his right elbow.

With wife Carole Lombard at the Atlanta Ball. Following "GWTW" premiere, 1939.

With newly-wed bride Carole Lombard
just before entering theatre for premiere
of "GWTW."

In the chicken coop on their Encino ranch.

bachelor again. But not for long.

Several months before "GWTW" completed production, Gable drove Carole Lombard to Kingman, Arizona, and married her in a quiet ceremony on March 29, 1939. Their marriage came as a surprise to no one. They had been seen together almost constantly for nearly three years. All of Hollywood had anticipated their elopement. MGM big-wigs and Selznick had feared that Clark might hold up shooting with a long honeymoon. But he was too conscientious for that.

Louella Parsons hailed it as "a match made in Heaven," much in the same manner that the Doug Fairbanks-Mary Pickford union had been embraced. Because both Clark and Carole were major stars, their marriage was headline news. Carole, who also was at her peak, was actually making twice Clark's salary. She was the world's highest paid actress and the first freelancing star to command $150,000 per picture; also one of the first to obtain a percentage deal, something that Clark would not be able to get for years.

There is no doubt that the Gable-Lombard marriage was a happy one, one that has since taken on such legendary proportions that it has become a symbol for the ideal relationship, perfection in almost storybook terms. A Gable-Lombard marriage is the kind to have.

They bought a ranch in Encino, California, and took great satisfaction in owning land and raising cows and horses. After having conquered the world of bright lights and glamour, Clark preferred a life that echoed his rural childhood. Carole took management of the household and their social life. And since Clark's second home was in the mountains, desert or wherever studio bosses couldn't reach him, Carole became a hard-drinking, rugged, outdoorsy companion to her husband. She went on his hunting trips, learned to handle a shotgun, and slept on the ground like the men.

One evening at dusk as Carole and Clark stood on their porch of their ranch house, he exclaimed: "Look at that beauty, look at those flowers and trees. They're all ours. What else could two people want? What else do we need?" To which Carole sassily replied, "Another load of manure for the alfalfa field."

Their happiness was cut short in January, 1942. Carole was returning from the first War Bond selling tour immediately following the attack on Pearl Harbor when the plane crashed into the side of a mountain near Las Vegas. The flames from the wreckage could be seen fifty miles away. There were no survivors.

"For months after her death, Clark was almost out of his mind with grief," observed writer Adela Rogers St. Johns, a close friend who visited Gable often during his bereavement. "I'd go to his house and he'd be having dinner alone in the dining room with Carole's dog and Siamese cats at the table. He refused to touch her room and left it just the way it was when she left. I asked, 'Why don't you go out? Why don't you call your old friends like Vic Fleming?' And he'd say, 'Carole used to make the calls when we wanted to go out.' "

With all his grief, though, he worried about the family of the MGM press agent, Otto Winkler, who was also killed in the crash. He withdrew his claim against the airline with the provision that they pay $100,000 to Winkler's widow. He also helped pay for a house for Mrs. Winkler. Some say that he felt responsible for Winkler's death because he had requested that a Metro publicist accompany his wife on the tour. Winkler was assigned but had not wanted to go.

The picture Clark was working on at the time, ironically titled *Somewhere I'll Find You,* was two-thirds finished. When Gable dropped out of sight for several weeks and production was suspended, no one knew if the actor was coming back to finish it. But Clark was too much of a professional ever to have thought about not returning to work. He never missed a call, was never late, even if he had spent the whole night before drinking, and always labored diligently on the set. And now, after suffering the greatest blow of his life, he returned to complete the film.

His first day back, he announced that as soon as production was wrapped up, he was retiring from the screen to join the Army Air Corps as a buck private. The last word he had had from Carole was a telegram that urged: "Hey Pappy, you'd better get in this man's army."

Upon entering the service in August, 1942, Clark Gable, age 41, declared, "I don't want to make speeches, I don't want to sell bonds, I don't want to entertain. I just want to be a machine gunner on a bomber and be sent where the going is tough." Many took this statement as an indication of his desire for action to help forget his deep sorrow.

But the anonymity and the hardship Gable sought were largely denied him. As had been agreed upon prior to his enlistment, he was assigned to Officers Candidate School in Miami, Florida. On the way there his train was mobbed by well-meaning fans several times, delaying it considerably. Then

Gable and Carole Lombard at the Hollywood Race Track (1938)

Visiting the set of "Idiot's Delight," Carole Lombard brings a dozen roses for Gable who surprised everyone with his hoofing ability (1938).

Celebrating their wedding day with a cake at the MGM commissary (March 29, 1939).

49

Capt. Gable walking with fellow officers at Army Air Corps Base in England, 1943

Most notable about this imposing stellar gathering surrounding MGM boss Louis B. Mayer is Gable's absence in the service. Left to right, first row: Capt. James Stewart (on leave), Margaret Sullavan, Lucille Ball, Hedy Lamarr, Katharine Hepburn, Mayer, Greer Garson, Irene Dunne, Susan Peters, Ginny Simms, Lionel Barrymore. Second row: Harry James, Brian Donlevy, Red Skelton, Mickey Rooney, William Powell, Wallace Beery, Spencer Tracy, Walter Pidgeon, Robert Taylor, Pierre Aumont, Lewis Stone, Gene Kelly, child actor Jackie Jenkins. Third row: Tommy Dorsey, George Murphy, Jean Rogers, James Craig, Donna Reed, Van Johnson, Fay Bainter, Marsha Hunt, Ruth Hussey, Marjorie Main, Robert Benchley. Fourth row: Dame May Whitty, Reginald Owen, Keenan Wynn, Diana Lewis, Marilyn Maxwell, Esther Williams, Ann Richards, Martha Linden, Lee Bowman, Richard Carlson, Mary Astor. Fifth row: Blanche Ring, Sara Haden, Fay Holden, Bert Lahr, Frances Gifford, June Allyson, Richard Whorf, Frances Rafferty, Spring Byington, Connie Gilchrist, Gladys Cooper. Sixth row: Ben Blue, Chill Wills, Keye Luke, Barry Nelson, PFC Desi Arnaz, Henry O'Neill, Bob Crosby, Rags Ragland.

in Florida he was constantly hounded by reporters. He insisted on taking the normal course of instruction to win his commission and his wings as an aerial gunner, but still he stood out in the ranks.

Competing with classmates who had a more extended formal education was a distinct disadvantage for Clark. Yet he graduated in the upper third of the class. That was accomplished, he explained, "by committing the manuals to memory." His instructors were certain that the former actor had studied during many of the hours assigned to sleeping. His classmates chose him to give the graduation address on October 28, 1942. "Our job," Lieutenant Gable said then, "is to stay on the beam until—in victory—we are given the command to fall out."

Overseas with the Eighth Air Force in 1943, Gable volunteered and flew on five bombing missions over Germany. Since Carole's death, just being in an airplane frightened him, but some despairing impulse impelled him into combat. Returning with Gable from a raid on the Ruhr Valley was Andrew McIntyre, who had enlisted with him. McIntyre said, "Gable did his job. The Army didn't give him a thing."

When the German high command learned that Gable was in Europe, Air Minister Hermann Goering added him to the preferred list of Americans he wanted dead or alive. Goering wanted Colonel Hubert Zemke and Lt. Colonel Francis Gabreski, two of our leading fighter pilots. Gable he hoped to get alive because he was Hitler's favorite American movie star. For Captain Gable, he offered $5,000, a furlough and an immediate promotion.

Zemke and Gabreski scored twenty-eight fighter kills each and were both shot down in 1944. Gable was the only one of the trio to escape.

Officially Clark's job was to make a training film. But the picture was obsolete by the time it was finished and never widely shown. After seven frustrating months in England, Gable was ordered home. Just before his return, in October, 1943, Captain Gable received the Distinguished Flying Cross and Air Medal, the latter for "exceptionally meritorious achievement while participating in five separate bomber combat missions." In June, 1944, he was promoted to the rank of major and discharged. Though the war still raged, the Army Air Corps had no further use for him.

His military service brought him new admiration and respect from the public and his fans. Huge crowds turned out to welcome Major Gable back from the fighting. According to MGM

Being sworn into the Army Air Corps as a buck private in the Los Angeles recruiting office, August 12, 1942. He is 41 years old.

As a machine gunner on a bombing raid from England over the Ruhr Valley, 1943

AIRMAN GABLE—Clark Gable, now an Army Air Forces lieutenant, arriving here on a military mission, talks with E. J. Mannix of the M.G.M. studios.

Lieut. Clark Gable Arrives on Special Military Mission

Every inch a fighting man, Lieut. Clark Gable of the Army Air Forces visited friends in the Hollywood film colony yesterday while in Southern California on a special military assignment.

Now enrolled in the Air Forces

Gable, who enlisted Aug. 12, was graduated from the officers' training school Oct. 28 with the single gold bar of a second lieutenant. He was spokesman for his class of 2500 Air Corps offi-

Newspaper clipping of Gable's stopover in Hollywood on his way to England, 1943.

Lieutenant Clark Gable as a machine gunner, just before a bombing raid on the Ruhr valley in 1943.

On leave before going to England, Lt. Gable compares notes with another MGM star who had just earned his bars, but as a pilot—Jimmy Stewart (1943).

publicist Eddie Lawrence, "Richard the Lion-Hearted didn't get a better reception when he came back from the Crusades."

Returning to his still vacant spot at Metro, Clark began work immediately. His first post-war picture was *Adventure* (1945) with Greer Garson. Although a forgettable romance, the picture made money because everyone was eager to see Gable again. The national advertising campaign announced: "Gable's back and Garson's got him!" It couldn't have been farther from the truth. Emil Torchia, the publicist on *Adventure,* said, "Gable and Garson never hit it off. He'd look at her as if she wasn't even there. It was the same with Jeannette MacDonald in *San Francisco.* With warm, earthy girls like Jean Harlow, Ava Gardner, and Lana Turner, he was his usual charming self. With others he could be cold as ice."

Perhaps most indicative of her rapport with Clark was Miss Garson's own version of the *Adventure* publicity slogan: "Gable's the guy who put the arson in Garson."

Although the momentum of his great days in the thirties and the early forties carried the King through a new series of mediocre MGM films, the first eight or nine years after Gable's return to private life were unhappy ones. His old zest and good humor were gone. His mood was due to a combination of things, including recurring personal grief, the lingering shock of war and the death of his father. His nerves seemed shot; he would get the shakes on camera, making long scenes and closeups extremely difficult; he drank and ate to excess without regard for what it was doing to him. The once vital concern for himself and his appearance was gone. The added poundage and dissipated looks seemed to mirror his unhappy mental state. He seemed bent on destroying himself, as though he no longer cared about anything. Even as he took several escapist trips to Europe alone, life appeared to be a chore, a day-to-day ritual that was getting to be tiresome.

It was during this period that he had his drunken driving accident; and was unjustly arrested on a game law violation which, because of his pride as a sportsman, depressed him greatly. His numerous dates all seemed casual and unimportant. And to a widower in his late forties, it sometimes seemed an unreasonable strain to be the dashing Clark Gable. These years aged him fiercely.

It was a long time before Clark married again, and his seven-year period between marriages extended itself to nine years, prolonged perhaps by the war. Among the many women he was seen with, only one stirred him to action. It was Lady Sylvia Ashley, a vivacious blonde who was gay, sophisticated, cosmopolitan, and most importantly, bore a striking resemblance to Carole Lombard. Born Sylvia Hawkes the daughter of a London pubkeeper, Lady Ashley began a career as an actress only to discover that her best talents embraced drawing rooms and men of distinction. With her first marriage, she acquired a title she never relinquished, despite three succeeding husbands. She became Lady Ashley and never forgot it.

Lord Ashley was the son of the Earl of Shaftsbury. His marriage to Sylvia ended in divorce, and she, now an international society figure, began another adventure. In 1934, she cruised the world with Douglas Fairbanks, Sr., who was then married to Mary Pickford. Fairbanks was a broken man, his days as a swashbuckling film hero long since gone. He was even jealous of the rising successes of his own son, Doug, Jr. Miss Pickford reluctantly divorced him, a shocking action that destroyed the fable of supreme happines and fairy tale charm connected with their marriage. Fairbanks then married Lady Ashley.

The Pickford-Fairbanks breakup led to the great significance attached to the ideal public success of the Gable-Lombard marriage, intensifying that Hollywood legend to its present magnitude. Many writers in recent years have singled out the Gable-Lombard relationship as the only one that had true meaning, the sole one to survive in the plastic community of filmdom. Like a contemporary Romeo and Juliet story, it has become part of our modern-day mythology.

After Fairbanks died in 1939, tired and beaten, his widow soon wed Baron Stanley of Alderly. When Sylvia divorced him in 1948, she ignored his name, bypassed Fairbanks and became Lady Ashley again.

She was forty-two when she met Clark Gable in Hollywood. The idea of getting married came up at a party late at night on December 21, 1949. In good spirits induced by much champagne, Gable took Sylvia to Santa Barbara and married her, with Howard Stricking and Gable's secretary, Jean Garceau, as witnesses. Three weeks later, his close friends say, Gable knew he had made a mistake.

Lady Sylvia was ultra-genteel. Quite soon, her affectations and her disdain for outdoor life came between them. On a fishing trip while on location for *Across the Wide Missouri,* (1951), Lady Sylvia wore high heels and complained about discomfort in the rowboat even though she had taken several cushions along

A poster advertising Gable's first post-war movie—with the now classic line: "Gable's back and Garson's got him"

Gable and bride Lady Sylvia Ashley are showered with rice following their marriage at the Alisal Ranch, an exclusive resort just north of Santa Barbara. December 21, 1949.

Lady Sylvia Ashley, Gable's fourth wife,
reluctantly roughs it with him on location
for "Across the Wide Missouri."

Gable's beard tickles director William
Wellman's daughter, Cissy, on the
Colorado location site of "Across the Wide
Missouri," 1950.

Lady Sylvia paints pictures on the location
set of "Across the Wide Missouri."

on which to lounge. Around their temporary cabin she wanted to plant trees for privacy, and she hung frilly curtains on the windows. Life in the open was too coarse for a creature as delicate as she.

In 1951, Lady Sylvia sued for divorce. Among other indignities, she charged that Carole Lombard's ghost was always there. Their Encino house, she stated, was full of mementos that Clark and Carole had gathered together. She won her suit with a large property settlement, even though Clark had also filed for divorce in Reno, where he had attempted to set up a new residence and move as much of his estate as possible to escape the California divorce laws, which give women a strong edge. In addition, she was also granted a ten per cent lien on Clark's salary for one year. Following the settlement in April, 1952, Sylvia became Lady Ashley again and returned to the European nobility to which she was accustomed, much wealthier than when she had left it.

If Gable's life is viewed in its totality, it becomes obvious that his regrettable marriage to Lady Sylvia was the logical conclusion to his post-war grim period which began to take a different direction only after the sobering experience of his third divorce. The frustrations in Gable's private life were paralleled in his professional life. The films Clark was now making for MGM compared unfavorably with the great pre-1942 productions. Movies in general had hit the skids during the war, when talent and money were tight and the demands of the movie-goers were casual. Now the studios were sluggish about returning to pre-war form.

There were a number of reasons for this. The emergence of television, which only a decade before had been regarded with scorn and amusement, cut theatre attendance sharply. Motion picture production costs soared, partially because price ceilings were removed and union activities increased. Then on the final day of 1946, the courts ruled that film companies could no longer distribute and exhibit their movies in wholly-owned theatre chains. Monopoly booking and the profits connected with it became a thing of the past.

In addition, the House Un-American Activities Committee investigations of Communist Party members, supporters and sympathizers in Hollywood had shaken the industry. Film makers proceeded with caution, returning to tried and true formulas rather than attempting new things for fear of being labeled "pink" or "red."

*With Gene Tierney in "Never Let Me Go,"
1952*

*On the European location for "Betrayed"
with Victor Mature, 1953*

*His famous picture with Jean Harlow,
"Red Dust," was remade in 1953 under
the title of "Mogambo." Ava Gardner
played Harlow's role and the company
went to Kenya for location photography.
Gable was still the ultimate hero, playing
the same role convincingly after twenty
years.*

Because of executive confusion and inefficiency bred by earlier extravagant years, MGM experienced great difficulty in adjusting to the new conditions. Indicative of this was the balance sheet of Loew's, Inc., Metro's parent company, which in 1946 had declared $18 million net revenue and two years later reported only $4.2 million.

On June 22, 1951, Louis B. Mayer, who had slowly lost his grip on studio control because of a conflicting interest in horseracing, was replaced as MGM studio head by Dore Schary. Schary, whose earliest contact with Metro dated to 1933 when he was hired as a writer, had been contracted by Mayer in 1948 to be MGM production head. The company's product improved considerably and Schary, who had produced pictures for Dave Selznick and had standing offers from most of the other studios, was hailed as the new Irving Thalberg. Then when continued clashes between Mayer and Schary forced a showdown, the New York office sided with Schary, and Mayer resigned.

Schary was faced with lowering the expenses of running a studio while at the same time making better pictures. The answer seemed to lie in releasing the large stable of talent (actors, writers, directors, producers, etc.) and giving them single picture options on a yearly basis so that Metro wouldn't have to carry the cost of their services when they weren't working. At the time, MGM had nearly four thousand people under exclusive contract, while turning out an average of twenty-five to thirty movies a year. It didn't seem to make sense. The lion's share of stars had to be sacrificed.

Among the first to go were temperamental favorites like Mickey Rooney and Judy Garland. Wallace Beery died; Mario Lanza was dropped; Greer Garson was released from her contract; Spencer Tracy departed by mutual agreement.

And Gable? His contract, which expired in 1954, was not renewed. Although still popular, the King was too expensive to retain at $520,000 a year. It was just as well, because the studio had changed so much it no longer seemed like home to the veteran actor. And on one occasion, he had locked horns with Schary about a script and was suspended temporarily. "Imagine that," raged Gable. "Suspending a guy for the first time in his life after twenty-three years with the studio."

After Gable was gone, his last two MGM films were released: *Betrayed* and *Mogambo,* both in 1954. *Mogambo* was such a box office champ that Metro courted the King again, but nothing would bring him back. Stories have it that Gable would sometimes have his agent feel Metro out and push them for the best possible arrangement they would give him for a one-picture deal, only to turn them down.

Mogambo, a fine adventure film reflecting Schary's talent as a producer, was a remake of *Red Dust,* one of Gable's earliest pictures with Jean Harlow. In the new version, every member of the original cast was replaced, except one. A little battered and graying, Gable was still the ultimate romantic hero. He was still able to convey a strong charge of masculine magnetism toward Ava Gardner and Grace Kelly.

Overnight, Clark Gable became the most expensive free-lance actor in the industry. First to sign him was 20th Century-Fox. For a percentage of the gross, Gable made two pictures for them in 1955, *Soldier of Fortune* with Susan Hayward, and *The Tall Men* with Jane Russell. Both were fast-moving action films, helping to restore his image.

Clark's personal affairs also took a turn for the better. On July 7, 1955, he married for the fifth time. His bride was Kay Williams Spreckels, who had known Clark from the mid-thirties at MGM. When her early designs on him failed, she wed Adolph Spreckels, Jr., heir to a sugar fortune. Their marriage didn't last, but she had two children by him. After her separation, and following Clark's divorce from Lady Sylvia, they began to see each other again.

He was attracted to her because her background was similar to his. She had been raised on a farm, she had had a brief fling as an actress, and knew the industry. She was charming, and, even more so than the last Mrs. Gable, was a stunning blonde resembling Carole Lombard. And Clark, weary from the unfulfillment of recent years, longed for a family.

When Kay moved into Clark's Encino home, she didn't try to change anything. She brought her two young children and gave to Clark something he hadn't had before: a true home life. When Clark wanted to play golf, Kay played golf. When Clark wanted to go hunting, Kay went hunting. When Clark went anywhere on location, Kay and the children went with him. She devoted her life to making her husband happy. She helped him lose the weight that carelessness and neglect had put on.

A friend said, "Sometimes I would close my eyes and listen to Clark and Kay call each other Ma and Pa and exchange quips and insults, and I thought I was listening to a road version of the Gable-Lombard marriage."

After his profitable experience with 20th Century-Fox,

Gable and his fifth wife, Kay Spreckels, attend the premiere of "The Tall Men" in 1955.

Kay Gable gave him what he wanted badly: his first family life. She brought with her two children from her previous marriage, Joan and Bunker.

*Taking Melody out of the stables on his
Encino Ranch for an early morning ride,
1956*

Clark wanted to try producing his own pictures for a greater
share of the gross. He founded his own company, GABCO,
and made *The King and Four Queens* (1956) with Eleanor
Parker. The picture, a minor Western, didn't live up to the
promising title, nor to Gable's expectations. When asked if he
had plans to direct films, as so many stars were doing, he
answered, "Hell, I haven't learned to act yet."

Cured of wanted to produce his own pictures, Clark signed
with Warner Brothers to do *Band of Angels* (1957) with
Yvonne de Carlo and Sidney Poitier. This film emerged as a
miniature fascimile of "GWTW," but had neither the inspiration
nor the sensitivity of that classic.

Things improved when Burt Lancaster, another actor turned
producer, persuaded Gable to co-produce and co-star with him in
Run Silent, Run Deep (1958). The result was a well-conceived
and well-executed war drama. Then Paramount signed him for
three comedies: *Teacher's Pet* with Doris Day (1958); *But Not
for Me* with Carroll Baker (1959); and *It Started in Naples*
opposite Sophia Loren (1960). These were not outstanding
films, but they were reminiscent of the glossy humor of his
pictures with Claudette Colbert and Myrna Loy in the thirties.

Just before Clark finished *It Started in Naples,* producer
Frank Taylor sent him a copy of Arthur Miller's script for
The Misfits, a contemporary Western. He wanted Clark to play
Gay Langland, the male lead. Taylor later explained why. "We
had a great cast lined up—Marilyn Monroe, Montgomery Clift,
Eli Wallach and Thelma Ritter. And we had a great director
in John Huston. But I knew only one actor in the world who
could express the essence of complete masculinity and virility
that we needed for the leading role. And that was Clark Gable.
At 59 he was still a contemporary image of virility. Marlon
Brando is virile to women but not to men. Gable was virile to
both men and women. Brando is a symbol of both sexuality and
sensuality. Gable had no sensuality about him. His essential
maleness was right on the surface."

For $750,000 and a percentage of the gross, Clark Gable
signed with Taylor to do *The Misfits.* The contract also provided
that if the shooting ran over sixteen weeks, he was to receive an
additional $48,000 each week. With Miss Monroe's
procrastinations and chronic illnesses, the picture was so delayed
that Clark earned $1.25 million before one cent was taken in at
the box office.

Taylor confessed that he was "attempting to make the

*Publicity pose with Jane Russell for
"The Tall Men"*

*With Sophia Loren, the aging Gable is
still the romantic lead in "It Started In
Naples," 1960.*

*The people who made "The Misfits"
(1960) a special picture: producer Frank
Taylor (under ladder), playwright
Arthur Miller (top center), Eli Wallach,
director John Huston, Montgomery Clift,
Marilyn Monroe, and Gable.*

ultimate motion picture. This is not only the first original
screenplay by a major American writer, but the best screenplay
I have ever read."

The Misfits was truly significant in that this was the first
time that the two top sex symbols of the screen appeared together.
Marilyn Monroe, the young, neurotic sex goddess, was nervous
about the experience. As an orphaned child, she had kept a
picture of Clark Gable and told people that he was her father.
And now, many years later, she was playing his screen lover.

Gable, who admired Marilyn and at the same time detested
her irresponsible work habits, treated her with forced patience
and tenderness. All his professionalism boiled when Marilyn
would arrive at 11:30 A.M. for a 9:45 call. Huston specifically
set late starts, instead of the usual seven or eight A.M. calls for a
production unit, to allow for Marilyn's inability to begin working
much before noon. The interminable delays had Clark on edge
during most of the shooting. He bellowed once, "You'll probably
see a lot of fire and smoke before we're through with this
picture." Then, recalling when he worked with Jean Harlow,
who was always on time, he said, "It was a different era. In
those days when stars were late, they were fired."

But Gable held on through the calamities that beset *The
Misfits* production with outward calm and wry humor because
he believed in Miller's story and felt a real kinship to the man he
portrayed. Whatever their momentary differences, Gable, Miller
and Huston agreed on the major statement of the screenplay:
the necessity of personal dignity in a society bent on destroying
individuality.

Gable considered *The Misfits* his best picture since *Gone
With the Wind*. He was playing, in Miller's words, a Westerner
whose idea of living was: "You start by going to sleep. You get
up when you feel like it. You scratch yourself, fry yourself some
eggs, throw some stones at a can. Whistle . . ." In short, Gable
was playing himself.

On the *The Misfits* location in Reno, Nevadans stared in
admiration when Gable fixed a flat on his own car. They were
watching a man who did everything himself, and did it well. He
delivered eggs from his Encino farm one morning when his egg
man took sick. His friends included studio executives, bellboys,
contractors, mechanics; and with some of them he would
motorcycle through the San Fernando Valley at 100 miles an hour
in the early morning hours.

Halfway through production of *The Misfits*, Gable learned

*The top female sex symbol and the top
male sex symbol together for the first time
for "The Misfits," 1960—a strange, tragic
picture which proved to be the last one for
both great stars.*

Gable being dragged by a mustang in "The Misfits," one of the strenuous action sequences in that film that probably contributed to his death shortly after.

that his wife Kay was pregnant. The thing Clark regretted most about his previous marriages was that he didn't have any children. Now at fifty-nine years of age he had produced an offspring. "It's going to be a boy," he announced proudly. Although he was a man who usually didn't talk much about himself, he never ceased bragging about his child-to-be.

It *was* a son, but sadly, Gable didn't live to see him. Two days after the completion of *The Misfits,* the King suffered a heart attack, and on November 16, 1960, he died.

Kay Gable blamed production anxieties and Clark's headstrong insistence on doing all his own stunts as having been directly responsible. He did stunts that no man his age should have tried. He was overweight and out of condition, but he was a professional and the scenes required realism. He stood upright on the hood of a car, fell across it, tumbling to the ground. He ran 100 yards for the camera at a hgh altitude in 106-degree heat and repeated this action several times. In another scene, while wrestling with a wild stallion, he was tied to a rope and dragged along the ground face down.

Prophetically, he spoke these lines to Marilyn Monroe in a key scene: "Honey, we all gotta go sometime, reason or no reason. Dyin's as natural as livin'. Man who's afraid to die is too afraid to live, far as I've ever seen." And Gable had never been afraid to live. In the film, he repeatedly tells the others, "I'll teach you how to live."

Quite coincidentally, *The Misfits,* which evolved into a remarkable film with Gable giving one of his finest characterizations, was also Miss Monroe's final screen appearance. At the completion of the film, her marriage to Arthur Miller fell apart and she entered a sanitarium. She had been sickly and on the verge of a total nervous collapse. Following her release from the mental hospital, she began another picture but never finished it. On August 4, 1962, she took her life with an overdose of sleeping pills.

There was more genuine regret over the death of Clark Gable than any other star since Rudolph Valentino. Everyone in the world knew him. They'd seen him eat, fight, make love, smile, howl with pain, go to bed, get up. His jaunty walk and his ears were trademarks. Milton Berle called his ears "The best ears of our lives." His death left a void which the film industry has been unable to fill. No one today could play Rhett Butler as convincingly.

At his funeral, all the great stars of Hollywood gathered

silently to pay tribute. Gable used to say, "If anything happens to me, don't let them make a circus out of it." As in his lifetime, no one would have dared mar his final dignity and privacy. The small military funeral ended with burial beside his beloved Carole Lombard in a mausoleum at Forest Lawn Memorial Park in Glendale, California.

It marked the end of an epoch. His star had risen higher and stayed there longer than any other in the history of films. There was no one anywhere who approached the cumulative glamour and excitement of the King's life and career. "He's not a man, he's an institution," John Huston once said of him. Then after Gable's death, Huston declared: "Clark was one of the few holdovers from the days of the champs. His career in pictures had the same sweep and color as Dempsey's in the ring. Put his name on the list with the Babes, the Galloping Ghosts and the Flying Finns. He is the only screen actor I can think of who rated the sobriquet, the King."

And as with royalty, Gable in later life was regarded by many people as a personal friend, but few in the crowds that always surged around him dared touch him or call him anything but "Mr. Gable."

There was something about Gable's physical presence that indicated he had some mystical effect on people when he approached them. That Gable magic was there a long time before he became famous, almost from the first time he appeared before an audience.

Ralph Wheelwright, an MGM official who is unimpressed by most stars, said, "The first time I saw Clark, he was in one of the early pictures he did with Joan Crawford. He appeared in the doorway of the sound stage while they were making a scene down at the other end of that barnlike place. Yet everybody working there felt something and looked around." All of his life people turned around to look at Clark Gable.

Eleanor Harris, a national magazine writer, had a similar experience fifteen years later. She was attending a cocktail party at the Evelyn Walsh MacLean mansion in Washington. There were a number of celebrities present. "Suddenly, I had the curious compulsion to turn around," she reported. "So did everyone else in the room. Clark Gable had arrived and was standing between two opened French doors for a moment before coming in."

The King's personal magnetism was coupled with an ability to project the character he was portraying on the screen. The cynical dean of film critics, Bosley Crowther, who reviewed until recently for *The New York Times,* wrote: "Oddly enough, one simple notion was a long time entering anybody's head; that was that Mr. Gable could act like the top-notch pro he was. He played so naturally it looked simple. Don't believe it. Let's pay him the respect he's due."

But as big as Gable got in his final years, he never thought of himself as a great actor. He continued to be down-to-earth and, true to his early promise, he had not "gone Hollywood." One legend concerns some mementos from his early struggling days that hung in his walnut-paneled dressing room. To them he attached a note: "Just to remind you, Gable." He never ceased being grateful for his success. Once he told a reporter that on his tombstone they should put the epitaph: "He was lucky and he knew it."

Kay Gable with John Clark, the son Gable never saw.

His thirty-year career, during which he appeared in sixty-seven films, spanned the rise and fall of the Golden Age of Moving Pictures, and vaguely paralleled it. Beginning as he did in the silents, he experienced the painful transition to sound and the glorious realization of what could be done with talking pictures. He and the film industry grew together, developed and hit their peaks simultaneously in 1939-41. Production levels and movie attendance were at all-time highs; full-color, wide-screen and stereophonic sound had been introduced. Then World War II slowed everything down. In the post-war years, Gable's career and films in general struggled to their feet but failed to achieve the pace and glamour of the previous decade.

In leaving MGM in the early fifties to free-lance, Gable, once again representative of the industry as a whole, symbolized the death of the old star system upon which Hollywood was built. Actors and actresses refused to be tied to a single studio and could no longer be manipulated as they once had been.

Coinciding with Gable's death was the beginning of the black decade for film producers, with movie attendance falling sharply because of improved television programming. During Gable's lifetime, he only once consented to appear on TV, in a brief interview with Ed Sullivan. Being a movie actor of the old school, Clark felt that a star should not appear on television because it competed with films.

And now nearly a decade after his passing, as Gable begins a new life as the idol of a cult movement, there is a new hope for films. Fresh concepts in movie making and cinema techniques and a more adult approach to subject matter have created a tremendous upsurge in the motion picture industry. Films are also being produced directly for television now. And for the first time in years, new movie theatres are being built across the country.

Finally, the Golden Age, an important part of film history, lives on in the pictures produced in that era and continues to be revisited by old fans and those discovering it for the first time. That era's King, Clark Gable, though his kingdom crumbled after his death, rules on.

Gable as an MGM "featured player
(Springer/Bettman Film Archive)

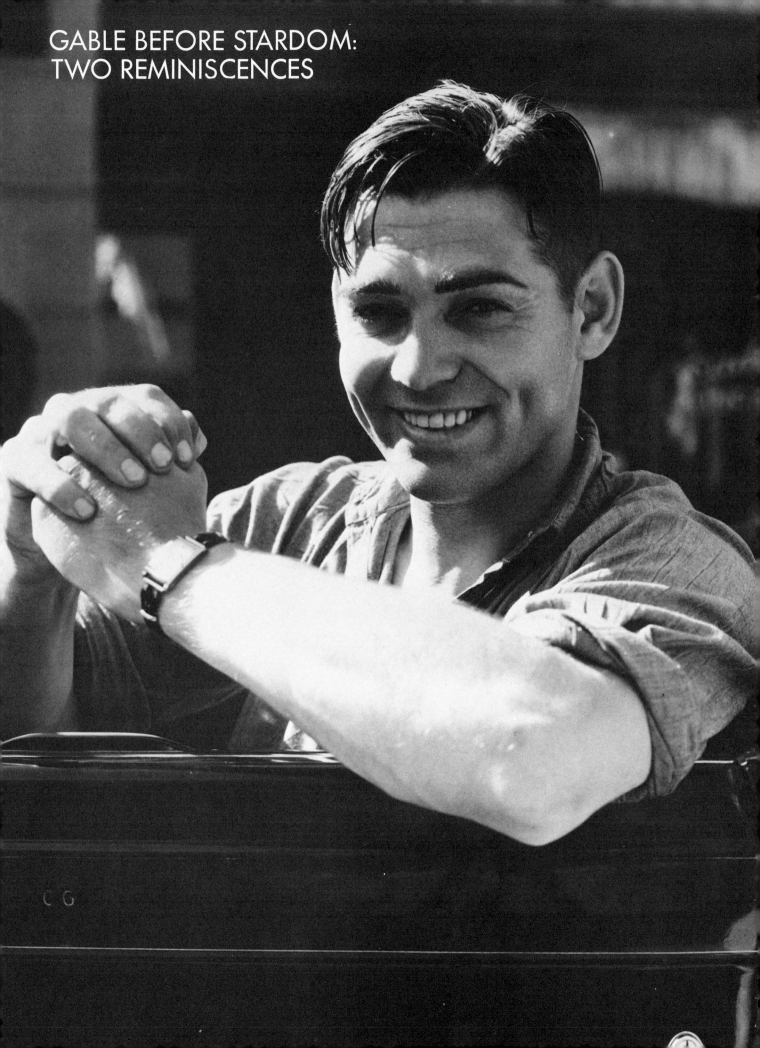

Franz Dorfler in a costume pose with the Astoria Stock Company in 1922.

I WAS BILLY GABLE'S SWEETHEART, BY FRANZ DORFLER

On Thursday, April 22, 1937, I testified in court on behalf of Clark Gable. He had been charged by an Englishwoman named Violet Norton with having fathered her then 13-year-old daughter, Gwendolyn. I think that she was misguided by those advising her because, of course, there was no truth to her claim.

During the months Clark was supposed to have been in England living under the name of Frank Billings, he was actually with me in Astoria, Oregon, in a small stock company on tour. He was called Billy Gable then and mostly played small comedy parts, while I did ingenue roles. And since there were very few members in our company we sometimes had to play parts to which we would not have been otherwise suitable. Occasionally I took a boy's role and Clark would have various parts, from a Negro mammy to a baby in a carriage. And since he wasn't self-conscious, he could be very funny. If he hadn't turned out so handsome, he would have made a marvelous comedian.

Having nostalgically saved some programs from our stock company days together in 1922, I was able to help clear Clark in that terrible trial. And poor, naive Mrs. Norton, who had written to Clark demanding money for child support, was indicted by the United States Post Office for using the mails to defraud.

The trial was bittersweet for me because it forced me to relive the wonderful lost relationship that Clark and I had enjoyed so many years before. When he was just a struggling, inexperienced actor, and I, a naive, aspiring actress, we discovered love through each other. We became engaged, but the conditions were such that our marriage was an impossibility.

I met Billy Gable in Portland during the auditions for the Astoria Players Stock Company, being organized to go on tour in July of '22. Billy was clumsy, unable to read lines, and seemed generally hopeless as a stage prospect. He had been brought around by Earle Larrimore, who sold ties with Billy in a men's store. Earle, a fine young actor, was signed to be the leading man in the group. And I was signed as the ingenue.

Billy hung around after he'd botched his reading and tried to make friends. I didn't like him at first. I thought him aggressive. But I had been raised in a convent, and although I loved it, I learned nothing about the world. I had never had a beau that I cared about before, so I resented him a little initially. But he was always as nice as he could be. A little forward, but charming.

By the time the company was ready to begin the tour, we had become close friends, and Earle and I went to Rex Jewell

GABLE PLOT CASE
Ex-Sweetheart Aids Film Star

Newspaper clipping of the Gable paternity case.

Snapshot of Billy Gable taken by Franz
Dorfler after the Astoria Stock Company
folded in 1922.

who organized the group. We insisted that Billy be taken along
on a trial basis. Mr. Jewell begrudgingly took him on. It meant
so much to Billy.

Billy brought with him his only Brooks Brothers suit and one
spare white shirt with French cuffs in a Gladstone bag. He
always wore French cuffs, even when he was penniless. For having
so little, he always managed to look immaculate. I could never
understand how he did it.

As the tour continued, we became closer and he began to
depend on me. He seemed insecure because of past hardships,
financial troubles, and had to be reassured that he was liked.
Once he confided to me that his mother had died of epilepsy,
and he was afraid of having inherited the disease. Normally,
he was jovial and outgoing.

One day he asked me if I would rehearse his lines and I did.
And so he leaned over and kissed me. This shocked me. I just
sat there because I wasn't accustomed to it. But then I thought
how wonderful this is. I've met somebody who lives to be an
actor and so do I, and wouldn't this be fun? So it didn't take me
long to become terribly fond of him. Soon I couldn't bear to
be away from him.

There were several times that the manager threatened to fire
him for bungling his part or tripping on stage at an inopportune
time. These incidents would send him into fits of depression.
But Bill's inexperience was only a small share of our troubles.
A few weeks after the tour began, one of the managers
absconded with all our receipts, and we were unable to pay our
bills. We tried to carry on as best we could, but without operating
capital it was difficult. Business grew worse. It seemed that the
people of Astoria were rather conservative patrons of the arts.
We began to eat less than three meals a day. A prop boy resorted
to stealing canned goods from the market. But within a month,
we gave up the struggle.

The female lead of the company, Lucille Schumann, had a
kind and gracious mother who lived in a resort town twenty
miles away called Seaside. Lucille invited Earle, Billy and me to
stay with her until a river tour we hoped for could be arranged.
Gratefully, we accepted her invitation, but since her home could
not accommodate all of us, we took turns at beachcombing.
Those of us who had to sleep out built a fire and wrapped
ourselves in blankets against the bitter cold nights.

One day when Billy and I walked with Lucille and Earle
on the Seaside waterfront, a clairvoyant called me over. She told

me that my boyfriend would go much farther than the more handsome fellow, meaning Earle. "He has something wonderful inside of him," she said, "something that others cannot see."
At the time, it seemed a little ridiculous because Earle appeared to have much more promise. When Billy learned of the prediction, he wanted to tell Mr. Jewell who was trying to arrange the new tour.

Neither Billy nor I had ever been at a seacoast resort before, and we took advantage of the romantic, although precarious, living conditions. Mrs. Schumann could shelter us in turns, but she couldn't afford to feed us. For a few days we were allowed to use credit at her grocery store, but when that ran out, we had to shift for ourselves.

Eventually the river tour was arranged and our director called us back to Astoria to begin work. We were to sail down the Columbia River, stopping at the little towns we passed for performances. We were never sure that there would be a performance or that we would get paid. But we took that chance with the local managers. It seemed better to do that than starve.

The journey was made on milk boats, as the cheapest means of transportation. These boats had no cabins and the company had to sleep on deck, rain or shine. It was early fall and the weather was not very pleasant. Billy was not very strong, despite his huge frame. And the ill effects of the hand-to-mouth situation began to tell on him. There was so little money in those days that we often had to choose between pie and soup for our meals when we could afford it.

And much to the manager's dismay, Billy had to be given more parts because several of the actors deserted the company and there was no one left to play their parts. In fact, after Earle was summoned by his aunt, Laura Hope Crews, to Broadway where he made quite a name for himself, Billy was pushed into several leading roles. It was either that or cancel the rest of the tour.

By this time, Billy and I had become engaged. We were so happy all that time, even through the hardest conditions, that everything seemed much better than it was. We were almost oblivious to much of the bitterness. We were always together. And in recollection, it seems that Billy behaved much as a schoolboy in love for the first time. I found it hard to take a walk by myself without having to explain to him where I'd been. It felt strangely wonderful to be loved so passionately.

I used to iron everything for him. He jokingly told me that

he actually fell in love with me when he learned how good I was with an iron. And once when I burned his only spare shirt, I felt miserable until he showed me how to bleach out the burn with peroxide. A hobo taught him that trick, he said.

When the tour ended, I invited Billy to my family's farm in Silverton, Oregon. He needed rest and some good meals badly. He was undernourished and sickly because he never had the money to eat properly. I worried about his unhealthy yellow color and all the weight he lost on the river tour.

My family awaited the arrival of my actor-fiancé with misgiving, expecting a ragged, broken-spirited ham. They were not fond of actors and reluctantly allowed me to pursue that profession only because they were unable to talk me out of it.

But Billy's charm, high spirits and friendly manner won them over from the start. He was a glowing light there on the farm with his dimpled smile, infectious laughter and a desire to please. They were a little taken aback because he called Mom and my sister "Hon" and "Sweetheart" at the start. But it didn't take them long to accept the idea that we were going to be married. However, they were a bit startled at his unhibited manner of seizing me and kissing me wildly at any time, without warning, in anyone's company. He seemed unable to restrain himself.

In short order, Billy and my family had adopted each other. Through the years that Billy kept contact with my parents, he called them mom and dad, as though they had been his own folks. I guess he substituted them for his dead mother and alienated father. He was pleasant and thoughtful, and seemed to want to belong to us.

Billy soon felt more secure than I'd ever seen him. Farm life agreed with him. He loved to put on some old jeans belonging to one of my brothers and wander with me through the fields and nearby woods. We'd climb trees, jump into the hay, tickle each other, laugh and giggle like we were ten years old.

Before long, he pleaded with me to marry him. But I knew that my family opposed the marriage at that time. To marry a penniless actor was out of the question. It wouldn't have been right to marry someone who couldn't support himself, much less a wife. I put him off because I still had my career to think of. And I was afraid of what poverty could do to two people in love. Billy complained but saw it my way when he realized that my mind was made up. He continued, however, to press me for a definite date.

Three weeks after our arrival, we went hop-picking to make

Gable worked for the Silver Falls Timber Company for $3.20 a day in 1922. Here is the ledger of the company and a cancelled check.

a little money. Billy and I took along an armful of books to study. If he expected to be a success, I told him, he would have to improve his grammar. Since he had an inferiority complex about his education, he studied hard, but was unable to stick with it. He just wasn't very intellectual.

When the hop-picking job ended, we returned to the farm and Billy and my younger brother, Fritz, went to Portland and got jobs on a surveying crew. For several weeks, they plowed through timber and mud swinging an ax. Finally the heavy rains forced them to return.

That winter, Billy went to work for the Silver Falls Lumber Company earning $3.20 a day in the loading department. He lived in a boarding house in Silverton, seven miles from the farm. He would walk the distance to the farm on the weekends to see me. The weekdays were depressing but didn't seem so bad when I thought of the weekends.

Something about Billy's character is evident in an incident on his first day at the lumber mill. He wore peg-topped breeches and riding boots to the mill because those were the only clothes he had other than his suit. It was the riding outfit he had worn in "Corinne of the Circus" and Mr. Jewell had let him have it after the show folded in Portland. He suffered much ridicule from the rugged Swedes who worked for the lumber company. He looked a bit like a clown, but he would have died before admitting that those were the only clothes he had to wear. After proving himself a capable worker, he was accepted.

In November, I decided to take singing lessons and moved to Portland where I lived with an older married brother. It was as easy for Billy to come see me there as it was at the farm and he continued to visit me on weekends. A few weeks after I arrived there, Rex Jewell offered me a job with a new musical show he was taking on tour through the Northwest.

When I told Billy that I would be going out of town for months, he didn't like it at all. He especially pouted because this meant that we would be separated at Christmas. But it would have been foolish not to have taken the engagement.

We promised to write every day. Sometimes I would receive two or three letters that had been written the same day. They were filled with how lonely he was without me. And mine were filled with the same sentiments. My only consolation was that he spent Christmas with my family.

During the holidays, storms delayed the mail trains and he didn't receive a single letter from me for over a week, nor I from him. His following letters were filled with chiding and hurt. He was certain that I was forgetting him. I replied quickly that he was never out of my mind for an instant.

In January, 1923, Billy wrote that he had quit the mill and moved to Portland where he found a job as a want ad solicitor for the *Oregonian*. He quit this in March, and worked in a garage and other odd jobs. In the meantime, I had convinced him to study voice, hoping this would revitalize his interest in the theatre, which he seemed to be drifting away from. He began singing lessons with Lawrence Woodfrin, whom I had recommended, and by June had progressed enough to sing in a recital.

My sister Bertha was getting married that same week so I returned from Seattle, where the tour was playing, to attend the wedding and to hear Billy sing. His voice wasn't outstanding but I felt like I was going to burst with pride. This time when he asked me when we were going to get married, I answered "at the end of the year." We spent every moment together before I had to return to Seattle.

A few months later, a friend in Portland informed me about a little theatre that was being opened by Josephine Dillon, a distinguished Broadway actress, who had taught dramatics in New York. Upon hearing this news, I lost no time writing Billy an enthusiastic letter about her work, advising him to get in touch with her immediately. I hoped that she would be able to find a spot for him in her new theatre group.

During his interviews with Miss Dillon, she listened to his ambitions and told him the truth as she saw it. The first thing he would have to do was forget all the eye-catching, attention-getting tricks he'd picked up, and start from the beginning. Then he would have to acquire perfect body control. His eyes, voice, gestures, hands and arms, legs and eyebrows, must become tools for him as a master craftsman of the stage.

She gave him hope, but explained that he was starting late in life and what he had to learn would take years of hard work. She, or someone like her, could teach him, but if she accepted him as a pupil, studying under her must become the only important thing to him in the world. She pointed out that even if he followed all instructions faithfully, it was still a gamble. She could only guarantee that he could be able to make the most of a break when it came along.

He wrote excitedly to me about beginning to study under her. For the first time in over a year, he was once more a part of the theatre, with greater hope than ever before. That revolutionized his whole existence. I was terribly happy for him.

Miss Dillon sent Billy on a three or four week vacation to a ranch to recover his failing health. She got a doctor to prescribe a diet for him, and sensing that Billy had no money, paid for everything herself. Upon his return, she had him take a physical culture course.

After Billy's vacation I noticed that his letters were beginning to lose their intensity. I wrote him that I would be home for Christmas and that we could be married then as I had promised.

I arrived in Portland on Christmas eve, telephoned Billy to meet me at my brother's house where they were having a party. Our reunion was a bit more formal than I had expected, and when I began to tell him about the wedding plans I'd made, he stopped me.

"I don't love you anymore," he said gruffly. "I never believed that this could happen to me. But I'm going to study with Josephine Dillon for the next few years. Without her help, I'll never get anywhere. Working with her has come to mean everything to me."

That shattered me. I felt great physical pain. Unable to answer him, I quickly turned and ran away. The next four days, I could neither eat nor sleep. I would burst into tears each time, my brother or sister-in-law tried to talk to me. Wanting to only die, I withdrew to the security of my parent's farm.

On New Year's Eve, Billy telephoned me there and was terribly apologetic about the other night. He said he didn't mean a single word of what he said, and that he wanted to marry me. He asked to see me.

When I saw him, he took me into his arms and said exactly what I wanted him to say. But somehow it was different. He seemed like a man carrying out an obligation. All his thrilling urgency was gone. Unable to endure it, I made some excuse to put it off. He seemed relieved rather than disappointed. So I told him that under the circumstances, it might be best to break off the engagement and leave things the way they were. He later said that a doctor had told him that he could never get married. It seemed so preposterous that I didn't ask him to explain. I simply said that I didn't think I was ever going to get married either.

In the meantime, I began work with the Forest Taylor Stock Company in Portland. Billy continued to see me, but not as often as he used to. He complained about working days with the telephone company and nights at the theatre.

The boarding house where Gable lived during late 1922 and early 1923.

A newspaper clipping from 1923.

WILLIAM GABLE

Who will be presented by Josephine Dillon at the MacDowell Club on Tuesday.

• • •

MacDowell Programme.

The MacDowell Club has prepared a special programme for the next regular meeting on Tuesday at 3 o'clock in the Woman's Club building for members and guests, presenting Mrs. Carlos Cooper Close and Miss Helen Martin, harpists. The programme follows:

The Ballet of Despair..........Bewberg
Under the direction of Miss Josephine Diffon
The Spirit ....Alice Price Moore
The Poet................William C. Gable
Accompaniment
Piano............Mrs. Helen Van Houten
Violin.............Miss Gertrude Hoeber
Cello................Miss Prospera Pozzi
ORTLAND.

The next of this number is from the poem "La Ballade du despspire," by Henry Murger, and tells of a young poet in direst poverty who, having lost love, refuses fame, wealth and royalty, but welcomes death, which brings him surcease from his earthly woes.

Mrs. Close and Miss Martin will give two groups of harp duets.

Gable snapped by Franz Dorfler in front of a music practice studio they rented together in Portland, Oregon (1924).

One of my worst nights came when Billy and Miss Dillon dropped in at the theatre where I was working. They wanted to borrow some scenery. He introduced me to Miss Dillon who turned her nose up at me. I could tell she was in love with him. But I didn't hate her.

Miss Dillon upstaged me that evening. And what was far more important was that Billy did too. That was one lesson, upstaging, he learned from her that he hadn't told me about.

I never saw Miss Dillon again, except when she came into the little Hollywood dress shop where I was working in the early thirties. She bought a blouse from me and paid for it by check as "Mrs. Clark Gable." I remember thinking then that she did it just to spite me because she knew who I was, even though she didn't acknowledge the fact.

To my astonishment, Billy kept seeing me and renewing my hope for us with every visit. In fact, he would get intensely jealous whenever he saw me with another man.

That summer, Miss Dillon left for Los Angeles to open a drama school and before leaving she got Billy a job with the same stock company I was with. But working together on the same stage awoke in Billy no glowing memories of Astoria or the nights on the milk boat. It was quite the opposite. He seemed to be avoiding me. Once or twice when I accidentally encountered him backstage, I came close to telling him off. Each time, I was just able to run back to my dressing room.

Billy remained with the company for only two weeks. Forest Taylor gave him only minor roles, that of Chang Lee in *East is West,* and Harry Haydock in *Main Street.* In those two shows, Billy had himself billed as W. C. Gable. It was so unnerving working with him in a dressing room a couple of doors down that I was almost glad when he left to join Miss Dillon in Hollywood, presumably to continue his lessons. At that time, Hollywood and Los Angeles were the theatrical center of the west coast, and the home of motion pictures as well. If he drew attention on the stage, then perhaps films would follow.

I stayed on in Portland, working in a musical show. When that folded, I got a chance to go to San Francisco. The city had always fascinated me, so I went. In the meantime, I had decided to concentrate on dancing. I approached it with enthusiasm and met with more than a fair amount of success, finally being fortunate enough to open my own school across from the Gerry and Curan Theatres.

The next time I saw Billy was a year later when he came to

San Francisco with a road company. Through a mutual friend he found out where I was and called me. He left a ticket for me at the box office and asked to meet me after the show. I agreed and was excited and nervous about seeing him again. That evening he asked me what I thought about his performance. I told him that he still seemed to lack polish but that Miss Dillon had helped him enormously. He said so too, but mentioned nothing about being married to her at the time.

In the following months he returned to San Francisco with different shows and always came to call on me. He appeared glad to be with me and so I continued to see him. We'd kiss goodnight but didn't get more involved, even though he remained the love of my life. He was still underfed and haggard but the dental work he had done had improved his looks considerably. And he was slowly improving as an actor. The last play he came to San Francisco with was *The Last Mile,* in 1930. And by that time he had changed his name to Clark.

That same year, I decided to move southward. I wanted to get some sun. I loved San Francisco dearly, but it is quite cold and foggy there. Moving to Hollywood, I took an apartment on Gower Street with Dorothy Fox, a girl friend who came down with me.

Somehow Clark found out where we were staying and would come over for dinner. I still didn't know that he was married to Miss Dillon. One evening he mentioned casually that he was getting a divorce. It surprised me, to say the least. During all of our meetings in San Francisco, he had said nothing. And he said nothing now about his plan to marry an even older woman as soon as the divorce became final.

He didn't speak too highly of Josephine. I didn't like that about him. Perhaps he was trying to justify his divorce. We both knew why he had married her. He said that she "is a fine woman. And she sure helped me in my work. But she can't stop playing teacher. She is just too domineering. Sometimes she acts like she's Mrs. God."

I still hoped that we could be reconciled, but I guess I knew that it was impossible. From our conversations, I knew that his career was too important. But I found no one else, so I kept on hoping. I'd already gone through the worst years of hell after our breakup and now found myself falling in love with him every time I saw him. Sometimes I wished that I hadn't met him because I was unable to accept any of the other proposals I'd had. I couldn't marry someone else while I still loved Clark.

Franz Dorfler in the early 1940's, when she was under contract to MGM.

Some evenings when he came over he would play the piano and we would all sing. We were enchanted with him. Sometimes when he talked of the progress he was making, I sat there just looking and listening, with mouth open and thinking "Oh, you wonderful thing!" which was, I suppose, what he wanted.

More often he discussed his fears of not making good. While making *The Easiest Way,* his first picture for MGM, he complained that "neither Constance Bennet nor the director know I'm alive." And he added, "You're the only friend I have in this town. I hate everybody at the studio, everybody I work with. And nobody at MGM likes me." He felt lost and out of place as a newcomer at the big studio, even after he got his contract.

Once he started making good in films, I didn't see him anymore. In fact, I didn't see him again till his lawyers found me for that trial in 1937.

The evening of the trial, Clark threw a dinner party and invited me. We reminisced and talked about old times. He knew that I wasn't doing so well financially and asked MGM to hire me for their stock company. I did a little singing and dancing and stock work in short subjects.

At the studio, Clark would walk right past me, pretending that he didn't see me. Once he became important, he forgot his old friends. I never saw him again on a friendly basis.

I stayed with MGM through the first few years of World War II. Then there were a lot of layoffs because fewer pictures were being made. And eventually, I got the ax. I suppose that if I had gone to Clark, he would have made them keep me on, but I was too proud for that.

Once I left the studio, I never saw Clark again. I never went to his pictures because I knew him. I knew all of his expressions, his gestures, the raising of one eyebrow, the crooked smile, his dimples and wink. He never really changed. A bit polished, but still the same.

In the final analysis, Clark got what he wanted, but he had to work hard for it. He married two women he didn't love to further his career, and that's something I couldn't have done. But then he did a number of things that I didn't think were right. He had a lot of hard times, and he drank a lot, but he managed to win in the end. He never took advantage of me and I've always respected him for that. I just wish that things had worked out better for us.

CLARK GABLE, THE STAGE ACTOR
BY PAUL FIX

I came out from New York in 1922, a real dewy kid with a
bride, just to see what California was all about. The climate made
me stay. It was beautiful country then. There was nobody
around, no smog. It was a paradise. This area started to go to
hell following World War II when all the GI's coming through
here discovered it. Right after the war, people began moving
here by the thousands and everything changed.

But in 1922, Hollywood was just a sleepy little town. We
were on an extended honeymoon, living off some money I had
inherited. We rented a bungalow from a man named Webster
Collison, who had already retired from the picture business, if
you can imagine that. We became friends and talked about the
movies. It wasn't very promising, I remember him saying. The
pictures already had a lot of talent and weren't interested in
getting more. At the time, there were only two casting agents
in town.

Anyway, he introduced me to Neal Hart, who eventually
called me to do a picture. I played a young smart-alecky kid who
comes out West with his sister to live on a ranch they inherited.
The hero, who was played by various actors like Hart, Ken
Maynard, Col. Tim McCoy, and a lot of others through the
years from 1922 to 1936, would always have to save my neck
and would always fall in love with my sister. I must have made
over forty one- and two-reelers like that.

But making silent pictures wasn't real steady employment
so I also became active in stage work. I met Clark Gable when
I went to audition for a part in a play by Sidney Howard called
Lucky Sam McCarver. Pauline Fredericks was the female lead.
At the time she was the top West Coast tragedian; her tour
de force was *Madam X*. John Cromwell was her leading man
and also directed *Lucky Sam McCarver*.

In the play she was an exhibition dancer in a night club of
which Gable was the manager. I played a young kid who shoots
her boy friend in a jealous fit. Cromwell as Lucky Sam covered
up the crime and ended up marrying Pauline.

Stu Erwin was the stage manager and he, Gable, and I
became good friends. We used to bum around together. Clark
was married to an older woman named Josephine Dillon. She
tried to help his career. I guess she was his acting coach, but
couldn't get him anything good in the movies. I'd get a few jobs
once in a while, but Clark never got anything.

Clark had an old automobile that he was real proud of.
It was a Roamer and had no top on it. It was designed after

the Rolls Royce. Clark would drive it over to my place on Sunset Drive. Stu would take the bus over. I owned a putter and Clark had a driver or an iron. We'd go out to Griffith Park, where they'd put in a golf course, and look around the roughs for stray balls. Then with the two clubs we'd play golf all day. We'd flip to see who went first.

I did quite a few shows with Clark. *Madame X, Chicago, The Last Mile. Chicago* was a big hit, with Nancy Carroll, a picture star of those days. It played eighteen weeks in Hollywood. Usually a good show lasted four weeks. *The Last Mile* was the play that catapulted Clark into films.

But before *The Last Mile* came along, things became so tough around here that Clark left for Tucson with a stock company. Soon after he was gone, I met a producer here who was going to do *Hit the Deck* in Los Angeles. He didn't have a part for me, but he had one for Clark. I wrote him, but he wired back that he had a pretty good guarantee there at $150 a week. And it was too good an offer to turn down.

That was a good salary then—if you could get it every week. I guess it would be equal to about $300-$350 now. Remember that in those days you could get a shot of good whiskey for a quarter. Makes a difference.

But Clark didn't stay in Tucson very long. With the stock company, he soon went to Texas, where he met a divorced gal with a lot of money. In the meantime, he had separated from his wife. He went to New York to crash Broadway and later married this Texas dame. In New York he did a great job in a play, *Machinal,* but it didn't amount to anything.

A few years later, he was asked to play "Killer" Mears in *The Last Mile* here in Los Angeles. Clark came out for it and we were reunited in that production after about three years. That play made it for him. We went on tour with it up to San Francisco, where we played for six weeks.

Although it was an Equity show, all the actors had signed salary guarantee waivers because the producer, Louis MacLoon, had asked us to. We had all signed waivers with him before, so nobody had any doubts about being paid. The payroll was always handed out between the first and second acts of the Saturday matinee. But that sixth Saturday, there was no payroll. MacLoon sent somebody over to let us know that we would be paid that night. So nobody got excited.

That afternoon, I stopped into Clark's dressing room and told him that we hadn't been paid. He said that he was going

82

Two scenes from the 1925 Los Angeles production of "Chicago"

Paul Fix, Nancy Carroll, Gable, and Art Minor

Gable, Barry Townley, Paul Fix, Nancy Carroll, and Kay Campbell

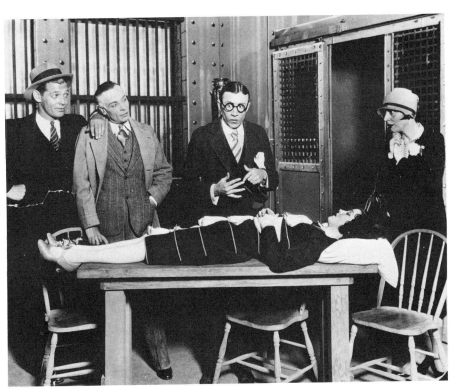

over to see MacLoon. So I went with him. MacLoon had been expecting Clark, but was stunned to see me.

"What's he want?" MacLoon asked Clark.

"He wants to borrow some money," Clark said.

"How much?"

"$150," I answered. That was my weekly salary.

"Keep this under your hat," he pressed me while counting out the cash. "Otherwise everybody'll be over here."

"Sure," I said. I knew how to play that.

We got our dough. But that night after the show there was no payoff to the others. MacLoon had split with all the money. It was like a riot. Somebody said that there was cash at the box office, but Louis had raided that too between the second and third acts.

His wife, Lillian Albertson, had directed the play and MacLoon had always produced for her. But their marriage was breaking up and this was going to be her last play with him. So he made a killing at the expense of a lot of people. He hit out for Connecticut and never produced again. Last I heard, he went into the yacht business, but that collapsed. He died some years ago.

While the third act of *The Last Mile* was playing the night he took off with our money, one of his assistants, Vic Mole, a sweet little guy, came back stage off the street. He walked along the dressing rooms, and mine was the first one he passed. So I pushed him into mine and said, "I wanna see you."

He had the tickets to L.A. for the company in his hands. At least MacLoon did that much for us. When some other guys saw that I had shoved Vic into my room, they started coming down to see what was up. I ended up behind him where he had the tickets and I managed to grab two. One for me and one for Clark.

Before long all the tickets were gone. When I saw Clark, he already had one. So I had an extra ticket. There was this one guy who came up empty-handed. We were all teasing him about how he was the only one stranded in San Francisco. He could probably hitch a ride in a couple of days if he thumbed real hard, we told him. He became despondent.

Clark knew I had the extra ticket, and he finally growled, "For Chrissakes, give him the ticket."

That was the play that established Clark on the West Coast. He had a lot of screen tests right after, but none of them were any good. Everybody turned him down, Zanuck at Warners,

Fox, everybody. Then finally he played a heavy in a Bill Boyd picture that got him a break at MGM. They eventually gave him a good role in an Adela Rogers St. John story about her father, in which Clark pushed Norma Shearer around. That film was as famous at that time as Cagney's squashing the grapefruit into Mae Clark's face. He was off to the races.

When I think of all the stage productions we'd done together, it's kind of strange that we never worked in the same film.

I continued to see Clark to the end, but not as much as in the old days. And it was understandable. Whenever I was at MGM for anything, I would ask to see him. I used to have a helluva time getting to him. Often my messages would never reach him. *Everybody* wanted to see Clark Gable. And if you tried, they thought you were some kind of crackpot. Finally, he put them straight about me and I didn't have trouble after that.

A lot of people say that he was highbrow, but that's a lot of shit. He didn't change much after he became a star. He only became a little more refined, smoother. For example, his ears stuck out and he got them fixed. Christ almighty, they stuck out like barn doors and he was sensitive about them. They did it after he was established at Metro.

By this time, he had already had his teeth recapped. They were in terrible shape when he first came to Hollywood. His first wife helped him some, but it was Pauline Fredericks who paid for most of it. She liked him, and he liked her. But it was quite a respectable affair. In fact, very few people ever knew it was going on. And later he got an entire new set of teeth on Metro.

But no matter how successful or famous he got, he never let it go to his head. He never became too good for his old friends. He had two marvelous expressions that he used all the time: "Well, chew me up and spit me out," and "Christ, it smells like a flicker's nest." I don't know what a flicker was. I don't know if he knew, but he used it to express contempt for the smell of a room or something. He's the only one I ever heard use these expressions.

Paul Fix today

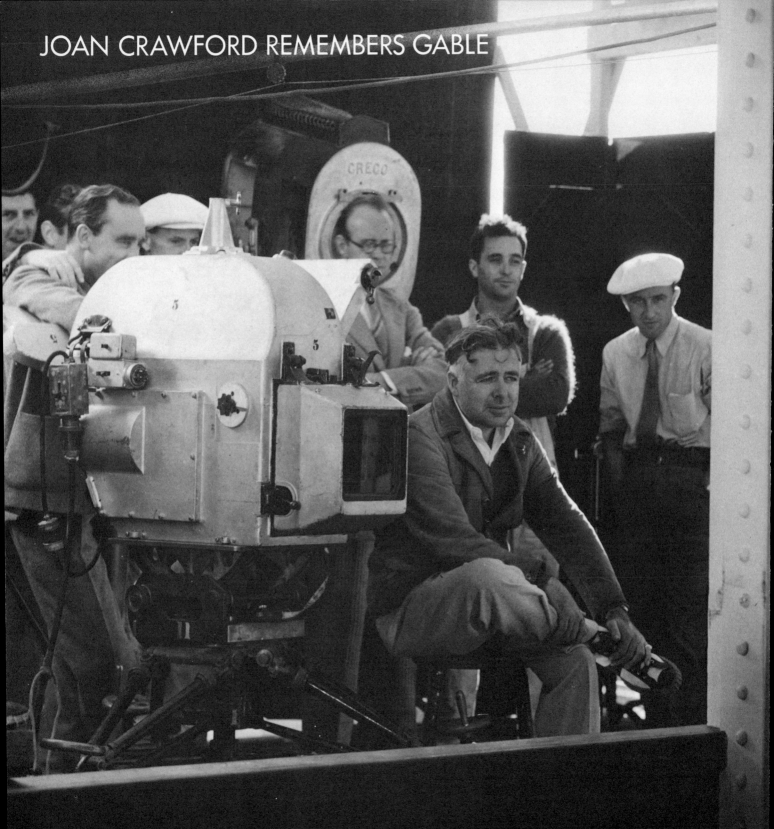

Preceding page:
Clarence Brown, who first recognized
Gable's physical quality, directs him and
Joan Crawford in a scene from "Chained"
(1934).

Gable and Miss Crawford on the set of
"Possessed" (1931).

Dance Fools, Dance (1931) . . . based on the shooting of Jake
Lingle and the St. Valentine's Day Massacre . . . was memorable
for the presence of an electrifying man, one who couldn't miss
stardom—Clark Gable. He played Jack Luva, the gangster heavy,
and in one scene where he grabbed me and threatened the life
of my brother, his nearness had such impact, my knees buckled.

If he hadn't held me by both shoulders, I'd have dropped.
I wasn't the only one who noticed Clark. Every girl on the lot
noticed him. So did Mr. Mayer with his unerring eye for talent;
and the consequence was fairly unique in the industry.

My next picture was *Complete Surrender,* with Johnny Mack
Brown as the Salvation Army man who restores this cabaret girl's
self-confidence. After the preview, Mr. Mayer called us back for
a total remake. Johnny's performance was excellent, but Mr.
Mayer had seen the chemistry between Clark and me and thought
he scented box-office dynamite. This time the picture was called
Laughing Sinners and Clark Gable was the Salvation Army man.
We didn't have too many scenes together, but they were powerful
ones and went well.

It had taken my career a long time to start rolling, but it was
on its way like some lovely snowball. Everything we did made
money. Occasionally, we even made a good picture. *Possessed,*
for example. In this film, Clark and I hit our stride. In spite of
the fact that I was emotionally distraught. The shadow of divorce
colored my mood.

Here I was, lonely, dejected over the failure of my marriage,
and every day Clark Gable walked onto the set—earlier than
necessary. We took to arriving earlier just to have a little more
time with each other. In the picture, we were madly in love.
When the scenes ended, the emotion didn't—we were each
playing characters very close to our own. It was a love bounded
by the flats on the set. Perhaps twice a week, we lunched together
—he couldn't absent himself oftener from the publicity table
where he and Spencer Tracy always ate, without being
conspicuous. Occasionally we'd break away early, go for a quiet
ride along the sea. And all day we'd seek each other's eyes. It
was glorious and hopeless. There seemed nothing we could do
about it. There was no chance for us.

Clark insisted that I was wrong, that there was hope, that we
could marry. We talked of marriage, of course. But I dared not
ruin the dreams. I'd rather live with them unfulfilled than
have them broken.

Outside the studio we never even held hands, never held

more than a momentary glance. Clark was married. I was often
in groups with him and Ria socially. She was a charming lady,
so happy in Clark's success, so anxious not to intrude on his
glamour, and you felt like a heel cherishing this emotion for her
husband. I wouldn't have hurt her for the world. Neither would
Clark. And yet the rumors were rampant. "What star is interested
in her leading man?" "There's a top actress and a grand gal who's
running a couple of risks. She's wide-eyed in another hubby's
direction."

I'll never forget lunching at a popular restaurant with
Ria Gable. A writer rushed up to the table and gushed, "I just
saw you in *Possessed*. Joan, you were wonderful, inspired, the
way you look at Clark, anyone can tell you're crazy about him."

I blanched, turned quickly to the writer and said, "May I
present my good friend, Mrs. Clark Gable?"

It was like living over a lighted powder keg, but it was
worth it. I've said that Clark could melt you with a look.

He was extremely sensitive, but like most physically big
guys, afraid to show it. There is probably only one other man of
our time whose personality incorporated the same blend of
toughness and tenderness, the same ability to be a woman's man
and a man's man—Ernest Hemingway.

Much as I cared for Clark, the deep conviction that we could
last was lacking within me and I knew it. I settled for friendship.
We always worked well together, and harmoniously . . . our
only argument when I refused to do *Parnell* . . . we met often
socially . . . Carole Lombard and I were good friends.

After Carole's death, it was a long while before Clark came
back to work and when he did come to the studio, he was solitary.
He wouldn't even go to lunch in the commissary; his set was
closed; and with policemen standing guard to insure his privacy,
he'd occasionally sit out in the sun. I'd check with his secretary
to ask how he was. Finally one day I wrote a note and asked if
he'd like to stop by the house for a cocktail. He wrote back
saying he'd be there.

That night he talked for hours, talked and talked and talked.
He'd listened to me once, now I listened to him, knitted, listened,
and filled the ice bucket. The next day I received twelve-dozen
red roses with the longest stems I'd ever seen. From then on for
the next four or five months, Clark stopped by the house every
single day. He wasn't the gay romantic Clark I'd first known,
he wasn't the easy-going Clark, he was a moody man who
needed friendship.

Gable and Joan Crawford in "Dancing Lady"

"You're living in the past," I told him. "You have a guilt complex because you didn't go with Carole on that trip. You couldn't go, you were working! You've had your grief, Clark, now pull yourself out of it."

Gradually, he did.

And no one was more pleased than I when he married Kay (1955). I love Kay, she's wonderful and she made him happier than he'd ever been in his life. They made each other happy. There had been many men in love with Kay, many girls adored Clark, but when the two got together, it was just right . . . the kind of close harmony that makes for deep contentment. I'm glad "the King" had that.

A condensed extract from "A Portrait of Joan," by Joan Crawford, with Jane Ardmore

A 1934 portrait by Clarence Sinclair Bull.

Gable and Rosalind Russell on the set of "China Seas" (1935), their first film together.

ROSALIND RUSSELL

"The nicest thing about working with Clark Gable was his humor, and by that I mean not only his personal witticisms, but his humor about himself. He was one of the few actors I ever knew who had genuine humor about himself. He actually, I believe, considered himself rather ludicrous at times, having to do certain things that he considered awkward or possibly unnatural. He was a totally natural human being. He was a rarity in many ways, but perhaps the rarest of all his characteristics was that at all times he was himself—Clark Gable. . . .

"I met him on the set of *China Seas,* our first picture together, and he made a comment about feeling silly about having to be madeup. He didn't like makeup and wouldn't let it be put on him. I know that he had tremendous influence on bringing about the fact that actors today wear little or no makeup. Only perhaps for character work. Clark just wouldn't have it. He had the attitude that it was not natural.

"I don't believe that he really considered himself an *actor,* per se. I think that he thought of himself purely as a man, and that his work was acting. He did a job and did it with heart, professionally, without cheating. He was direct with an honesty from within. So many people try to be something other than what they are, rather than developing their own resources. Clark merely developed his own resources possibly better than any other actor. This was one of the secrets to his success.

"I don't believe that he was a manufactured personality. I think it was the other way around. He was himself, and the studio, MGM, was wise enough and smart enough to realize that they had a wonderfully vibrant and natural personality in this man. And they created his public image from himself. This is something you don't see very often, and this is what his true greatness was.

"Years later when we did *They Met in Bombay,* he was just as real and natural as he had been years before. And so wonderfully helpful. He again was very generous in working. He always shared, never upstaged his marks or the other performers. There was nothing small or petty about him. He was as big as he was physically.

"So many things were said about Clark being 'Ze Great Lover', when he was just tremendously graceful. No director ever had to give him directions in a love scene. There was never any toe-to-toe for a screen kiss. He was a very graceful person with his body, and there wasn't all this enormous clinching and awkwardness. Much like a ballet dancer in a sense, he had rhythm and timing. He was beautiful to play a love scene with.

"He certainly lived his life and colored it with experience. He filled his horizons with other things than just his work. And that's another reason for his success, I think. The balance between the private and the professional. He had a great deal more to give to his work."

LANA TURNER

"The first thing that comes to mind when I think of co-starring with Clark Gable in *Honky Tonk* in 1940 is that I was completely terrified. I was still in my teens and this was my first starring role. And to find myself playing opposite the King was most devastating. So I was nervous. But I wasn't afraid of him. I think I was more in shock—an 'Is this really me?' and 'Somebody pinch me' kind of thing.

"But God bless Clark. I'm sure that he, as well as the rest of the cast, the director, and the crew, could see me trembling whenever I would have to go into a scene with him. And it was only after we had finished the picture that I realized how very much this man had helped me. Knowing how frightened I was, and in awe of him really, he would kind of tease me out of it and joke with me, trying to put me at ease. And it was really important to me, not only for the film, but in my life.

"He was very kind and considerate to me. Whenever I fluffed a line, he'd say, 'That's all right, Baby. Now don't you worry about it.' And you know what he'd do? He'd blow a couple lines just so I wouldn't feel so bad. And he used to play practical jokes on me because, he said, I was a good sport."

JOAN BLONDELL

"It was the joy of your life to know Clark Gable. He was everything good that you can think of. He had delicious

Gable and Turner, a photograph by Clarence Sinclair Bull.

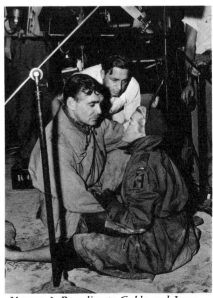

Mervyn LeRoy directs Gable and Lana Turner in a scene for "Homecoming" (1948).

Gable chats with Joan Blondell on the set of "Adventure."

humor; he had great compassion; he was always a fine old teddy bear. He was a man that guys loved, women loved, and children loved. Somehow, he just made people grin. Perhaps it was because he was so unaffected. In no way was he conscious of his good looks, as were most of the other men in pictures of that time. Clark was very un-actory.

"The difference between Clark and other actors was that he was able to see himself objectively, and he always did it tongue-in-cheek. It kind of amused him when the girls knees would cave in around him. He was flattered, of course, but mostly he was gentle and tender about it, and amused. It was like he was sitting aside, looking at someone else being worshipped by the pretty little girls. He had a very sweet attitude about it.

"And he never took advantage of that marvelous appeal he had. He handled himself very well. I guess that's why men liked him so. He was completely real in every sense of the word. He was just a helluva guy."

EDWARD DMYTRYK

"When assigned to direct Clark Gable in *Soldier of Fortune* in 1955, I was a little apprehensive at first because I was afraid there might be a little trouble getting a performance out of him. I knew him as a great personality on the screen but personalities, in Hollywood particularly, have a reputation usually of not being very good actors. Often false, as I found out in Gable's case.

"He was a wonderful guy to work with, like most of the oldtimers. The one noticeable thing about the older actors, those who grew up in the early days of motion pictures, is that they were so very well disciplined. Actors like Gable, Spencer Tracy, Bogart, Van Johnson, all of them were always on time, and very rarely did any of them complain about anything.

"Gable was never late on the set. He only had one rule. He always quit at five—I think so he could start drinking. Gable was quite a drinker. In fact, most of the older actors were; and Gable did as well as any of them. Never, of course, on the set. He always came to work ready and clear. But in the evening he was a very heavy drinker. As a matter of fact, he told me once that if he couldn't drink he'd just as soon die.

"He drank quite a bit but I don't think it affected his abilities as an actor. Late in life, he had problems with long scenes but that was due to something else which may or may not have had anything to do with the drinking. In the last few years, under tension—not normally, strangely enough, just under tension—he used to shake. For instance, he wouldn't do it during a rehearsal but as soon as we started shooting, almost as soon as you said action, he would start a slight tremor and then if the scene went for any length of time it would get to be a decided shake, so that I used to have to cut the scenes down to three or four lines, no more than that. In the long shots, it didn't matter of course because it wasn't noticeable, but in the close shots it was.

"I imagine the tension was due to nerves. Part of it may have been physical. I don't know. It may have been due to his having been such a good solid drinker most of his life. It could have been just nerves, but God knows he'd made pictures for an awful long time. I think he felt fairly secure as an actor. He believed in himself as an actor. He didn't have the doubt that some people had about him.

"We had an interesting experience in Japan. We went to one of those theatres where they have nothing but women performers; and after watching the show for a little while we were taken backstage by the manager to meet the star of the production. She was in a Kabuki outfit and her face was all made up with rice powder. She took one look at Gable who towered above her. He held out his hand and she took it and tears streamed out of her eyes down through her makeup on both cheeks, making little rivers right down to her chin. She didn't say a word. All she did was look at him and cry. Now obviously a man who has that kind of thing happen to him must know that he affects people, that he affects women. He also affected men, I must say, because as you know he was a man's man and I never knew a man's man like Gable.

Dmytryk and Gable on the Set of "Soldier of Fortune," on location in Hong Kong.

"Gable just had a great deal of personality. He had it to the nth degree, more than anybody else I can remember, with the possible exception of Valentino. But it was a different kind of thing in Valentino. Valentino did appeal specifically to the women, whereas Gable appealed to everybody, affected everybody. I think he had a great effect on styles, on thinking, on everything else of his generation."

LARRY BARBIER

"A Free Soul" (1931): Director Clarence Brown blocks out a scene in miniature with his stars, Leslie Howard, Gable, and Norma Shearer.

"I was in charge of the MGM still department when we met on the set of *A Free Soul*. They were trying to tape his ears back. The director, Clarence Brown, sent him over to makeup, and Jack Dawn pinned his ears against his head with fish skin. Clark went along with it for a couple of days. Then suddenly he ripped off the tape and said that they were going to film him the way he looked or he was going back to New York, to the theatre. He was determined, and they let him have his way. In those early days they considered his big ears drawbacks, but they became one of his best-known trademarks.

"I guess Clark thought that pinning his ears back was a compromise, going Hollywood. You know, pretending to be something you aren't. He was too natural to try to fool anybody. I sometimes suspected that he really wasn't altogether satisfied about being an actor. After he returned from serving overseas in World War II and seeing the boys that served with him getting killed, and himself in a couple of close matches over there, he thought this was kind of a silly business to get back into.

"A lot of people will tell you he was pretty tight. But this was a carryover from the days when he was down and out and didn't have two coins to rub together. He was afraid that his luck would end and he would be poor again. Because he was always insecure, he was constantly saving. Every once in awhile, he'd say to me, 'Larry, I'm sure a lucky sonuvabitch.' That's the way he approached it. To him it was all luck. And he figured it could suddenly change.

"He usually didn't give presents, he was so thrifty. And a lot of times he just didn't think of it. I remember that one of the few presents I ever received from him came from his wife, Carole Lombard. For Christmas, one year she got me an expensive robe. When I saw Clark, I thanked him for the Christmas present. 'Oh,' he said. 'What'd I give you?' That's when I knew that Carole had bought the gift and signed his name to it.

"Another time, he gave me a car that he had gotten as a St. Valentine's day gag from Carole painted white with red hearts all over it. Clark spent some fifteen hundred fixing it up and repainting it black. He got a belt out of passing Cadillacs and Lincoln Continentals in that old rattle-box. But after about eight months he became bored with it. And whenever I went over to see him, I'd see it sitting in the yard. So one day I told him that I had a kid sixteen years old going to high school and I had to buy him a car. I asked if he would sell me his old car.

" 'Hell, no,' he said. 'Do you think I want him to wrap himself around some telephone pole and kill himself?' I didn't argue. You learned not to argue with Clark. He was stubborn as they came.

"But a few weeks later, after I promoted him a new Dodge station wagon with special gear for hunting, he drove me to the nearest Department of Motor Vehicles. Then he asked me for a buck. 'What for?' I asked. He said that he was going to sign his old black car over to me, but damn if he was going to pay the buck transfer fee, too. That was just like him.

"When I told the boys on the set about the car, they said, 'You must have hypnotized him. That's the first thing he ever gave away.'

"We took that car on a trip once and got it up to 102 mph. No wonder he thought my son might get hurt driving it. It seemed that everything Clark owned went fast. He loved to race. One of his favorite hobbies was racing motorcycles in the valley with Keenan Wynn, Al Menasco and a couple other guys. They'd have a couple of drinks and then fool around on those bikes like kids. At 90 mph they'd play tag. They'd have to tag each other with a wheel or something. I never rode with them, but I did ride with Clark in his Jag a couple times. And, believe me, he liked speed.

"Another typically Gable characteristic was that he expected to be met halfway. If he could show up on time for a special photography session, he expected his co-star to be there too. Once, after waiting for an hour and a half for Vivien Leigh to arrive, he fumed out of the studio saying, 'Time and Gable wait for no actress.' She finally showed thirty minutes later and was furious that Gable hadn't waited. When I set the thing up again and both were on time, Clark, knowing that I was the one responsible to the Studio for the pictures, pulled me aside and asked if I got in trouble for what had happened. I told him no. 'Okay,' he said. 'I just didn't want you holding the bag.' That was the sort of guy he was, always looking out for the little man. He never forgot that he had once been a little guy himself.

"There was little that disgusted him more than to see other stars lording it over less important people. Once he and I walked by a set just as Spencer Tracy was bawling out everyone near him in rage. As we passed by, Gable said, 'Larry, if I ever start acting like that, do me a favor and kick me in the butt.' I promised to and would have, but it never became necessary.

"But after he left MGM, his home studio for 25 years, I noticed that he had grown a little bitter. He was unhappy about Dore Shary, who had replaced Louis B. Mayer as studio boss. He thought it unfair that MGM did not cut him in on the millions that they made with *Gone With the Wind*.

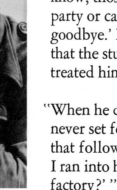

A 1934 study by Clarence Sinclair Bull.

"I remember his last day on the lot. I walked him out to his Jag after he finished the picture he was working on. He said, 'You know, those bastards in the front office didn't give me a farewell party or cake or anything. They didn't even bother to say goodbye.' It's not that Clark expected a party, but he felt bad that the studio whose reputation he helped build in the thirties treated him shabbily because of economic difficulties.

"When he drove off the lot that day, Clark vowed that he would never set foot on it again. He never did. And I guess in the years that followed he became more cynical about Metro. Whenever I ran into him, he'd ask me if I was 'still out at the goddamned factory?' "

CLARENCE SINCLAIR BULL

"Generally, Clark was easy to photograph because he didn't have a preconceived idea of what he should look like in stills. He didn't try to tell me which was his best profile; in short, he didn't tell me my business. Spencer Tracy was easy to photograph, too, once you got him in the gallery. But it was like pulling teeth to get him to come down. He wasn't as easy-going. He didn't seem to care about the pictures.

"On the other hand, Clark went out of his way to co-operate and make himself available. He knew that I had to have certain pictures of him and that it would go easier if we both wanted them. I think Clark liked having his picture taken because he was so photogenic. The photographs always looked like him, even flattered him. He often said that he liked my work, but I don't believe that he was ever deeply concerned about his pictures. He just wanted to make the whole business more pleasant.

"From the photographer's point of view, it was easy to shoot Gable because he was so natural. He didn't try to give you static, dry poses. He'd just move and try different things. He could always tell when he struck a pose or expression that was good.

"Normally, I had to pick up the stills and portraits of the stars while a film was shooting and as the principals became available. I was lucky to get them for even a short time. And if I didn't get all the necessary pictures during production, then the star had to be called back to the studio, and in most cases put back on the payroll. This could get very expensive. Clark had a pay waiver put in his contract that allowed a certain amount of time for still photography. Clark once told me that he considered himself very fortunate to be doing so well and didn't mind giving of his time when needed.

"When I introduced retouching to MGM, and this takes me back a few years, a lot of the stars had certain retouching requirements written into their contracts. But Gable? He couldn't have cared less. 'Whatever you think' was his usual reply to questions about this. The only thing that he was ever anxious about were his ears. During one sitting after the studio had made a big thing about his ears, he asked, 'What am I going to do with these flops?' I told him to forget them. 'In their prominence, they're a bit like Valentino's nostrils,' I said. 'If nostrils can become sex symbols, so can ears.' He never said another word about them to me."

A publicity shot for "Red Dust" by Clarence Sinclair Bull. Gable was sensitive about this one for a while because of the way it shows off his ears.

As "Killer" Mears in "The Last Mile

FORBIDDEN PARADISE

1924. Paramount.

Directed by Ernest Lubitsch. From the stage play by Lajos Biro and Menyhert Lengyel. Adapted by Agnes Christine Johnston and Hans Kraly.
Release date: November 30, 1924.

CAST: Pola Negri, Rod La Rocque, Adolphe Menjou, Pauline Stark, Fred Malatesta, Nick De Ruiz, Mme. D'Aumery. (Cark Gable in his first motion picture as an extra.)

In "What Price Glory?"

WHAT PRICE GLORY?

1925. West Coast Road Company.

A drama in three acts by Maxwell Anderson. Directed by Lillian Albertson. Produced by Louis O. Macloon in May, 1925.

COMMENT: Lillian Albertson

"My husband, Louis Macloon, and I brought *Romeo and Juliet* to the West Coast with Jane Cowl and we needed some tall players for soldiers. A big, awkward boy came walking down the aisle of the half-lit theatre toward the stage where we were rehearsing. Jane and I were talking over some stage details at the time. He inquired for me. Both of us were struck simultaneously by his height—which was one of the necessary qualifications for the new extras needed as soldiers. Jane said, 'Look at that boy. He'll do. What's his name? He looks like he has something.' That was Clark Gable and we engaged him. At that time, Clark was terribly thin and he was awkward . . . but he had a rugged quality of physique and personality that was arresting. I wasn't particularly interested in his potentialities until he appeared in *What Price Glory?* for us. His voice was high-pitched. We worked with him to help him lower it; it wasn't quite heavy enough to match his general makeup.

"In *What Price Glory?* we gave him a chance as one of the three roughnecks, known as Kiper. The role was that of a fellow who knows he is somebody and tells the world about it in tough, humorous language. It was Clark's first real part with us and established him in our minds as a hardy, virile type. And when Hale Hamilton who played Sergeant Quirt in the first Los Angeles production left the troupe, we gave Clark the chance to follow him in the role. He had fifteen weeks with that engagement. And within a year, he had appeared in two other productions of the play. The last one starred the late Louis Wolheim as Captain Flagg.

"Then in succession Clark did six other plays for us, mostly in minor roles with one exception, the role of the reporter in *Chicago,* in the spring of 1927 showed him off well. He also did *The Copperhead* with Lionel Barrymore, whom he greatly admired. He was an old judge with a long white beard in *Madame X* with Pauline Frederick; character roles of old men in *Lucky Sam McCarver* and *Lady Frederick;* and a drunken sailor in *Lullaby. Chicago* was the last play he did with us before going to New York and returning to 1930 for our production of *The Last Mile* which led to films for him. In between plays, he did bits in pictures to get him through the air pockets so to speak."

William Haines shows George O'Hara how to hold a baseball in "The Pacemakers." Gable, an extra, sits on the left.

THE PACEMAKERS

1925. F. B. O.

Twelve chapters, two reels each. Directed by Wesley Ruggles. Scenario by Beatrice Van, based on the original stories of H. C. Witwer. Photography by Lee Garmes. Release dates: March 1 to August 2, 1925

CAST: Alberta Vaughn, George O'Hara, Al Cooke, Kit Guard, Stanley Taylor, William Haines. (Clark Gable as an extra.)

An extra, Gable, with his hair plastered down and parted in the middle, watches Albert Vaughn squirt soda on another extra in "The Pacemakers."

As extra soldier, Gable salutes, standing behind Roy D'Arcy in "The Merry Widow."

THE MERRY WIDOW
1925. Metro-Goldwyn-Mayer.

Directed by Eric Von Stroheim.
Screen adaptation and scenario by
Eric Von Stroheim and Benjamin
Glazer, based on the musical comedy
by Victor Leon and Leo Stein and the
operetta by Franz Lehar.
Release date: September 14, 1925.

CAST: Mae Murray, John Gilbert, Roy
D'Arcy, Tully Marshall.
(Clark Gable as an extra.)

THE PLASTIC AGE
1925. F. B. O.

A Bud P. Schulberg Production.
Directed by Wesley Ruggles. Based
on Percy Marks' novel of college life.
Release date: October 4, 1925.

CAST: Clara Bow, Donald Keith,
Henry B. Walthall, Gilbert Roland.
(Clark Gable as an extra.)

NORTH STAR
1926. Associated Exhibitors.

A Howard Estabrook Production.
Directed by Paul Powell. Based on
the novel by Rufus King.
Release date: February 7, 1926.

CAST: Strongheart, Virginia Lee
Corbin, Stuart Holmes, Ken Maynard,
Harold Austin, William Riley, Marte
Faust (Clark Gable as an extra.)

An extra in dance scene, Gable is pinpointed by arrow in this scene from "The Merry Widow," with John Gilbert and Mae Murray.

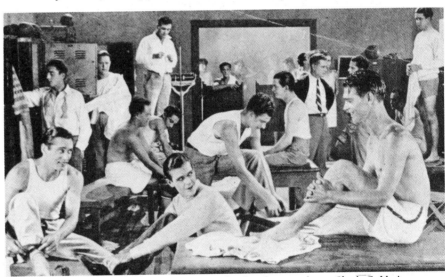

Donald Keith (second from left), Gilbert Roland and extra player Clark Gable in locker room sequence from "The Plastic Age."

Gable and two other extras with Virginia Lee Corbin and Strongheart in "North Star."

MACHINAL

1928. Plymouth Theatre, N.Y. City

A play in two parts and ten scenes by Sophie Treadwell. Settings designed by Robert Edmond Jones. Presented and staged by Arthur Hopkins at the Plymouth Theatre, September 7, 1928.

CAST: (In order of appearance) Zita Johann, Millicent Green, Grace Atwell, Leopold Badia, Conway Washburn, Jean Adair, George Stillwell, Otto Frederick, Nancy Allan, Monroe Childs, Hal K. Dawson, Zenaide Ziegfield, Jess Sidney, Clyde Stock, Clark Gable, Hugh M. Hite, John Hanley, Tom Waters, John Connery, James MacDonald, Charles Kennedy.

REVIEWS:

The New York Times: Clark Gable played the casual, good-humored lover without a hackneyed gesture.

The Morning Telegraph: He [Gable] is young, vigorous, and brutally masculine.

George Carpozi, Clark Gable: Gable became an overnight sensation of the legitimate stage and *Machinal* had a reasonably long run, although it was not in itself one of Broadway's more enduring hits. There followed a succession of other plays after *Machinal* closed, but in these Gable appeared competently yet without distinction—mainly because they all turned out to be flops: *Blind Windows, Gambling, Hawk Island* and *Love, Honor and Betray.*

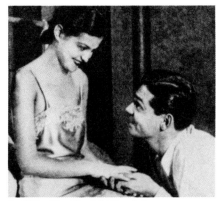

In "Machinal" with Zita Johann.

"Love, Honor and Betray" with Alice Brady.

LOVE, HONOR AND BETRAY

1930. Eltinge Theatre, N.Y. City

A play in three acts. Adapted by Frederic and Fanny Hatton from the French play by Andre-Paul Antoine. Staged by Lester Longergan; settings by Yellenti. Produced by A. H. Woods, at the Eltinge theatre, March 12, 1930.

CAST: (In order of appearance) Robert Williams, Mark Smith, Alice Brady, Clark Gable, Lucille Ferri, Wilton Lackaye, George Brent, Glenda Farrell.

REVIEWS:

Stewart Beach, Theatre Magazine: This has been one of those unfortunate seasons for Mr. Woods. He has produced lavishly only to find that the public was not interested in his offerings. *Love, Honor and Betray,* the latest of his productions, was scheduled to close something like a week after opening. Then it took on a new lease of life, and as these lines are written, it is still faring forth nightly at the Eltinge. Whether it will still be on view as you read this, I shall not prophesy but would judge that it will not . . . I found almost nothing in *Love, Honor and Betray* to persuade me that it was anything but tedious, heavy, somewhat bewildered; and hovered between satire and comedy, occasionally slipping into farce. Most of its action take place in a cemetery, and two of its characters when the play opens are already dead, brought to their ends by the unconcerned passion of a woman whom one man has desired, the other married. Before the play is over, a third is added to their company— the lover [Gable] who had been laid low by the insistence of this same lady's love. . . One does not know during most of the love scenes whether they should be considered as satire or farce or more serious business. And in consequence, one does not much care. Miss Brady, with the leading role, does not enhance her reputation greatly.

COMMENT:

Elza Schallert, Los Angeles Times: Following *Machinal,* Gable opened in *Blind Window* for David Belasco in New York. Later there followed brief Broadway and off-Broadway engagements in Howard Irving Young's *Hawk Island,* in which he played a boat skipper; *Gambling,* a George M. Cohan play; and, *Love, Honor and Betray,* with Alice Brady. None of these plays had runs of any length or made even mild hits.

Love, Honor and Betray" with Alice Brady.

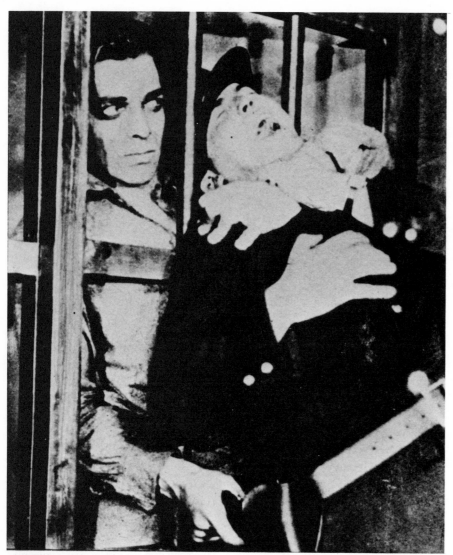

As "Killer" Mears in "The Last Mile."

THE LAST MILE

1930. West Coast Road Company.

A drama in three acts by John Wexley. Directed by Lillian Albertson. Staged and presented by Louis O. MacLoon, in Los Angeles at the Belasco Theatre, June 7, 1930.

CAST: (In order of appearance) Edward Woods, Clark Gable, Earl Dwire, Paul Fix, John Lester Johnson, Russell Hopton, Bruce MacFarlane, Kingsley Benedict, William Wagner, Adrian Morris, V. Talbot Henderson, Mike Spooner, James Gordon, George La Mont, Hernando Rodriquez, George Hoffman.

REVIEWS:

Harold Waight, The Hollywood Filmograph: Stark, terrific and stunning are adjectives beloved by critics, but never have they been used with more right than in the description of that strange and bitter outpouring of human emotions known as *The Last Mile.* One fancies that actively participating in an electrocution and prison breaks would be no more fraying on the nerves than the realism of this medodramatic thriller. It is propaganda perhaps, opposing legalized murder—but we have since learned that propaganda can make magnificent theatre fare. We leave the rights and wrongs of the case to those who wish to debate. *The Last Mile* is much too interesting to allow ourselves to be led astray from its discussion . . . There is no question in our mind as to whom the acting honors go. Edward Woods, as the young boy who goes to the chair in the first act, gives a performance that one will remember always. Clark Gable's role is more coarsely drawn. As "Killer Mears," the role that Spencer Tracy is now essaying in the New York production, he portrays the leading character in the last two acts with verve and force . . . Lillian Albertson directed and it is her finest here in Los Angeles.

COMMENT:

Elza Schallert, Los Angeles Times: I saw every one of Gable's early performances locally. It was my business to view them with critical eyes, in fact. Yet it is still almost impossible to identify him with any of his early Los Angeles theatre work. It simply was not outstanding. However, in the role of convict "Killer Mears," who waits behind bars to walk his "last mile" to the chair, Gable literally knocked everyone in the audience between the eyes with the fierce, bloodthirsty, vindictive and blasphemous way he tore the part open.

Following page:
Sam Wood directs Gable and
Jean Harlow in a romantic scene for
"Hold Your Man" (1933).

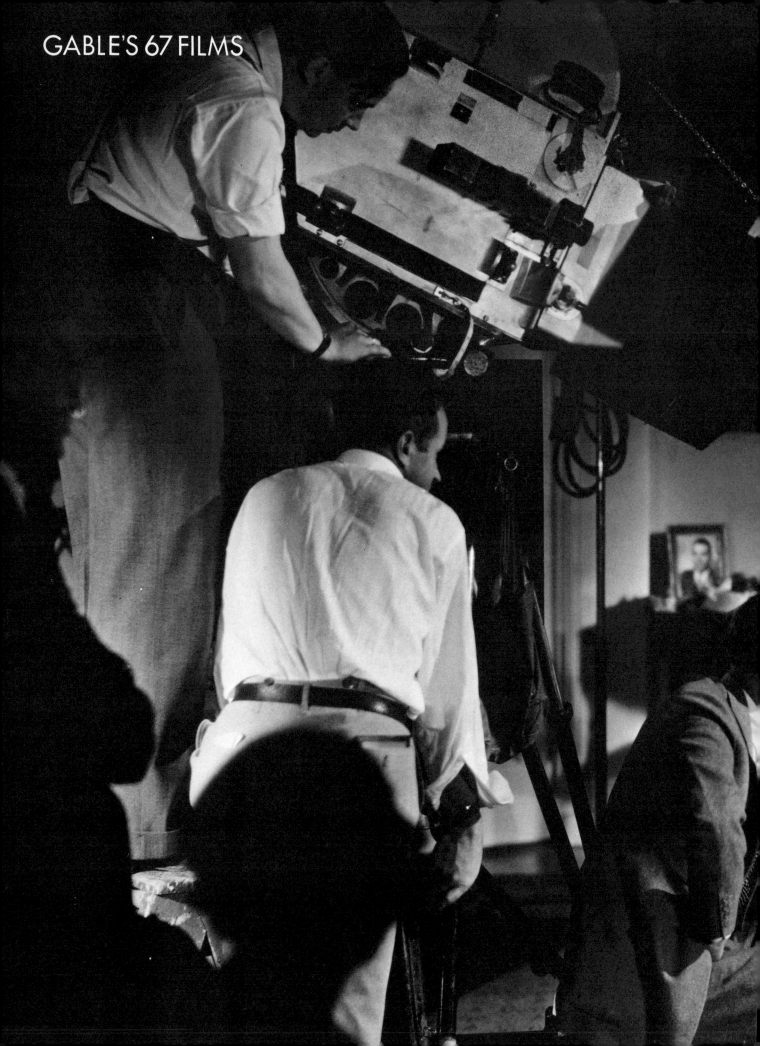

With William Farnum

With William Boyd

THE PAINTED DESERT

1931. Pathé.

Directed by Howard Higgin.
Original screenplay and dialogue by Howard Higgin and Tom Buckingham.
Cameraman: Ed Snyder.
Editor: Clarence Kolster.
Release date: January 18, 1931.
Running time: 80 minutes.

CAST: William Boyd, Helen Twelvetrees, William Farnum, J. Farrell MacDonald, Clark Gable, Charles Sellon, Will Walling, Guy Edward Hearn, Wade Boteler, William LeMaire. With Cy Clegg, James Donlon, Richard Cramer, George Burton, James Mason, Brady Kline, Jerry Drew, Hugh Allen Adams.

SYNOPSIS: A baby is found in an abandoned covered wagon on the desert by two old prospectors, Jeff Cameron (*J. Farrell MacDonald*) and Cash Holbrook (*William Farnum*). Both want to adopt the infant, but Cash takes the baby from Jeff. This causes a rift between them and their resulting feud is carried on for over thirty years, for Jeff never lets Cash forget. Jeff and his pretty gun-toting daughter, Mary Ellen (*Helen Twelvetrees*), keep Cash's cattle from the waterhole at the point of a gun.

The foundling grows up to sturdy manhood and is known as Bill Holbrook (*Bill Boyd*). After returning from an Eastern engineering school, he dedicates his life to patching up the quarrel between the bitter old men. Also he falls in love with Mary Ellen. With his engineering knowledge he decides to mine tungsten to become wealthy and then resolve the feud by marrying Jeff's daughter.

In wooing Mary Ellen, Bill has to contend with Brett (*Clark Gable*), a young tough in town who is also a suitor for her hand. Brett plays on the feud in order to aid his case and finally resorts to dynamiting Bill's mine. Upon discovering Brett's involvement, Bill forces a showdown and emerges victorious, and also wins Mary Ellen. The subsequent wedding brings Cash and Jeff together again and they are reunited.

With William Boyd

REVIEWS:

Film Daily: He [Clark Gable] wasn't a very good cowboy but the lady fans liked him. His brutish mannerisms were appropriate to the role.

Hollywood Reporter: The picture is filled with lovely views of mountains and the grim stretch known as the Painted Desert. Toward the end there are a number of effective scenes of a mountainside crumbling under the impact of a dynamite charge set by an unsuccessful suitor (*Clark Gable*) for Miss Twelvetrees' hand to destroy Bill's mine . . . Much of the dialogue is unconvincing and serves chiefly to slow up the action.

Variety: Of the picture's three featured people, Helen Twelvetrees contributes much toward its superiority over other Westerns. She's a name now in the first-runs, which can't harm this non-first runner. William Farnum's presence, in grey hair, should attract some old-timers. Bill Boyd was handed one of those honest, but misjudged hard-riding hero parts that less experienced others often grapple with. Boyd just strolls through and nothing more was necessary . . . Director Howard Higgin moved his players carefully through the great outdoors in such a way that they didn't take too much away from some excellent camera views of the fantastic beauty of the bleak California desert.

Photoplay: You'll like this Western, which makes no pretenses other than entertainment. It's far above the average, with Bill Boyd (uh-huh, the movie actor), as just the sort of virile guy he does best, and J. Farrell MacDonald and William Farnum, swell as two old Westerners who quarrel but almost kiss and certainly make up. Helen Twelvetrees is the girl. You'll find it a nice show.

With J. Farrell MacDonald and Helen Twelvetrees

THE EASIEST WAY

1931. Metro-Goldwyn-Mayer.

With Clara Blandick, Anita Page, Constance Bennett, and J. Farrell MacDonald

Directed by Jack Conway. Screenplay by Edith Ellis, from the play by Eugene Walter. Photography by John Mescall. Editor: Frank Sullivan. Release date: March 1, 1931. Running time: 86 minutes.

CAST: Constance Bennett, Adolphe Menjou, Robert Montgomery, Anita Page, Marjorie Rambeau, J. Farrell MacDonald, Clara Blandick, Clark Gable.

SYNOPSIS: Laura Murdock (*Constance Bennett*), a hard-working child of the slums, is discovered in a department store by Morris Gensler (*J. Farrell MacDonald*), who whisks her away to be a model for the Brockton Advertising Agency.

Before long, she becomes Brockton's (*Adolphe Menjou*) mistress, improving the Murdock family fortune considerably, but is ostracized by the family for her morals. Peg (*Anita Page*), the older sister, who marries

Nick (*Clark Gable*), a laundry man, would welcome her to their home. But Nick objects.

Then Laura falls in love with John Madison (*Robert Montgomery*), a wealthy Argentine rancher who must hurry back to Argentina because of a revolution. He asks Laura to wait for him. Laura is torn between Brockton and Madison, but stays with Brockton while Madison is away.

When Madison returns and finds her living with Brockton, he leaves her desolate. Since she and Brockton hadn't been getting along, he leaves her too. A figure of loneliness, she becomes a prostitute as the only thing left for her to do.

With Constance Bennett and Anita Page

REVIEWS:

Film Daily: They probably did the best they could with this old stage play by Eugene Walter that has become outmoded, with its theatrical plot of the girl who chose the easiest way. It fails to hold conviction with the artificial plot. Constance Bennett as the girl who chose the easiest way gives an indifferent performance . . . But the screen adaptation fails to build any real suspense when the fiancé returns from South America to find his sweetheart again living with the rich man she once gave up. The modern sophisticated screen plays of this type make it look very much outdated. The ending is weak and unsatisfactory.

Motion Picture Herald: Montgomery is unsympathetic; Menjou does his usual good job; Constance Bennett is superb; Rambeau is precious; Anita Page is good; and newcomer Gable shines briefly in this mildly entertaining adaptation of a slightly dated stage play which lacks conviction on the screen.

Photoplay: This one is modern, sophisticated, beautifully directed,

With Anita Page

superbly acted as Constance Bennett, Adolph Menjou, Bob Montgomery, Anita Page and the rest, and stunningly costumed. It wasn't important enough to be a great picture, but it's certainly worth its celluloid weight in entertainment. In it, Connie Bennett is a child of the slums, who after two lovers desert her must return to the dirt she once left.

With Anita Page

DANCE, FOOLS, DANCE

1931. Metro-Goldwyn-Mayer.

With Natalie Moorhead and Joan Crawford

Directed by Harry Beaumont. Screen play by Richard Schayer, from an original story by Aurania Rouverol. Dialogue by Aurania Rouverol. Photography by Charles Rosher. Editor: George Hively. Release date: February 1, 1931. Running time: 82 minutes.

CAST: Joan Crawford, Lester Vail, Cliff Edwards, William Bakewell, William Holden, Clark Gable, Earl Foxe, Purnell B. Pratt, Hale Hamilton, Natalie Moorhead, Joan Marsh, Russell Hopton.

SYNOPSIS: Bonnie (*Joan Crawford*) and Rodney Jordan (*William Bakewell*) are spoiled by their wealthy father (*William Holden*), who dies when the market crashes. Bob Townsend (*Lester Vail*) with whom Bonnie had been having an affair, wants to marry her, but she refuses. Rodney goes to work for Jake Luva (*Clark Gable*), a bootlegger, telling his sister that he is going to sell stock. Bonnie, through a friend, gets a job on a newspaper.

When Luva stages a gangland

killing of seven men, the papers are sure he did it but lack proof. Scranton (*Cliff Edwards*), a reporter friend of Bonnie's, discovers damaging information on Luva. On a threat of death, Luva forces Rod to kill Scranton.

To find out who killed Scranton, Bonnie becomes an entertainer to worm her way into Luva's mob. She becomes his favorite and finds out the horrid truth about her brother. Luva discovers the truth about Bonnie and decides to "take her for a ride." Rod interferes and they kill each other. Bonnie escapes and reports the story, exposing the rest of Luva's gang. She then finally consents to become Townsend's wife.

REVIEWS:

The New York Times: Probably *Dance, Fools, Dance* is a good title as motion-picture titles go, but a metaphysician might exhaust his learning trying to reconcile it with the melodrama of newspapers and gangdom in which Joan Crawford is featured at the Capitol. Outside of that and a number of incredible turns in a strictly made-to-order plot, the new picture is a brisk and lively entertainment of its sort, and it brought scattered applause from a thin audience at its first showing yesterday. The scenes of a city room in a mentropolitan daily are authentic.

Photoplay: Again Joan Crawford proves herself a great dramatic actress. Again Billy Bakewell turns in a fine performance as her weak younger brother. The story, which concerns a one time wealthy girl, who must work for her living, and a brother who falls in with gangsters, is hokum—but it's good hokum and Joan breathes life into her characterization. It's fast and thrilling entertainment.

Variety: Clark Gable's characterization of the gang chieftain is a vivid and authentic bit of acting, and Mr. Edwards makes an interesting reporter. Miss Crawford's acting is still self-conscious, but her admirers will find her performance well up to her standard. William Bakewell never loses sight of the fact that his part calls for a hard-drinking weakling. On the whole, Harry Beaumont, for his direction, deserves most of the applause for *Dance, Fools, Dance.*

With Joan Crawford

With Earle Foxe and Joan Crawford

With Earle Foxe and Joan Crawford

THE SECRET SIX

1931. Metro-Goldwyn-Mayer.

With Johnny Mack Brown and Wallace Beery

Directed by George Hill. Screenplay and dialogue by Frances Marion. Photography by Harold Wenstrom. Edited by Blanche Sewell. Release date: April 18, 1931. Running time: 83 minutes.

CAST: Wallace Beery, Lewis Stone, John Mack Brown, Jean Harlow, Marjorie Rambeau, Paul Hurst, Clark Gable, Ralph Bellamy, John Miljan, DeWitt Jennings, Murray Kinnell, Fletcher Norton, Louis Natheaux, Frank McGlynn, Theodore Von Eltz.

SYNOPSIS: During the prohibition era, Scorpio (*Wallace Beery*), Mizoski, the "Gouger" (*Paul Hurst*), and Johnny Franks (*Ralph Bellamy*) start a bootleg liquor business. When their activities spread to the big city, rival gangster leader Colimo (*John Miljan*) becomes anxious. Franks and some underlings pay a visit to Colimo's brother at his club. Franks kills Colimo's brother and places the blame on Scorpio. Scorpio is wounded and, learning that Franks has pulled a doublecross, kills him. Colimo is also rubbed out.

Hank (*John Mack Brown*) and Carl (*Clark Gable*), two reporters, set out to investigate the gangland killings. When Scorpio sees them hanging around his café he hires Anne(*Jean Harlow*), a lusty blonde, as a cashier to distract them.

Six leading businessmen, a group of reformers known only as "The Secret Six," ask Hank to get evidence against the gang. He locates Scorpio's gun. Anne learns he has the murder weapon and that he is being followed by Scorpio's men. On a subway train her attempts to warn him are useless and he is murdered.

Anne goes to the law, and Scorpio is brought to trial but acquitted by a fixed jury. Scorpio has Anne

With Jean Harlow

kidnapped and Carl goes to her rescue but is also made prisoner. The reformers and police raid the hideout while Carl gets Anne to safety. Scorpio tries to escape with Newton (*Lewis Stone*), his lawyer and the brains of the gang. In an argument over splitting up the cash they are carrying, Scorpio shoots him; but Newton, before he dies, kills Scorpio.

REVIEWS:
Mordaunt Hall, The New York Times: Jean Harlow, the ash-blonde of several other such tales, once again appears as the girl in the case . . . The picture moves along swiftly and the dialogue is quite well written . . . Clark Gable, who has been seen mostly as a gangster, undertakes the part of a newspaper writer named Carl . . . does valiant work. Mr. Gable is another whose acting is forceful, and the same might be said of John Mack Brown, who appears as Hank.

Photoplay: You will see exactly how liquor is made; you will witness the most thrilling gangster chase ever filmed. Beautifully produced and directed by George Hill. Cast is splendid. . . . No; gangster pictures are not dead—not as long as they produce thrillers like this!

Thornton Delehanty, New York Post: Jean Harlow plays Berry's girl friend, a plausible character softened by love for the reporter . . . *The Secret Six* is another neat gang melodrama, genuinely thrilling . . . The picture is unusually well directed and it moves with a pulsating speed. The acting, too, is generally on a high level.

London Film Weekly: A more appropriate title for this ruthless underworld story would be *Slaughterhouse*, the grim nickname of Scorpio the killer, whose rise to gang leadership and even more precipitate fall it traces. Wallace Beery's magnificently repellent study of the brutish gunman dominates the film, even though such capable actors as Lewis Stone, Clark Gable and John Miljan are in the cast. It is a splendid, uncompromising performance in which nothing has been spared to achieve realism.

THE FINGER POINTS

1931. First National.

Directed by John Francis Dillon.
Screenplay by Robert Lord, based on
a story by John Monk Saunders and
W. R. Burnett. Dialogue by
John Monk Saunders.
Photography by Ernest Haller.
Editor: Leroy Stone.
Release date: April 11, 1931.
Running time: 90 minutes.

CAST: Richard Barthelmess, Fay Wray,
Regis Toomey, Robert Elliott, Clark
Gable, Oscar Apfel, Robert Gleckler,
Noel Madison, Mickey Bennett.

SYNOPSIS: A green Southern boy,
Breckenridge Lee (*Richard
Barthelmess*), takes on a job as a
reporter with a big-time newspaper.
New to the big city, he is the only
one on the paper's staff who takes a
gangland story suppression order
seriously. Within a very short time,
he is transposed into a hard-boiled
newshound, not only familiar with
the inner circles of gangdom, but
dictating from his $35-a-week
reportorial desk thousands of dollars
for suppressing news of its activities.

Marcia Collins (*Fay Wray*), who
works on the same paper develops
romantic interest in him. When she
learns of his grafting, she pleads with
him to free himself from the
underworld. His intentions are good
but he cannot turn his back on the
money.

When the gangland leader, Louis

With Richard Barthelmess

Blanco (*Clark Gable*), orders two men
killed, he also orders Lee to suppress
the story. But things go wrong and
the story is published. Blanco believes
he has been double-crossed because his
gang is implicated. That night as he
leaves the office building, Lee is
mowed down by machine guns as the
fulfillment of the finger having been
pointed at him by the gang leader.

REVIEWS:

Film Daily: As a gangster-newspaper
talker it doesn't hold much. Where

Barthelmess stands well and where
the gangster fever is in high, plus the
phase of the reporter who runs the
underworld of the town, this picture
should do well. In other spots it calls
for support . . . Regis Toomey is
excellent as a fellow reporter unaware
of Barthelmess' activities and who
admires him as his ideal, while Clark
Gable again scores with his fine voice
and magnetic personality.

Variety: The leading characterization
must have been a tough one for the
writers. Even when the reporter goes
bad the script attempts to keep him
clean, if not of hand at least of heart.
This permits a sob-sister angle. Fay
Wray interprets this assignment,
constantly remonstrating with the lad
to get out of the blood money class
. . . A breezy and booze-loving
reporter, also enamored of
Barthelmess' girl, is excellently
interpreted by Regis Toomey. Story
takes the conventional twist by having
him get the gangster yarn which
cleans up the local situation, but not
before he is paid in full with
machine gun bullets by the gangland
czar, portrayed characteristically by
Clark Gable.

As Louis Blanco

With Richard Barthelmess

LAUGHING SINNERS

1931. Metro-Goldwyn-Mayer.

Directed by Harry Beaumont.
Screenplay by Bess Meredyth, from "Torch Song," a play by Kenyon Nicholson. Dialogue by Martin Flavin. Photography by Charles Rosher. Edited by George Hively.
Release date: September 5, 1931.
Running time: 71 minutes.

CAST: Joan Crawford, Neil Hamilton, Clark Gable, Marjorie Rambeau, Guy Kibbee, Cliff Edwards, Roscoe Karns, Gertrude Short, George Cooper, George F. Marion, Bert Woodruff.

SYNOPSIS: Ivy Stevens (*Joan Crawford*), an entertainer, is given the brush-off by a traveling salesman, Howard Palmer (*Neil Hamilton*). Her life is pulled out from under her; she feels that all purpose in living is gone. She is befriended by a Salvation Army worker, Carl Loomis (*Clark Gable*), who tells her that she must believe in God and leads her to the mission. She joins the group that goes singing on streets.

While singing in a hotel, she notices Howard in a poker game sitting with a slut named Edna (*Gertrude Short*). Howard has since

With Joan Crawford

With Neil Hamilton and Joan Crawford

gotten married and Ivy pleads with him to be faithful to his wife. He palms Edna off on Cass Wheeler (*Guy Kibbee*). Ivy wants him to see the light as she has. When the group sings a ribald parody on a sacred hymn, she, with Howard's help, drives them out of the room. Now

that they are alone, Ivy gives in to Howard, and sleeps with him. In the morning she hates herself. She only wanted to help Howard. God cannot be proud of her anymore. Ivy becomes hysterical and begins screaming, bringing everyone, including Carl, into the room.

When Carl enters, there is a hush. Howard clears the room and he and Ivy tell Carl what has happened. She tells him to find another girl for her uniform; it doesn't fit anymore. But

rather than give her up, Carl turns his back on the Salvation Army. Leaving the past behind, he finds real happiness with Ivy.

REVIEWS:

The New York Times: New leading man Clark Gable is rather unconvincing as the saviour of fallen Joan Crawford, who is better than usual in a film that is less than average in its overall scheme. It doesn't live up to its publicity.

Photoplay: Adapted from the stage play *The Torch Song* and not so good, but if you're a Joan Crawford fan you may like it. Clark Gable, as a Salvation Army worker, causes Joan to go straight after Neil Hamilton, the cad who does her wrong. Hamilton's work is splendid in a dirty-dog role. The title came out of a grab-bag.

Film Daily: Better than average screenplay with Neil Hamilton giving the outstanding performance. As a cad of a traveling salesman, he is quite strong when the moment of truth demands it. The Salvation Army worker, Clark Gable, doesn't have the high moments that Hamilton does, but is more consistent, however average. He has done better. So has Miss Crawford.

With Joan Crawford

With Joan Crawford

A FREE SOUL

1931. Metro-Goldwyn-Mayer.

With Lucy Beaumont, Norma Shearer, and Leslie Howard

Directed by Clarence Brown. Screenplay and dialogue by John Meehan, based on the novel by Adela Rogers St. John. Photography by William Daniels. Edited by Hugh Wynn. Release date: June 20, 1931. Running time: 91 minutes.

CAST: Norma Shearer, Leslie Howard, Lionel Barrymore, Clark Gable, James Gleason, Lucy Beaumont.

SYNOPSIS: Stephen Ashe (*Lionel Barrymore*), brilliant criminal lawyer, is generally disapproved by his family for his drinking and unconventionality. When drunk, he brings Ace Wilfong, (*Clark Gable*), gambler and underworld leader, to his mother's (*Lucy Beaumont*) birthday gathering. Being unwelcome, they leave, together with Jan (*Norma Shearer*), Stephen's motherless daughter.

Jan becomes Ace's proud mistress. When Ace wants to marry her, Steve refuses to let him, saying that it would be no life for his daughter.

During a raid that night, while trying to hide, Steve discovers Jan and Ace together. She agrees not to see Ace anymore if he will stop drinking.

But Steve cannot stop and Jan goes back to Ace who has changed and has become brutal. He tries to molest her and Dwight Winthrop (*Leslie Howard*), Jan's ex-fiancé, interferes. Winthrop kills Ace and is arrested.

Frantically, Jan gets her father to save Winthrop. When Steve realizes what anguish he's caused Jan, he confesses to the murder of Ace and is gunned down by one of Ace's mob. He dies with a prayer for forgiveness and the happiness of Jan and Winthrop.

With Norma Shearer

With Norma Shearer

With Norma Shearer

REVIEWS:

New York Herald Tribune: Clark Gable is a fascinating villain who will convince the female customers that he is naughty but nice. Although not as prominent as Leslie Howard in this photoplay, he does stand out in one's mind as the major character. His acting, however, is nowhere on the same level as the superb Mr. Barrymore. Mr. Gable would do well to sit back and take a lesson.

Motion Picture Herald: Clark Gable and Leslie Howard are both grand. The story concerns a modern girl, brought up by her clever but erratic father to do exactly as she pleases— to be a "free soul." She pleases to have a sordid affair with a gambler, whom she discovers to be a cad.

London Film Weekly: Both Leslie Howard and Clark Gable were relatively unimportant players, at the threshold of their subsequent fame . . . It marked Lionel Barrymore's return to the screen as an actor after a long period of direction.

1932 ACADEMY AWARDS
BEST ACTOR: Lionel Barrymore

With Norma Shearer and Leslie Howard

With Lionel Barrymore

NIGHT NURSE

1931. Warner Brothers.

Directed by William A. Wellman. Screenplay by Oliver H. P. Garrett, based on the novel by Dora Macy. Dialogue by Oliver H. P. Garrett and Charles Kenyon. Photography by Chick McGill. Editor: Ed McDermott. Release date: August 8, 1931. Running time: 72 minutes.

CAST: Barbara Stanwyck, Ben Lyon, Joan Blondell, Clark Gable, Charles Winninger, Vera Lewis, Blanche Frederici, Charlotte Merriam, Edward Nugent, Rolf Harolde, Walter McGrail, Allan Lane.

SYNOPSIS: Lora Hart (*Barbara Stanwyck*), a young nurse, is hired by Mrs. Ritchey (*Charlotte Merriam*), a wealthy and drunken widow, to act as a private nurse to her children. Mrs. Ritchey's past indifference to their welfare has allowed the other members of the household to hatch a plot to starve the two little girls to death, thereby getting possession of a trust fund left to them through marriage of the chauffeur, Nick, to the mother.

When Lora discovers the scheme she seeks the help of a breezy bootlegger, Mortie (*Ben Lyon*), whom she had attended to when he had been shot in the shoulder. He comes to her rescue after she is pretty badly man-handled by the rough chauffeur (*Clark Gable*), who warns her that she will be killed if she tells what she knows.

Maloney (*Joan Blondell*), a close nurse friend to whom Lora confides, tells her to tell the police, but she is afraid and leaves the situation to Mortie. The bootlegger is in love with Lora and with a few gangland friends disperses the scheming mob. The grateful Lora confesses her love to Mortie as he resolves to give up his illegal business.

REVIEWS:

Sidney, Variety: Clark Gable goes through socking everybody, including Miss Stanwyck, and is finally done away with by inference. What legitimate performances crop up in the footage seem to belong to Miss Blondell and Charlie Winninger as the hospital head. Miss Stanwyck plays her dancehall type of girl on one note throughout and is shy of

With Ben Lyons and Barbara Stanwyck

shading to lend her performance some color . . . Production is adequate, but Wellman has 'way overplayed the indifference to the welfare of her children, as done by Charlotte Merriam, who is the wealthy and drunken mother.

Hollywood Reporter: The best things about *Night Nurse* are its title and cast names plus the Misses Stanwyck and Blondell stripping two or three times during the picture. Otherwise, it's a conglomeration of exaggerations, often bordering on serial dramatics.

With Barbara Stanwyck

Film Daily: Strange but amusing mixture of hospital drama, crook activities and comedy, with good work by fine cast . . . Joan Blondell, in the role of a sister nurse to Miss Stanwyck, walks off with a big slice of the honors as a result of her

With Mildred Harris, Walter McGrail, and Barbara Stanwyck

wisecracking and comedy antics, all of which register solidly. Lyon's bootleg role also is in a comedy vein, and there are plenty of laughs throughout.

SPORTING BLOOD

1931. Metro-Goldwyn-Mayer

Directed by Charles Brabin. Screenplay and dialogue by Willard Mack and Wanda Tuchock, from the novel *Horseflesh,* by Frederick Hazlitt Brennan. Photography by Harold Rosson. Editor: William Gray. Release date: August 8, 1931. Running time: 82 minutes.

CAST: Clark Gable, Ernest Torrence, Madge Evans, Lew Cody, Marie Prevost, Harry Holman, Halam Cooley, J. Farrell MacDonald, John Larkin, Eugene Jackson.

SYNOPSIS: Jim Rellence (*Ernest Torrence*), who sells the fast horses he breeds instead of racing them himself, reluctantly sells "Tommy" to rich Jerry Hardwick (*J. Farrell MacDonald*). Jerry wins a lot of money with Tommy but is forced to sell the horse to Angela (*Marie Prevost*) and Phil Ludeking (*Harry Holman*), a gambler.

With Madge Evans

With Madge Evans and "Tommy"

His new owners overwork Tommy, who loses a race he should never have run. Angela is furious about losing and Phil goes to Tip Scanlon's (*Clark Gable*) gambling place to win the money back. He loses heavily and is forced to give the horse to Tip as payment.

Tip races Tommy honestly for a while, then has Tommy pulled to win big on the loss. Ruby (*Madge Evans*) and Warren (*Lew Cody*), dealers at Scanlon's gambling joint, object to Tip's intention to use dope to spur Tommy to win under great strain. When the horse loses, unplanned, Tip is in big trouble with dangerous mobsters who bet heavily on him. To cover himself Tip transfers Tommy to Ruby who takes the horse back to Jim Rellence. Under Jim's care, Tommy goes on to win the Kentucky Derby, despite all crooked attempts to stop him. Warren, who brought warning of the "fix," takes Ruby for his wife.

REVIEWS:

Time: Horses and nonsense. With a plot that one can nearly guess the turns and happenings; only the race sequences offer any promise to the fan. This one is indubitably not Mr. Gable's best work, though far from his worst.

Films In Review: Clark Gable heads the cast, but Torrence, as the head of the family of horse breeders, steals the show. Mr. Gable should not take it hard to be up-staged by so fine an actor in a show where even the horses feature prominently. The screenplay is just barely adequate, carried almost entirely by the high grade of acting and direction of Charles Brabin.

With Lew Cody

SUSAN LENNOX—HER FALL AND RISE

1931. Metro-Goldwyn-Mayer.

Directed by Robert Z. Leonard. Screenplay by Wanda Tuchock from the novel by David Graham Phillips. Dialogue by Zelda Sears and Edith Fitzgerald. Photography by William Daniels. Edited by Margaret Booth. Release Date: October 10, 1931. Running time: 84 minutes.

With Greta Garbo and Ian Keith

CAST: Greta Garbo, Clark Gable, Jean Hersholt, John Miljan, Alan Hale, Hilda Vaughn, Russell Simpson, Cecil Cunningham, Theodore von Eltz, Marjorie King, Helene Millard, Ian Keith.

SYNOPSIS: A brutal farmer named Ohlin (*Jean Hersholt*) wants to marry his illegitimate daughter, Helga (*Greta Garbo*), to a low-class wealthy farmer, Mondstrum (*Alan Hale*). In order to escape the undesirable marriage, she runs away and comes upon the mountain cabin of an engineer, Rodney Spencer (*Clark Gable*). He hides her from her angry father and they fall in love. When Rodney leaves for work, Helga's father returns to the cabin and she flees again.

When night falls, she manages to get aboard a carnival train. In order to stay with the traveling show she has an affair with the owner, Burlington (*John Miljan*). She finally gets away from the carnival to find Rodney, who learning of her affair rejects her. She changes her name to Susan Lennox and with the money she's saved, she buys new clothes and becomes the mistress of a rising politician, Mike Kelly (*Hale Hamilton*). But when his enemies find out, his career is ruined and he forces her to leave.

All hope gone, she takes a boat to South America to look for Rodney who has continually rejected her. She finds him down-trodden and working on a jungle construction project. He refuses to believe that she has changed. But when she has a chance to leave with a rich man, Robert Lane (*Ian Keith*), and elects to stay with Rodney, they are reconciled and begin a new life.

With Eddie Kane and Greta Garbo

REVIEWS:

Richard Griffith: Susan Lennox approaches an honest treatment of the male response to the streetwalker heroine; and Miss Garbo does a superb job in bringing this type of female to the screen, alive and running with and afoul of our due sympathies. She more than betters the able performance of her rugged co-star, Clark Gable, who shines under stress but occasionall lapses into moments of amateur play-acting.

Variety: Once more she [Garbo] achieves an acting effect by means that baffle while they provoke interest. Teaming with the great

With Greta Garbo

Garbo, of course, marks the peak of Gable's vogue.

James Agate, Motion Picture Herald: The picture is good for the reason that it covers a lot of ground and refreshes the eyes with circuses, cabarets and the like while our minds are resting. It is good because Mr. Gable is excellent as the king of job who is Rodney.

London Film Weekly: Garbo makes up for a great deal [of the picture's weaknesses] by a clever study in alternating moods, while Clark Gable gives a strong, if straightforward, performance as her lover. Even though a bit scrappy and unpalatable, it is worth seeing for the acting and personalities of the leading players . . . The novel on which the film is based was written in 1917 by David Graham Phillips, who was shot some years later by a crank who objected to his treatment of women in the book. His work aroused a storm of protest in America.

With Greta Garbo

POSSESSED

1931. Metro-Goldwyn Mayer.

Directed by Clarence Brown. Screenplay adaptation by Lenore Coffee, from the play, *The Mirage,* by Edgar Selwyn. Photography, by Oliver T. Marsh. Release date: November 29, 1931. Running time: 76 minutes.

CAST: Joan Crawford, Clark Gable, Wallace Ford, Skeets Gallagher, Frank Conroy, Marjorie White, John Miljan, Clara Blandick.

SYNOPSIS: An employee in a box factory, Marian Martin (*Joan Crawford*), determines to make a better life for herself, and resolutely refuses the proposal of Al Manning (*Wallace Ford*), a cement worker in the same factory. She runs away to New York, where a friend, Wally Stuart (*Skeets Gallagher*), introduces her to Mark Whitney (*Clark Gable*), a wealthy young lawyer who has a political future. After several engagements, Mark realizes he is in love with Marian, proposes to her and they are married. She insists, however, that it be kept a secret until she can educate herself to fill the position of his wife in the proper manner.

The night they are to announce their marriage, Travers (*Frank Conroy*), the man responsible for a large part of Mark's political success comes to their apartment. He tells Mark it must be kept secret for at least another month because Mark is being groomed for a political job of

With Joan Crawford

As politician Mark Whitney

With Joan Crawford and Frank Conroy

great importance and their enemies will start a whispering campaign against him concerning the sudden marriage. Mark says he is through with politics and that his wife's happiness comes first. After Travers leaves, Marian refuses to let Mark sacrifice his career and pretends that she has been insincere in her love and plans to marry Al Manning, now a successful contractor. Mark believes her, tells her to go and takes up the political campaign for governor.

At a large rally some hecklers interrupt Mark to ask about Marian, and he is so shocked he can make no defense. But Marian, who is in the audience, rises and makes a wonderful speech, insisting she is not in his life any more and that he belongs to the people, and turns the murmurs of disapproval into a rousing demonstration of good will. She rushes out of the auditorium during the uproar, but Mark finds her on the street, takes her in his arms and says he might win and he might lose, but whichever way it goes, it will be with her.

REVIEWS:

Film Daily: This man, Gable, that we've been watching for little over a year has come a long way from his villain roles. His performance suggests that he may become a solid actor. A personality he already is; but so much talent . . . will take him a good deal farther than just good looks.

Variety: Gable again is the stiff, cold-blooded, manly leading man. Since graduating from gangster parts he has failed to register any strong emotion. Happy or sad, it's always the same Gable. Only when the script calls for a snarl or for him to slap Miss Crawford in the face, to call her a "little tramp" and, to tell her to scram, did anything register on the Gable horizon. One *Variety* sobbie said that in Gable's face there is cruelty. So maybe that's what they like.

Mordaunt Hall, The New York Times: Through Clarence Brown's able direction, handsome settings and fairly well written script, *Possessed* is gratifying entertainment. . . . Miss Crawford adds another excellent performance to her list and Mr. Gable delivers a performance that is nicely restrained.

With Wallace Beery

With Dorothy Jordan and Marie Prevost

HELL DIVERS

1931. Metro-Goldwyn-Mayer.

Directed by George Hill. Screenplay and dialogue by Harvey Gates and Malcolm Stuart Boylan, based on a story by Lt. Comdr. Frank Wead. Photography by Harold Wenstrom. Editor: Blanche Sewell.
Release date: December 5, 1931.
Running time: 100 minutes.

CAST: Wallace Beery, Clark Gable, Conrad Nagel, Dorothy Jordan, Marjorie Rambeau, Marie Prevost, Cliff Edwards, John Miljan, Landers Stevens, Reed Howes, Alan Roscoe.

SYNOPSIS: Two petty officers in the Naval Air Force, Windy (*Wallace Beery*) and Steve (*Clark Gable*), are rivals and constantly bickering. In a barroom fight, Steve beats Windy, incurring the hard-boiled, yet good-hearted, older petty officer's hatred. Windy gets even by temporarily busting up Steve's matrimonial prospects with his blonde girl friend, Ann (*Dorothy Jordan*).

Later, during a sham air attack, Steve's plane buckles, killing his pilot and he becomes isolated on a rock formation off-shore which he reaches by parachute. Duke (*Conrad Nagel*) as pilot and Windy as observer in another plane, spot the accident. A difficult landing on a treacherous beach allows the two men to plunge through a raging surf to reach the injured Steve.

Once on the beach, the three men are marooned for days, the fog spoiling their chances of rescue. Windy finally gets their damaged plane off the shore and goes for help, but crashes when trying to land. Shortly after he is pulled out of the burning plane, he dies but only after he tells about Duke and Steve. This final noble gesture closes the breech between Steve and Windy and the younger officer gives him an appropriate burial at sea.

REVIEWS:

Film Daily: An intense study and celluloid display of naval aviation. Unusually long on footage and short on entertainment. Women will not like it, despite the Gable inclusion, and there have been so many naval pictures on, under, and over the water

With Marjorie Rambeau

that even the new sidelights George Hill has uncovered won't fully compensate the male patrons.

Hollywood Reporter: There is no story. What composition is present has a *What Price Glory?* basis from which springs the formula that has governed such pictures as *Cockeyed World, Flight,* etc. As it stands, it's a matter of squadron after squadron of planes, the mechanics attached thereto, the cutting in and around newsreel material, which Metro does so well, and Wallace Beery's excellent personal performance. Clark Gable and Dorothy Jordan provide what love interest is present, with Miss Jordan eliminated from the picture by the end of the third reel.

With Wallace Beery

John Gammie, London Film Weekly: Clark Gable, although not altogether overshadowed, has his work cut out to rival Beery, and is inevitably relegated to second place.

With Reed Howes

Variety: No one other than Beery and Gable is important on performance. The women concerned have but bits, while Gable is not placed to advantage in this assignment. With Miss Jordan having given promise she's coming along in prior films, here she is meaningless and practically forgotten by the time the picture is over . . . So it boils down to the air stuff and Beery. There has been much of both recently, which, as a combination, doesn't promise much.

131

POLLY OF THE CIRCUS

1932. Metro-Goldwyn-Mayer.

With Marion Davies and C. Aubrey Smith

Directed by Alfred Santell.
Screenplay by Carey Wilson, based on the play by Margaret Mayo.
Dialogue by Laurence Johnson.
Photography by George Barnes.
Editor: George Hively.
Release date: February 27, 1932.
Running time: 72 minutes.

CAST: Marion Davies, Clark Gable, C. Aubrey Smith, Raymond Hatton, David Landau, Ruth Selwyn, Maude Eburne, Little Billy, Guinn Williams, Clark Marshall. With Ray Millande, Lillian Elliott, Phillip Crane.

SYNOPSIS: While performing her act, trapeze artist Polly Fisher (*Marion Davies*), falls and is hurt. She is taken to the house of the local minister, Reverend John Hartley (*Clark Gable*), a warm and gentle man who is taken by the circus star's beauty. They fall in love and secretly become man and wife. John decides that Polly will not return to the circus because of the danger involved.

When they announce their marriage, Rev. Hartley loses his position because of the pressure from the congregation regarding Polly's distasteful background. John tries to find work but fails. When Polly goes to the straight-laced bishop, Rev. James Northcutt (*C. Aubrey Smith*), to get John reinstated in the ministry, he refuses. She decides to leave John and return to the circus because she feels that it is the only way he can regain his congregation and return to his beloved profession.

When the bishop changes his opinion of Polly, he goes to John but finds out Polly has left. The two rush to the circus grounds, where they find her already on the high wires about to try the act which caused her previous injury. She is not sure of herself, but the sight of John below gives her courage and she performs to the thunderous applause and later gets a warm kiss from her husband and a knowing nod from the bishop.

With Marion Davies

REVIEWS:

John Gammie, London Film Weekly: Opinions differ on the wisdom—or folly—of casting the forceful Mr. Gable as a minister of the gospel in *Polly of the Circus.* American critics favour the view that the screen's fashionable heavy lover is wasted in a role which gives him absolutely no scope for cave man tactics. I disagree. I think Gable makes a much better minister than a "typed" actor of the milksop variety would have done. He rubs the rough edges off his film personality and turns in a characterization that is virile without being "tough." Compare his Reverend John Hartley with his Ace Wilfong (the uncouth gangster of *A Free Soul*) and you will surely admit that his reputation as an actor is enhanced by the comparison. At the same time I am afraid that this picture, although pleasant, is a curious throwback to the early screen romances, and as such will not create much of a furor in the West End.

Film Daily: Comment is favorable on the camera work in the circus tent, where unusual angled shots are achieved. In fact much of the photography is good, serving as excellent background for the stars, Clark Gable and Marion Davies. Miss Davies suffers in a shallow role but comes across with greater credibility than Mr. Gable, who will disappoint his many fans. Well received in the support are Raymond Hatton as the drunken attendant at the minister's home, David Landau as the circus manager, and Maude Eburne in a minor role as the girl's nurse.

Motion Picture Herald: Sell Miss Davies all you want to; she'll need it in this one. But don't try to foist Mr. Gable as a preacher. This because of past roles, which he has so admirably filled, and because he simply doesn't register as a member of the clergy. True, the picture has its moments, but these are few and far between. Not even the suspense in the aerial sequences will atone for what is obviously gross carelessness in production, from casting right down the line.

132

With Marion Davie

RED DUST

1932. Metro-Goldwyn-Mayer.

With Jean Harlow

Directed by Victor Fleming.
Screenplay by John Lee Mahin,
based on the play by Wilson Collison.
Cameraman: Harold Rosson.
Editor: Blanche Sewell.
Release date: October 22, 1932.
Running time: 83 minutes.

CAST: Clark Gable, Jean Harlow,
Gene Raymond, Mary Astor, Donald
Crisp, Tully Marshall, Forester
Harvey, Willie Fung.

SYNOPSIS: Dennis Carson (*Clark
Gable*) is in charge of a rubber
plantation in a remote area of Indo-
China, where he and two assistants,
McHarg (*Tully Marshall*) and Guidon
(*Donald Crisp*), oversee the native
workers. Returning from Saigon,
Guidon arrives on the same boat as
Vantine (*Jean Harlow*), a prostitute
on the run from the police. Carson
and McHarg find her kicking the
drunken Guidon out of her bed.
Carson is forced to let her stay until
the next boat arrives.

At first indifferent to her, he
discovers she is sensitive and kind
despite her profession and succumbs
to her charms and presses her to
accept money for a stake, when the
boat arrives bringing Gary Willis
(*Gene Raymond*), an engineer, and
his bride, Barbara (*Mary Astor*). On
the trip, Willis has been stricken with
fever. While Carson nurses Willis
back to health, Vantine returns
because the boat has broken down.
Carson igonres her. He has fallen in
love with Barbara and decides to send
Willis with McHarg and Guidon to
supervise the building of a bridge in
the jungle. During his absence Carson
and Barbara become lovers.

When Willis returns Carson feels
ashamed because Willis thinks him a
great guy. He also realizes that Barbara
could never share his plantation life.
To turn her against him, he takes up
with Vantine. Barbara shoots him in
a jealous rage. Willis runs in at the
gunshot but Vantine covers up for
Barbara by telling him that Carson
made advances and his wife was only
protecting herself.

Willis quits his job and prepares
to leave with his wife. Vantine digs
the bullet out of Carson's belly, and
in this painful moment, he realizes
she is the woman for him, regardless
of her past. She stays on with him
in the jungles.

REVIEWS:

London Film Weekly: Gable is
perhaps more gruffly virile than ever
before. He and Jean Harlow make an
excellent team. Mary Astor is good
enough as the primly unfaithful wife,
and Gene Raymond is suitable for the
part of the colorless husband.

McCarthy, Film Daily: Gable, tough,

With Jean Harlow and Donald Crisp

With Donald Crisp, Gene Raymond, Tully Marshall, Mary Astor, and Jean Harlow

With Jean Harlow

With Mary Astor

ruthless, hardboiled, yet
retaining a sense of decency that
makes him sympathize with the
innocent husband. Miss Harlow,
voluptuous, smart, wise and wise-
cracking, making liberal use of her
charms to take Gable's mind off Mary
Astor. The climax has Gable flattened
by a gunshot wound, with Miss
Harlow reading him Peter Rabbit
bedtime stories.

*Richard Watts, Jr., New York Herald
Tribune:* The flagrantly blonde Miss
Harlow, who hitherto has attracted
but intermittent enthusiasm from this
captious department, immediately
becomes one of its favorites by her
performance in *Red Dust* . . . In the
new film she is called upon to go in
for the playing of amiably sardonic
comedy and, by managing it with a
shrewd and engagingly humorous
skill, she proves herself a really deft
comedienne . . . You know, too, that
these tales are, as a rule, things to
be questioned, if not avoided.
Thereupon, to everyone's surprise—
including possibly, the producers'—
Miss Harlow's comedy, which supplies
a running commentary on the course
of the story, came along and

With Mary Astor

transformed *Red Dust* into an
entertaining photoplay.

Time: Given *Red Dust's* brazen moral
values, Gable and Harlow have full
play for their curiously similar sort
of good-natured toughness. The best
lines go to Harlow. She bathes
hilariously in a rain barrel, reads
Gable a bedtime story about a
chipmunk and a rabbit. Her effortless
vulgarity, humor, and slovenliness
make as noteworthy a characterization
in the genre as the late Jeanne Eagle's
Sadie Thompson.

With Tully Marshall and Jean Harlow

STRANGE INTERLUDE

1932. Metro-Goldwyn-Mayer.

Directed by Robert Z. Leonard. Screenplay and dialogue by Bess Meredyth and C. Gardner Sullivan, based on the play by Eugene O'Neill. Photography by Lee Garmes. Editor: Margaret Booth. Release date: December 30, 1932. Running time: 110 minutes.

CAST: Norma Shearer, Clark Gable, Alexander Kirkland, Ralph Morgan, Robert Young, May Robson, Maureen O'Sullivan, Henry B. Walthall, Mary Alden, Tad Alexander.

SYNOPSIS: When World War I threatens, Professor Leeds (*Henry B. Walthall*) prevents the marriage of his daughter Nina (*Norma Shearer*) to Gordon Marsh (*Robert Young*), convinced that it would be best to wait. When Gordon is killed two days before the Armistice, Nina becomes bitter toward her father for having robbed her of her marriage. To escape from his rule, she marries faithful Sam Evans (*Alexander Kirkland*), a hopeless impotent who is all but repulsed by physical love.

Realizing that her marriage is a failure, Nina takes on a lover, Dr. Ned

As Dr. Ned Darrell

Darrell (*Clark Gable*) and becomes pregnant by him. Sam, thinking it is his child, is overjoyed. The baby is called Gordon after Nina's first sweetheart. He becomes the focus of his mother's passionate and possessive affection, even through his manhood. She becomes furious when she learns he is engaged, wanting to keep him for herself.

Nina attempts to frighten Gordon's fianceé, Madeleé (*Maureen O'Sullivan*), by telling her of the inherited insanity of the Evans family. Darrell stops her lies and comforts the girl, who is sympathetically tolerant of Nina's outbursts. Sam then suffers a stroke and, as they realize his helplessness, Darrell and Nina know that they must continue to set aside their own feelings, honor-bound to care for this man who has ignorantly trusted them so implicitly.

REVIEWS:

John Gammie, London Film Weekly: From the filmgoer's point of view, the outstanding thing is the acting of Norma Shearer, Clark Gable and May Robson. . . . Clark Gable's powerful personality shines steadfastly through the misty atmosphere of mixed psychology. . . . Norma Shearer's response to the demands of an extraordinarily exacting part shows that she has a far greater range as an actress than one would have suspected, even after her fine work in many intelligent talkies. *Strange Interlude* is a film that will be widely discussed. It must be set down as a cinematic novelty to be seen by discerning audiences.

Terry Ramsaye, Motion Picture Herald: Those elements of the play which are so poignantly O'Neill have

With Norma Shearer and Alexander Kirkland

for the screen, somewhat in the movie fashion, been subdued, sandpapered and varnished toward euphemism. There was in the making of *Strange Interlude* an evident awareness that it was strong meat. A borrowing from the stage though it is, it is a stepping out for the motion picture.

Photoplay: Clark Gable and Norma Shearer age beautifully within the short span of an hour and a half and, like vintage wine, they improve with each year.

With Norma Shearer

With Norma Shearer Alexander Kirkland and Ralph Morgan

With Norma Shearer

NO MAN OF HER OWN

1932. Paramount.

Directed by Wesley Ruggles. Screenplay by Maurine Watkins and Milton H. Gropper, based on a story by Edmund Goulding and Benjamin Glazer. Cameraman: Leo Tover. Release date: December 31, 1932. Running time: 85 minutes.

CAST: Clark Gable, Carole Lombard, Dorothy Mackaill, Grant Mitchell, George Barbier, Elizabeth Patterson, J. Farrell MacDonald, Tommy Conlon, Walter Walker, Paul Ellis, Lillian Harmer, Frank McGlynn, Sr.

SYNOPSIS: A big-time card shark, Babe Stewart (*Clark Gable*), takes it on the lam in a small midwestern town until the heat of one of his recent jobs cools off. On a bet with Vargas (*Paul Ellis*), one of his accomplices, he marries the town beauty, Connie Randall (*Carole Lombard*). Shortly thereafter, he finds that not only did he win his bet but that he is in love with the girl.

Taking his bride to New York, he discovers that there is a lot about him that his naive wife doesn't know. And he wants to keep it that way. He covers up his gambling and gets rid of most of his old girl friends.

Then under the guise of a South American business trip, Babe does a ninety-day jail stretch. Finally Connie

With Carole Lombard

With Carole Lombard

catches on to the whole scheme when Kay Everly (*Dorothy Mackaill*), one of Babe's discarded mistresses, tells her what Babe is really like in order to get even with him. When he returns, she pretends to give him a bad time, but realizing that he did the whole thing for her, she goads him into explaining everything so that she can fully appreciate it and him.

REVIEWS:

Variety: Gable is close to the whole picture himself as a swank card-gyp who hits the trail heavy for the women, but in his supporting company, from Miss Lombard down, Paramount hasn't cheated him at all. It is largely the good cast, direction and some of the comedy arising mostly out of the wisecracks that makes *No Man of Her Own* acceptable film fare.

Film Daily: Just about everything that the ordinary picture fan looks for in screen entertainment is included in *No Man of Her Own:* drama, romance, comedy, strong build-ups, exciting climaxes, a fine line of human interest. The story is easily understood, yet clever directorial touches endow it with a novelty which, aided by exceptionally pleasing work by the entire cast, provides a sparkle that should appeal to young and old.

Motion Picture Herald: Lots of prolonged howls of laughter and loads of action that presents Gable at his present best, sophisticated comedy. Luscious Carole Lombard is appropriately the object of his tomfoolery and frustrations. Both are magnificent in this modern fairy story of love and games that gaily flits across the screen too quickly, leaving the audience in want of more. Plan on it for a light, carefree evening's enjoyment.

London Film Weekly: Gable's impudently confident love-making exactly fits the character he is playing. Carole Lombard, cool, sincere and intelligent, makes the perfect heroine.

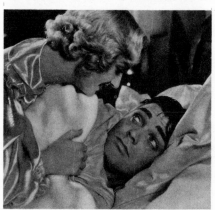

With Carole Lombard

With Carole Lombard and Dorothy Mackaill

GABLE AND LOMBARD

Even in Hollywood's golden era they were a legend: two glamorous stars whose life together was as romantic—and as much fun—as their movies, until it ended in heartbreak
BY WARREN G. HARRIS

The romance started during a leap year, on Saturday night, January 25, 1936. The Mayfair Club of Hollywood was holding a formal ball called the White Mayfair, for which Carole Lombard was serving as hostess. All the women were requested to dress in white gowns, the men in white tie and tails.

Lombard was famous for parties, such as the one for which she turned her house into a hospital ward and served dinner on an operating table. They were always as wacky as she was. By taking on the White Mayfair, she hoped to prove that, if she wanted to, she could give a party just as grand as those of Marion Davies's and other self-appointed Hollywood social arbiters.

Three hundred and fifty people were expected, and they all seemed to be arriving at once—David Niven, Merle Oberon, Gloria Swanson, Spencer Tracy, Jeanette MacDonald, Henry Fonda, Humphrey Bogart....

Clark Gable walked in as part of Marion Davies's group. Lombard rushed over to greet Miss Davies. Gable flashed one of his honey-and-hemlock smiles at Lombard and winked. She winked back and gave him a reserved but friendly hello. It was the first time they'd met since making "No Man of Her Own" together four years before. That encounter had resulted in a case of mutual dislike. He had objected to her boisterous behavior and profane vocabulary, while she thought he was too stuffy and reserved.

Now he seemed to be having a change of heart. She was tantalizing in a filmy, white silk gown and seemed much more mature and self-assured.

She was back at her table listening to Cab Calloway's orchestra when she noticed Gable heading toward her.

"I go for you, Ma," he said, grinning. Lombard stared at him, then suddenly realized that he was using one of the nicknames they had given each other during "No Man of Her Own."

"I go for you, too, Pa," she said, though it didn't sound as if she meant it. Assuming he wanted to dance, she got up before he even asked her.

Marion Davies, probably the most dedicated matchmaker in Hollywood, was watching them dance. Finally, she turned to Louella Parsons and said, in her customary stammer, "Th-those two were m-made for each other. W-wouldn't it be g-great if they f-fell in love?"

But at a table across the room, another woman was seething at the sight of Gable and Lombard together. She was Ria Langham Gable, his matronly second wife, from whom he was now legally separated. Ria was trying to forestall a final break by demanding a divorce settlement that would ruin him financially.

Gable said he needed some fresh air and offered to take Lombard for a drive in his Duesenberg convertible. When they had been out a few minutes, she noticed that they seemed to be circling around the Beverly Wilshire Hotel.

She asked him why and he said he lived there. Would she like to come up for a drink?

"Who do you think you are—Clark Gable?" Lombard quipped, aware of his image as the great lover who could have any woman he wanted. At her sarcasm, he slammed his foot on the accelerator and drove back to the White Mayfair at 90 miles an hour.

Later on he tried once more to persuade her to leave the party with him, but she had invited friends to her house for breakfast after the ball. She told him he was welcome to come home with her to help prepare for them.

It was around 12:30 when Gable and Lombard left for her house on Hollywood Boulevard. Gable didn't stay very long. Lombard wanted him to serve as a combination butler and bartender, which was not what he had in mind. He made an excuse and left in a huff.

The next morning, Gable was awakened by a strange cooing sound. He opened his eyes to find a plump white dove perched on his chest. On the table opposite him was a bird cage, with the gate wide open. There was another dove roosting on the chandelier. After he had left Lombard's house, she decided she had been too hard on him. She called up a pet shop and had them send a pair of doves as a peace offering. She then bribed one of the hotel clerks to release the doves in Gable's suite while he was still asleep. / turn to page 115

Left: Gable and Lombard in "No Man of Her Own," the only picture they made together. Right: After their marriage they eschewed Hollywood high life for the rustic pleasures of their ranch in Encino.

COPYRIGHT © 1974 BY WARREN G. HARRIS. FROM THE FORTHCOMING BOOK, "GABLE AND LOMBARD," TO BE PUBLISHED BY SIMON AND SCHUSTER

LEFT TO RIGHT, TOP TO BOTTOM: CULVER PICTURES; MEMORY SHOP; U.P.I.; CULVER PICTURES; U.P.I.; SPRINGER/BETTMANN; CULVER PICTURES

European cooks have long known the secret of combining two or more meats in the same dish—the classic French *pot au feu* is a good example. It's economical, adds variety to the meal, and the flavors of the meats augment each other, so that in terms of taste the whole is greater than the sum of the parts. Pictured at right, Flemish hot pot, a plump broiler and a smoked pork butt, simmered together with wine and herbs and served with horseradish sauce. Beginning on page 108, other delicious combinations: baked spareribs and tongue, cooked with sauerkraut and beer; chicken-and-ham rolls à la Suisse, with a cheese-and-mustard sauce; chicken-and-beef cacciatore, in a delicious Italian sauce; and more.

IRWIN HOROWITZ

THE WHITE SISTER

1933. Metro-Goldwyn-Mayer.

Directed by Victor Fleming. Adapted for the screen by Donald Ogden Stewart, based on the novel by F. Marion Crawford and Walter Hackett. Photography by William Daniels. Musical score by Herbert Stothart. Editor: Margaret Booth. Release date: February 24, 1933. Running time: 110 minutes.

CAST: Helen Hayes, Clark Gable, Lewis Stone, Louise Closser Hale, May Robson, Edward Arnold, Alan Edwards.

SYNOPSIS: Prince Guido Chiaromonte (*Lewis Stone*), fearing that his flighty daughter, Angela (*Helen Hayes*), will follow in her mother's footsteps and disgrace herself for love, arranges for her to marry Ernesto Traversi (*Alan Edwards*), the smug son of a Roman banker. Although Angela cares nothing for Ernesto, she is resigned to her fate and never thinks of questioning her father's decision. But one day, during a religious festival, Angela meets Giovanni Severa (*Clark Gable*), an officer in the Italian Air Service.

A mild flirtation develops into a love affair. Giovanni objects bitterly to her forthcoming marriage and becomes an ardent suitor without Prince Guido's knowledge. Angela runs away to join him. Shortly thereafter, war breaks out and Giovanni is called to active service. Angela prays that he will come back to her.

Two years later, when she receives word that he has been killed, she enters a convent to become a nun. But Giovanni is not dead. For two

With Alan Edwards

long, terrible years he was confined in an Austrian prison camp unable to send word to her. At last he steals an Austrian officer's plane and flies triumphantly back to Italy to begin a search for Angela.

After weeks of frantic investigation, Giovanni finds her. But Angela has taken her final vows. She is doomed to the White Sisterhood for life. Only by special dispensation of the Pope can she be released. And she refuses to ask for it even though she loves Giovanni. Two years of suffering have transformed her into a noble, strong-minded woman. Giovanni pleads in vain, even abducts her and tries to take her by force. Suddenly, something makes him understand. He releases her and takes her back to the convent. And as he leaves her, a bomb from a raiding Austrian plane strikes him down. Angela is called to his side. He dies in her arms, reconciled to her decision.

REVIEWS:

Motion Picture Herald: Mr. Gable is forceful in a story that isn't. Neither he nor Miss Hayes even with their moving performances can make the picture the noble effort it pretends to be. There is an anticipation that is never fulfilled.

Hollywood Reporter: White Sister is a . . . great picture. Hayes and Gable

are already stars of the first magnitude. Their performances now equal anything of their brilliant past.

London Film Weekly: Although marred by a certain lack of emotional depth, and by occasional incongruities of accent and idiom, this is a lavish, striking production, with many fine scenes and interesting performances by the stars. . . . Clark Gable's work as Giovanni will please his admirers, but he scarcely succeeds in sinking his own personality in the part.

With Helen Hayes

As Giovani Severa

HOLD YOUR MAN

1933. Metro-Goldwyn-Mayer.

Produced and directed by Sam Wood. Screenplay by Anita Loos and Howard Emmett Rogers, from Miss Loos' original story. Photography by Harold G. Rosson, Edited by Frank Sullivan.
Release date: July 1, 1933.
Running time: 89 minutes.

CAST: Jean Harlow, Clark Gable, Stuart Erwin, Dorothy Burgess, Muriel Kirkland, Gary Owen, Barbara Barondess, Paul Hurst, Elizabeth Patterson, Inez Courtney, Blanche Friderici, Helen Freeman.

SYNOPSIS: Eddie Nugent (*Clark Gable*), a slick young confidence man, is chased by the police and dashes into a cheap apartment house, where he takes refuge in one of the apartments. Explaining his predicament to the occupant, a tough girl named Ruby Adams (*Jean Harlow*), he induces her to hide him. Ruby is paid in return but he manages to filch it back from her and later walks out on her.

Realizing that her hold upon his careless affections is not very strong, she tells him about a man named Mitchell (*Paul Hurst*), the owner of laundry who wants her to take a trip to Pittsburgh with him. Eddie's pal, Slim (*Gary Owen*), sees a chance to frame Mitchell with Ruby and make him the victim of a bunko game. Eddie, who is to pose as Ruby's brother, agrees to the scheme; but he is more in love with Ruby than he has realized. When he returns to the

With Jean Harlow

apartment and sees her struggling with Mitchell, he accidentally kills him.

Eddie then fades away and leaves Ruby to take the rap. She is sent to reform school where she presently discovers that she is going to have a child. The news is taken to Eddie by an Armenian girl named Gypsy (*Dorothy Burgess*), a discarded mistress of his, lately discharged from the reform school.

Though he has arranged to get out of the country and send for Ruby later, the news of the coming child has made him return to marry her. Recognized by one of the matrons who sends for the police, he is arrested at the close of a hasty marriage ceremony. But with aid of a smart lawyer, he gets off with a short term and comes out to find his wife and small son awaiting him. He is going to go straight now and Ruby tells him that Al Simpson (*Stuart Erwin*), an old friend, has a job waiting for him in Cincinnati.

REVIEWS:

Motion Picture Exhibitor: The title is somewhat unfortunate in its choice, since it has the rather definite implication of a highly sophisticated type of drama, especially in view of the fact that Clark Gable and Jean Harlow share the lead. As a matter of fact, the picture is anything but sophisticated in the expected fashion, though several of the dialogue passages, entirely in the earlier sequences, are slightly off-color, lending a sharp flavor in keeping with the story, yet susceptible of frowns in certain communities.

London Film Weekly: Being themselves is the job at which Harlow and Gable have made good. It may be that in private life the one is the essence of refinement and the other shy and introspective, but it is as a pair of charming toughs, hard as nails, and superbly imprudent, that we have come to know them on the screen . . . [the film] is hardboiled, cheekily smart stuff, just right for these two.

Frank S. Nugent, The New York Times: Sam Wood's direction is effective, and the action is fast, but the sudden transition from hardboiled, wise-cracking romance to sentimental penitence provides a jolt. Miss Harlow and Mr. Gable will not disappoint their admirers.

Time: Strong drama, occasionally reaching the point of drawing audience tears, an occasional interjecting of capably-handled comedy, a rather powerful story with a definitely different twist, and the two stars, serve to bring this picture into the category of salable pictures of rather unusual drawing power.

With Jean Harlow

With Jean Harlow and Dorothy Burgess

With Joe Sawyer and Jean Harlow

NIGHT FLIGHT

1933. Metro-Goldwyn-Mayer.

As the doomed Fabian

Directed by Clarence Brown.
Screenplay adaptation by Oliver H. P. Garrett, based on the story by Antoine de Saint Exupery. Cameramen: Oliver T. Marsh, Elmer Dyer and Charles Marshall.
Release date: October 4, 1933.
Running time: 84 minutes.

CAST: John Barrymore, Helen Hayes, Clark Gable, Lionel Barrymore, Robert Montgomery, Myrna Loy, William Gargan, C. Henry Gordon, Leslie Fenton, Harry Beresford, Frank Conroy, Ralf Harolde.

SYNOPSIS: Riviere (*John Barrymore*) General Manager of the Air Express Company, overrules the objections of the President of the Company and the Board of Directors that the night flights are too dangerous and insists that they go on. A man of iron will, he has instituted the most rigorous discipline. Pilots are fined for the least infraction of the rules; even if they are delayed by fog from taking off on time they are fined. Though he never shows it, it hurts him to dismiss an employee and the loss of a pilot cuts him deeply.

He severely rebukes his inspector, Robineau (*Lionel Barrymore*), for indulging in a friendly dinner with one of the pilots who is below Robineau in rank. And to re-establish the proper relationship, he forces Robineau to find some lapse on the pilot's part to punish him for.

Tragedy enters when Fabian (*Clark Gable*), the pilot on the Patagonia route, loses his life in a storm. At home his pretty young wife (*Helen Hayes*) is eagerly awaiting his return. Through the radio with which the plane is equipped, he manages to get word to Riviere that he has only thirty minutes' gasoline left. Then there is

John and Lionel Barrymore

silence and he is heard from no more. Riviere has to break the news to the widow, but he cannot show any softness, for the virus of fear must not be allowed to enter into the system. The night flights must continue, work must go on, and Riviere, the indomitable, must bear his heavy load of responsibility.

REVIEWS:

John Gammie, London Film Weekly:
. . . Although a clever director and talented stars have been straining to make you believe in the epic achievement of flying aeroplanes over dangerous territories by night instead of day, all that is really being achieved is the saving of a few hours— another slight acceleration of the pace of modern living, which doesn't, after all, seem such a triumph of high endeavor. . . . There are too many stars in little parts. Gable, for instance, sits in a plane throughout his performance. John Barrymore is never seen outside his office. The only piece of genuine human relationship which warms interest is the little scene between Myrna Loy and Gargan.

New York Herald Tribune: As far as names are concerned, this picture should have plenty of pulling power. Yet its entertainment values are hardly up to the standard and class ordinarily expected of such an imposing cast. Even though with the handsome Clark Gable who has a rather inconsequential role, there is little in *Night Flight* to hold feminine interest. Its greatest appeal will be found among aviation enthusiasts.

Abel, Variety: As to cast, the names are obviously a marquee hypo. Most of 'em are wasted in the playing. The sub-people are about on a par with the others as regards histrionic contribution. Gable is almost wholly superfluous as a flyer. Montgomery lends little more than color. The two women, apart from their mental travail for their husbands, likewise deliver at a minimum. John Barrymore this time is the more forceful of the frères, being importantly cast as the ruthless managing director of the air service. Lionel is altogether a vague characterization.

As the doomed Fabian

DANCING LADY

1933. Metro-Goldwyn-Mayer.

Produced by David O. Selznick. Directed by Robert Z. Leonard. Screenplay by Allen Rivkin and P. J. Wolfson, based on the novel by James Warner Bellah. Photography by Oliver T. Marsh. Music by Burton Lane, Harold Adamson, Richard Rodgers, Lorenz Hart, Jimmy McHugh and Dorothy Fields. Costumes by Adrian. Edited by Margaret Booth. Release date: December 2, 1933. Running time: 94 minutes.

CAST: Joan Crawford, Clark Gable, Franchot Tone, May Robson, Winnie Lightner, Fred Astaire, Robert Benchley, Ted Healy, Floria Foy, Art Jarrett, Grant Mitchell, Maynard Holmes. With Nelson Eddy, Moe Howard, Jerry Howard, Larry Fine,

SYNOPSIS: Poverty and lack of opportunity force Janie Barlow (*Joan Crawford*) to work in a cheap downtown burlesque house in New York. Tod Newton (*Franchot Tone*), a wealthy young rounder, takes a slumming party of friends down to the burlesque house and is immediately attracted by Janie's fresh young beauty. When the show is raided and taken into court on a charge of indecency, Tod pays Janie's $50.00 fine.

He persuades her to return home with him, where he attempts to seduce der. But Janie doesn't buy his line. She tells him that she will pay back every cent when she gets work. Tod informs her that a striptease on Second Avenue is "art" on Broadway. This fires Janie's ambition to crash Broadway.

She accepts Tod's help to reach Patch Gallagher (*Clark Gable*), the director for Jasper Bradley's (*Grant Mitchell*) musical shows. Patch, once a hoofer himself, is annoyed by the girl's importunity but is persuaded by Tod to hire her. He soon recognizes her talent but does not admit it. Janie wins his friendship by her devotion to hard work and he decides to feature her in the show.

Tod hadn't anticipated Janie's success and in an attempt to force her to marry him buys Bradley out and closes the show. When Janie finds out, she gives Tod the brush-off. She and

With Joan Crawford

Patch continue with the show, using Patch's savings. It is a great success and Patch and Janie discover they are in love.

REVIEWS:

Time: The versatile Mr. Gable is cast surprisingly as a stage director, instead of a gangster, and might make hoofing the rage. Perhaps the film should have been called "Dancing Man" to introduce the new Clark Gable. Although it would be a premature observation to say that Fred Astaire may have some future competition from Gable, it would not be invalid.

Variety: Saying it's a backstage show is hardly enough. There have been plenty of those, and the mere presentation of one more probably would not stir the paying public. But *Dancing Lady* is so basically different that it belongs in another category. Everything is built upon a fundamental story. What happens is only the result of working that story to its logical conclusions.

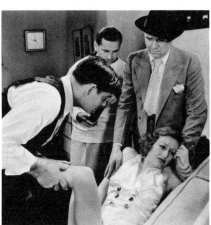

With Ted Healy and Joan Crawford

With Sterling Holloway and Art Jarrett

IT HAPPENED ONE NIGHT

1934. Columbia.

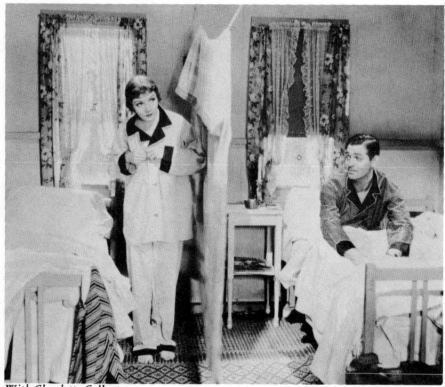

With Claudette Colbert

Directed by Frank Capra.
Screenplay by Robert Riskin, based on a story by Samuel Hopkins Adams.
Photographed by Joe Walker.
Edited by Gene Havlick.
Release date: February 23, 1934.
Running time: 105 minutes.

CAST: Clark Gable, Claudette Colbert, Walter Connolly, Roscoe Karns, Jameson Thomas, Alan Hale, Ward Bond, Eddie Chandler.

SYNOPSIS: Ellie Andrews (*Claudette Colbert*), an heiress traveling incognito, is running away from her tycoon father, Alexander Andrews (*Walter Connolly*). She boards a night bus on its way to New York. On the bus she meets Peter Warne (*Clark Gable*), a newspaper reporter who has just been fired for impertinence. They become friends and decide to travel together.

For financial reasons, their journey from Miami to New York finally resolves into hitch-hiking. They stay in tourist cabins at night and Peter properly hangs a blanket between them to give Ellie privacy. He calls the blanket "the Walls of Jericho."

While Ellie sleeps, Peter leaves her to rush ahead to New York to sell the story of her fabricated adventures to his ex-editor for $1,000. When she wakes, believing he has deserted her, she brings about a complication in which her father figures prominently.

He comes to her rescue and finds that their romance has patched itself up. The "Walls of Jericho" are blown down as Ellie's father is convinced that Peter is not just another of her

With Claudette Colbert

foolish fancies and that it would be futile to interfere.

REVIEWS:

Newsweek: Here is romance, garnished with lots of laughs. The formulas run askew as the stereotype heiress who takes it on the lam as no one has ever taken it on the lam before; with good fun and handsome Clark Gable.

The New York Times: Clark Gable's at his best, yet in winning new honors for himself, he steals nothing from Claudette. The picture has a rare quality of camaraderie with the audience—permitting those watching it to share the experiences and fun of the players. Skillfully directed by Frank Capra, whose insight into character relationships and reactions is brilliantly evident in the final analysis.

John Gammie, London Film Weekly: Clark Gable and Claudette Colbert hold the screen for fully three-quarters of the film's length—a test of personality and talent from which both emerge with honors. Gable is brilliantly impudent without being in the least unlikable. Miss Colbert acts with grace and humor and looks lovely. . . . Go and see for yourself how Capra and his players conjure amusement out of practically nothing. Note, especially the neat handling of the scenes in the cramped motor bus, the skill with which the daring yet utterly inoffensive bedroom incidents are done, the dissertation on the ethics of hitch-hiking, the sublime satire of the ceremonial wedding at the end, and many other instances of smart direction, writing and acting.

Film Daily: The finest of the year. Simply delightful and entertaining. Mr. Gable and Miss Colbert reach new heights, working together as though they have known each other for life. It will be a surprise if it doesn't win anything this year.

1934 ACADEMY AWARDS
BEST PICTURE: *It Happened One Night*
BEST ACTOR: Clark Gable
BEST ACTRESS: Claudette Colbert
BEST DIRECTOR: Frank Capra
BEST ADAPTATION: Robert Riskin

With Claudette Colbert

MEN IN WHITE

1934. Metro-Goldwyn-Mayer.

Directed by Richard Boleslavsky. Screenplay by Waldemar Young, based on the play by Sidney Kingsley. Photographed by George Folsey. Edited by Frank Sullivan. Release date: March 28, 1934. Running time: 80 minutes.

CAST: Clark Gable, Myrna Loy, Jean Hersholt, Elizabeth Allan, Otto Kruger, C. Henry Gordon, Russell Hardie, Wallace Ford, Henry B. Walthall, Russell Hopton, Samuel S. Hinds, Frank Puglia, Leo Chalzel, Donald Douglas.

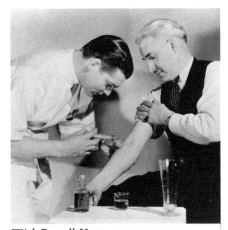

With Russell Hopton

SYNOPSIS: Dr. George Ferguson (*Clark Gable*) is an intern whose future has been laid out. Ambitious, brilliant, he is a protégé of Dr. Hochberg (*Jean Hersholt*), a famous surgeon. He expects to study in Vienna at the end of his internship, then to return to work under Hochberg. He is engaged to Laura Hudson (*Myrna Loy*), daughter of a wealthy man, who is to accompany him to Vienna.

Laura, spoiled by an indulgent father, loves Ferguson, but cannot understand his devotion to duty when it interferes with personal engagements.

With Elizabeth Allan

They quarrel when he is unable to keep a date with her, and that night he finds solace in the arms of Barbara Dennin (*Elizabeth Allan*), a student nurse who worships him. That night Barbara becomes pregnant.

Desperately ill because of an abortion, Barbara is rushed to the operating room in an effort to save her life. Hochberg and Ferguson are to operate. Laura, who has accompanied her fiancé to the hospital after their wedding rehearsal, is to witness the operation—a suggestion of Hochberg's who hopes she will realize the importance of Ferguson's work. And Barbara, who knows she will die, tells Ferguson she isn't sorry—that she loves him. Laura overhears her and understands everything. Barbara dies after telling Laura not to blame Ferguson.

REVIEWS:

Film Daily: Gable as a struggling doctor is very real and warm and unlike anything we've seen him doing before. It is unusual, yet very natural, not to see him batting the ladies around in a rough manner. This is the beginning, perhaps, of a "new" Clark Gable. Watch for him in "a new kind of hero" roles. We believe it will be a pleasant change.

Motion Picture Herald: It is a film long to be remembered—fine and honest. In the scene with the little sick girl, Gable does a remarkable acting job. And he has your sympathy all through the episode with the nurse who dies as a result of an operation that should not have been performed. Hersholt tops all previous performances. And what a trouper Elizabeth Allan is! Otto Kruger, C. Henry Gordon, too.

John Gammie, London Film Weekly: The principal asset of *Men in White* is indisputably the acting of Hersholt, closely seconded by the acting of Gable.

With Myrna Loy

With Elizabeth Allan and C. Henry Gordon

With Myrna Loy

MANHATTAN MELODRAMA
1934. Metro-Goldwyn-Mayer.

With Nat Pendleton and Myrna Loy

Directed by W. S. Van Dyke.
Screenplay by Oliver T. Marsh, H. P.
Garrett and Joseph L. Mankiewicz,
based on the original story by
Arthur Caesar. Photographed by James
Wong Howe. Edited by Ben Lewis.
Release date: May 2, 1934.
Running time: 93 minutes.

CAST: Clark Gable, William Powell,
Myrna Loy, Leo Carillo, Nat Pendleton,
George Sidney, Isabel Jewell, Murial
Evans, Thomas Jackson, Claudelle
Raye, Frank Conroy, Noel Madison,
Mickey Rooney, Jimmy Butler.

SYNOPSIS: Three East Side kids, thrown
together when their parents drown
in a boating disaster, grow up
together. Jim Wade (*William Powell*)
becomes assistant District Attorney,
Joe Patrick (*Leo Carrillo*) enters the
priesthood, and Blackie Gallagher
(*Clark Gable*) becomes the owner of
a gambling house with a dubious
reputation.

Blackie bribes the police and has
been involved in a number of gangland
killings. His mistress, Eleanor (*Myrna
Loy*), sick of the racket, pleads with

Blackie to get out. Blackie, however,
is content. He feels honesty is great
for guys like Jim. In fact, he has a
great deal of respect for Jim's
integrity, but wants no part of it
for himself.

A chance meeting between Jim and

As Blackie Gallagher

Eleanor causes them to fall in love.
Blackie does not object when Eleanor
leaves him because he considers Jim
the better man. Jim is elected D. A.
and fires his jealous assistant, Snow
(*Thomas Jackson*), for graft. Snow
sets out to ruin Jim's chances to be
nominated for governor. Eleanor
learns of his intentions and asks
Blackie to help. In a struggle Blackie
kills Snow and is caught.

Jim's integrity forces him to
prosecute his childhood pal, thereby
winning the nomination and election
to the governor's chair. Eleanor tells
him that it was for his sake that
Blackie committed the murder. Jim
rushes to the prison to commute the
sentence but Blackie won't allow his
friend to betray his principles. Blackie
walks bravely to his death with
Father Joe by his side.

REVIEWS:

Film Daily: Powell, Gable and Miss
Loy will get critical raves for their
superb playing. Powell unquestionably
topping his best past offerings. Gable
manages his exacting role with power
and appeal, Miss Loy represents a very
genuine and persuasive heroine—a
beautiful characterization. Leo Carrillo
as prison chaplain, Nat Pendleton
as a comic gangster, Isabel Jewell in
a nit-wit role and Muriel Evans
stand out.

Hollywood Reporter: Gable's back
to the type of role he does best: a
do-gooder gangster. And he comes off
great. Powell as the self-righteous
D. A. is dynamic. The story is
suspenseful. . . . Story, direction and
performance unit to give distinction
to the clash of love, ambition and
politics worked out of the lives of two
East Side waifs, told refreshingly.

London Film Weekly: Satisfactory
melodrama based on the highly moral
theme that the good little boy will
flourish, while the bad little boy will
come to a sticky end. William Powell
(as the model child) steals the
picture from Clark Gable, and by
clever acting saves it from lapsing into
sentimentality. Good entertainment.

1934 ACADEMY AWARDS
ORIGINAL STORY: Arthur Caesar

With Myrna Loy

CHAINED

1934. Metro-Goldwyn-Mayer.

Produced by Hunt Stromberg.
Directed by Clarence Brown.
Screenplay by John Lee Mahin, based
on an original story by Edgar Selwyn.
Photography by George Folsey.
Costumes by Adrian. Art direction by
Cedric Gibbons. Editor: Robert J. Kern.
Release date: August 31, 1934.
Running time: 74 minutes.

CAST: Joan Crawford, Clark Gable,
Otto Kruger, Stuart Erwin, Una
O'Connor, Marjorie Gateson, Akim
Tamiroff, William Deggar.

SYNOPSIS: Diane Lovering (*Joan
Crawford*) is Richard Field's (*Otto
Kruger*) mistress. It is the dignified,
quiet love of a rich elderly man for
his former secretary. Since Field is the
type of man who cannot bear
underhanded methods, he had discussed
the issue with his wife (*Marjorie
Gateson*) who refuses to give him a
divorce because of their children.
Field suggests a trip to Buenos Aires
for the frustrated Diane until things
can be worked out.

Aboard ship, she meets Mike Bradley
(*Clark Gable*), a wealthy Argentine
rancher. By the end of the voyage
she realizes that she is in love with him
but must never see him again because
of her ties with Field.

Upon returning to New York, she
learns that Field's wife has consented
to the divorce and Field has already
disclosed his wedding plans. She
writes Mike a curt note hoping that
he will hate her. He conceals his pain
and decides the whole affair was his
own poor judgment.

When on a business trip to New
York, quite by accident, Mike meets
Diane again. She breaks down and
tells him that she loves him but can
never be disloyal to her husband.
Convinced that he is right, Mike
follows Diane and Field to their
Placid lodge where he tells Field
everything. After considering the facts,
Field decides to set her free to seek
her happiness with Mike.

With Joan Crawford and Otto Kruger

REVIEWS:

Photoplay: Splendidly written, acted,
directed and photographed. The scenes
on board ship are especially well done.
. . . Joan Crawford in the moonlight
on the open sea appears quite seductive
and Clark Gable seems to agree. In
his role as the spurned lover we are
shown a new dimension of his ever
surprising acting skills. Stuart Erwin
turns in a grand comedy job and
Otto Kruger is superb as the dignified
New York businessman.

New Statesman: Under the current
circumstances, the film's moral
significance is one that only a
thorough understanding and appreciation
of local temper can evaluate. What
it is is a modernly premised romance
drama, without succumbing to any
temptation to make it a challenge
of any viewpoint.

John Gammie, London Film Weekly:
Joan Crawford and Clark Gable
naturally hold the screen most of the
time, and hold it well, but Otto
Kruger gets a fair chance to put in
some sound work as the oh-so-
sympathetic business man who has
no time to play. . . . Gable, of course,
adopts the particularly Gable-ish
attitudes of (a) regarding himself as
a sap for letting Joan play around
with him the way she does, and (b)
Joan as a sap for not telling Kruger
the truth.

With Joan Crawford

With Joan Crawford

FORSAKING ALL OTHERS

1934. Metro-Goldwyn-Mayer.

With Charles Butterworth, Billie Burke, Rosalind Russell, Robert Montgomery, Joan Crawford

Produced by Bernard H. Hyman.
Directed by W. S. Van Dyke.
Screenplay by Joseph L. Mankiewicz,
based on the play by Edward Barry
Roberts and Frank Morgan Cavett.
Photographed by Gregg Toland and
George Folsey. Costumes by Adrian.
Editor: Tom Held.
Release date: December 19, 1934.
Running time: 82 minutes.

CAST: Joan Crawford, Clark Gable,
Robert Montgomery, Charles
Butterworth, Billie Burke, Frances
Drake, Rosalind Russell, Tom Rickets,
Arthur Treacher, Greta Moyer, Ted
Healy, Lillian Harmer.

SYNOPSIS: Jeff Williams (*Clark Gable*)
returns from Spain to lay siege to the
heart of his childhood playmate, Mary
Clay (*Joan Crawford*), who has
always seemed to favor Dill Todd
(*Robert Montgomery*). Jeff arrives
just in time to be chosen by Aunt Paula
(*Billie Burke*) as the one to give the
bride away, for Dill and Mary are
getting married. Dill, however, leaves
Mary at the altar and runs away with
his mistress, Connie (*Frances Drake*).
This leaves Mary to be consoled
by Jeff.

A year of not much happiness for
anyone follows. Then a cocktail
party brings Mary and Dill together
again. They go on an outing on
bicycles and when it begins to rain

they take refuge in a cabin in the
Adirondacks. Storm-drenched and in
the clandestine atmosphere, they
renew their old love and plan another
marriage ceremony.

Again Jeff takes a back seat to
Dill in Mary's heart while the nuptial
arrangements are made. Before the
ceremonies, however, Mary realizes
that it was Jeff who did the many
nice things for which she had credited
Dill. In the meantime, Jeff,
disillusioned and disappointed, is on
his way back to Spain. This time it's
Mary who leaves Dill at the altar to

With Joan Crawford

scamper aboard ship where, after
finding Jeff, she pledges her undying
affection.

REVIEWS:

McCarthy, Hollywood Reporter:
Surrounding the adventures of the
trio (Gable-Crawford-Montgomery)
are the comedy situations in which
they involve themselves, all of which
is made more poignant by the jittery
affection of Aunt Paula and Uncle
Shep. One of the highlights
graphically identifying the picture's
comedy savor is a bicycle riding
sequence which culminates in
Montgomery and Miss Crawford
being catapulted into a pig sty.
Nothing so graphic befalls the
unassuming Mr. Gable and
appropriately so.

Variety: In the performances of
Crawford, Gable and Montgomery
there is scarcely a shade of preference.
All three are superb. . . . But they
alone are not the only interest-creating
qualities. The story is what one
would expect from such a cast. Clever
and smart, packing a lot of comedy
in action, situation and dialogue, it's
a unique light triangular dramatic
romance.

Time: Tastefully produced, with the
settings, costumes and air reflecting
the class of the cast, the picture comes
within the all grownup audience
category. Contrary to presumption,
sophistication is at a minimum. While
there is a continuous drawing room
flavor, comedy which sometimes
borders on the slapstick variety is
the element embellishing the premise.
Naturally the triple star value lead
names and the strength of the
featured support are the predominant
commercial assets of this picture.

John Gammie, London Film Weekly:
Clark Gable forgets all the he-man
stuff, and clowns and wisecracks his
way through the picture with an
unbridled sense of humor. He and
co-stars Joan Crawford and Robert
Montgomery have conspired with
Director W. S. Van Dyke to make
you laugh louder and longer than
you've done for ages. Put this down
on the "Must be seen" list right away.

With Joan Crawford

AFTER OFFICE HOURS

1935. Metro-Goldwyn-Mayer.

Produced by Bernard H. Hyman.
Directed by Robert Z. Leonard.
Screenplay by Herman J. Mankiewicz,
based on the story by Laurence
Stallings and Dale Van Every.
Photography by Charles Rosher.
Editor: Tom Held.
Release date: February 16, 1935.
Running time: 75 minutes.

CAST: Constance Bennett, Clark Gable,
Stuart Erwin, Billie Burke, Harvey
Stephens, Katherine Alexander, Hale
Hamilton, Henry Travers, Henry
Armetta, Charles Richman, Herbert
Bunston.

SYNOPSIS: Sharon Norwood
(*Constance Bennett*), a wealthy
socialite, gets a job working on a
newspaper, and Jim Branch (*Clark
Gable*), the managing editor, fires
her. That night he sees her at the
theatre, escorted by Tommy
Bannister (*Harvey Stephens*), a
wealthy young man about town.
Branch has been trying to find evidence
to substantiate the rumor that
Henry Patterson (*Hale Hamilton*),
middle-aged millionaire, is going
to divorce his pretty young wife,
Julia (*Katherine Alexander*),
naming Bannister as her lover. Branch
sees an opportunity of getting
information from Sharon, and so he
re-hires her.

The following evening is the
opening night of the River Club
and Jim knows that the Pattersons
are having a party there. He is sure
that Bannister will be among the
guests, so he asks Sharon to go with
him, telling her that he wants her
to cover the opening for the paper.

When Sharon sees Julia and
Bannister, she figures out why
Branch brought her here, and why
he took her back on the paper.
Bannister comes over to their table,
and when Branch is called to the
phone, Sharon leaves with Bannister.
They go to his place and Julia
Patterson follows them. He sends
Sharon upstairs and when Julia arrives
he kills her and hides the body. After
taking Sharon home, he takes the
body to the Patterson house.

Patterson is arrested for the
murder, but Jim knows it was
Bannister. With Sharon's help he

With Harvey Stephens

With Constance Bennett

tricks him into giving himself away.
Branch's paper is first with all details
of the case, and contains a full
confession by Bannister. Sharon and
Jim plan to marry, and take a few
days away from the paper for a
honeymoon.

REVIEWS:

Film Daily: Happy medium
entertainment for the mob as well
as the sophisticates and intelligent
fans. . . . Clark Gable as a
newspaperman crashing society in
order to get a lead on a murder
mystery. The clash between him and
Constance Bennett gives the story
a great kick. The dramatic solution
with excitement, a fine cast and great
production background makes this
one of the best balanced pix of the
season. It has practically everything.

McCarthy, Hollywood Reporter:
This picture moves fast. In most cases
the dialogue is crisp and the action
creates an atmosphere of bustle and
to-do. The time is modern, the locale
New York. . . . *Office Hours* has much
pep, with its more dramatic tensity
amply balanced by comedy and
romantic interest. Cast names,
however, appear to be the most

forceful asset, Clark Gable in
particular.

John Gammie, London Film Weekly:
Because we laughed at Clark Gable
in *It Happened One Night* and
Forsaking All Others, the idea now
seems to be that he should clown as
much as he possibly can. Which is
really a pity. This would have been
a better picture if Gable had been
allowed to do some more straight
acting. As it is, he is compelled
almost to burlesque his part of a
tough, New York newspaper editor.
. . . Constance Bennett is
overshadowed by the indomitable
Gable. What she has to do, she does
nicely, but that's about all. This is
the first time Clark Gable and Miss
Bennett have co-starred, but not the
first time they have appeared in the
same picture. They both played in
The Easiest Way four years ago.
Robert Montgomery and Adolph
Menjou were Miss Bennett's leading
men, and Gable came right at the
bottom of the cast list as Nick, the
milkman. Gable then went on to
The Secret Six and fame.

CALL OF THE WILD

1935. Twentieth Century-Fox.

Produced by Darryl F. Zanuck.
Directed by William Wellman.
Screenplay and adaptation by Gene
Fowler and Leonard Praskins, based
on the novel by Jack London.
Photography by Charles Rosher.
Editor: Hanson Fritch.
Release date: April 30, 1935.
Running time: 95 minutes.

CAST: Clark Gable, Loretta Young,
Jack Oakie, Reginald Owen, Frank
Conroy, Katherine DeMille, Sidney
Toler, James Burke, Charles
Stevens, Lalos Encinas, Tommy
Jackson, Russ Powell, Herman Bing,
George McQuarrie.

SYNOPSIS: An adventurous prospector,
Jack Thornton (*Clark Gable*), makes
a gold strike and then loses all his
dust on the gambling tables. When
trying to get another stake he saves
Buck, a seemingly unmanageable dog,
from being killed by a villainous
prospector named Smith (*Reginald
Owen*). He buys the dog and trains
him — winning the animal's love.

Smith wagers him a thousand
pounds that Buck cannot pull a sled
loaded with a thousand pounds for
a hundred yards. Thornton tells Buck
that it's up to him. The dog fulfills
the conditions of the wager and
brings Thornton the money to return
to the gold fields with his friend,
Shorty (*Jack Oakie*).

Prince, another sled dog, is jealous
of Buck. Whenever they meet he
tries to pick a fight. One night they
fight it out and Buck kills him. The
fight sets his wild blood pulsing in

With Buck

With Loretta Young

his veins. When he hears a pack of
wolves howling, he breaks his sled
harness and runs off to join them.
He mates with a she-wolf, but when
spring comes he remembers his master
and tries to find him.

Buck discovers a prospector named
Blake (*Frank Conroy*), who has been
robbed and left to die in the snow.
Upon locating his master, Buck
leads him to the dying man. In the
meantime, Jack Thornton has met
Blake's wife (*Loretta Young*) and
fallen in love with her. She had
believed her husband to be dead,
but when he is saved by Thornton,
she must dutifully give up the man
she really loves and return to her
husband. Thornton is left alone in
the wilderness. Buck, his wild spirit
subdued by his loyalty to his master,
stays with him.

REVIEWS:

London Film Weekly: Clark Gable
as Buck's bearded, gold-prospecting
master, has to conform more or less
to type. He is a figure compounded
of virility, stern silence and innate
nobility. Loretta Young is similarly
straitjacketed into a part which calls
for little beyond good looks, a certain
stubbornness, and a great deal of
charm. It is to Jack Oakie, in a
"friend of the hero" role, that the
plums fall. . . . With the exception
of four days' shooting, the whole film
was made on Mount Baker,
Washington, 5,000 feet above sea
level, the highest location ever chosen.
Expedition included one hundred
players and technicians. Snow ploughs
worked day and night over 65 miles
of road to make way for the equipment.
. . . Owing to blizzards, production
took three months instead of

anticipated six weeks. The unit was
cut off from civilization and, when
food ran short, had to forge to the
nearest town. The temperature, often
10 degrees below zero, was so cold
that it froze the oil in the cameras.

Film Daily: The romance in the film
is between Clark Gable and the lovely
Loretta Young, both of whom are
adequate. And it's a tenderly told
story on the screen. . . . But Jack
Oakie as the irrepressible jail-bird
and Reginald Owen as the evil Smith
are vividly stimulating in their roles.
. . . You will tell your friends about
those scenes where Oakie rolls the
bones.

Photoplay: Jack London's novel,
Call of the Wild, comes to the screen
a vigorous, red-blooded picture that

With Jack Oakie and Buck

you are sure to enjoy. The refreshing
backgrounds of deeply gleaming
snow, towering mountains and wild,
rushing rapids, are exciting in
themselves. And when you put four
fine actors, Clark Gable, Loretta
Young, Jack Oakie, and Reginald
Owen, against these backgrounds,
you have top-notch entertainment.

Time: The familiar story has been
changed in spots, but the revisions
make for stronger screen fare. And
all the humanness, the drama, of the
novel have been retained. The direction
of William Wellman deserves high
praise, and Charles Rosher's
photography is top-notch. . . . Gable
is no stranger to the rugged life that
Jack London depicted in his work.
His characterization in this picture
is appropriate and all that we have
learned to expect from him.

With Loretta Young and Jack Oaki

CHINA SEAS
1935. Metro-Goldwyn-Mayer.

Produced by Albert Lewin.
Directed by Tay Garnett.
Screenplay by Jules Furthman and
James Keven McGuiness, based on
the novel by Crosbie Garstin.
Photography by Ray June.
Music by Herbert Stothart.
Edited by William Levanway.
Release date: August 16, 1935.
Running time: 90 minutes.

CAST: Clark Gable, Jean Harlow,
Wallace Beery, Lewis Stone, Rosalind
Russell, Dudley Digges, C. Aubrey
Smith, Robert Benchley, William
Henry, Live Demaigret, Lillian Bond.
With Edward Brophy, Donald Meek,
Carol Ann Beery, Akim Tamiroff,
Ivan Lebedeff, Soo Yong.

SYNOPSIS: Captain Alan Gaskell
(*Clark Gable*) is skipper of the Kin
Lung on its way to Hong Kong with
a valuable consignment. Gaskell is
annoyed to find China Doll (*Jean
Harlow*), his mistress on board. She
has bought a ticket and intends to
sail with him. Then Sybil Barclay
(*Rosalind Russell*) comes on board.
Alan and she are engaged to be
married.

With Wallace Beery

When China Doll learns of
Gaskell's engagement to Sybil, she is
heartbroken. She consoles herself by
playing a drinking game with James
MacArdle (*Wallace Berry*), a
rascally China Seas trader. She drinks
him under the table and wins a
great deal of money from him.
Among the bills is a torn fragment
of a hundred-pound note which has
some Chinese characters written on it.

With Rosalind Russell

Gaskell brings the ship safely out
of the typhoon that strikes and when
he returned to his cabin, he finds
China Doll there. She suspects that
MacArdle is involved in a plot to
steal the gold, and tries to warn
Gaskell. But misunderstanding her
presence in the cabin, he orders her
out. Her temper up, she decides to
side with MacArdle. She steals the
key to the ship's armory for him and
he arms some Malay confederates. A
battle ensues, during which a Malay
pirate ship is signaled and comes
alongside. They board the ship and
demand the gold. Gaskell is tortured,
but refuses to tell.

Meanwhile, the third officer (*Lewis
Stone*), who has been branded a
coward, gets some bombs from the
captain's cabin and attempts to
throw them into the pirate junk. He
deliberately falls, a human arsenal,
into the junk. The junk is almost
totally demolished, and the Malays
on board the Kin Lung are taken
prisoner. MacArdle commits suicide.
Realizing that China Doll is the only
girl for him, Gaskell bids goodbye
to Sybil.

REVIEWS:

The New York Times: If any one
member of the cast were to be singled
out as outstanding, it would be
Clark Gable. As Alan Gaskell, an
Englishman, who like so many of his
countrymen, has heard the "East
a-calling," he is the two-fisted skipper
of the tramp steamer. It is a role

which demands vigor, an infectious,
devil-may-care philosophy and the
stinging passion of distempered blood,
and while Gable has displayed these
qualities before, it is one of his most
convincing portrayals.

Hollywood Reporter: Clark Gable
plays the captain of the ship with ease
and assurance that will win him
many new admirers (as though he
needed any new fans). The captain
is a natural for Gable, a kindly
fellow who hides his warm heart
with gruffness. It is a grand piece of
casting.

Photoplay: Action and thrills, striking
photography and the glitter of the
well-known team of Gable and Harlow
only partly obscure the sordidness of
this tale of a white man's deterioration
in the fetid moral atmosphere of the
Orient. It is not sufficiently adroit in
its handling to make its coarseness
and brutality even slightly palatable.

John Gammie, London Film Weekly:
The actors, as the setting demands,
are romantic rather than real. Beery's
calculated villainy is as true to the
"heroic" type as is Gable's dogged
silence when tortured with the fiendish
"Malay Boot." Rosalind Russell is
cool, poised and pleasing—a model
of self-disciplined English womanhood
in striking contrast to the emotionalism
and unrestrained hysteria of Jean
Harlow's "China Doll." . . . None
of them is called upon for any great
depth of acting. Their personalities
are distinct rather than subtle. The
constant threat of tempests, and piracy
makes the interest lie less in their
emotions than in their actions,
frequently subordinating them to the
boisterous excitement of the plot.

With Edward Brophy and Jean Harlow

With Lewis Stone

With Jean Harlow, Wallace Beery, Rosalind Russell, and C. Aubrey Smith

MUTINY ON THE BOUNTY

1935. Metro-Goldwyn-Mayer.

Produced by Irving Thalberg.
Directed by Frank Lloyd.
Screenplay by Talbot Jennings, Jules Furthman and Carey Wilson, based on the book by Charles Nordhoff and James Norman Hall.
Photography by Arthur Edeson.
Musical score by Herbert Stothart.
Edited by Margaret Booth.
Release date: November 1, 1935.
Running time: 132 minutes.

CAST: Charles Laughton, Clark Gable, Franchot Tone, Herbert Mundin, Eddie Quillan, Dudley Digges, Donald Crisp, Henry Stephenson, Francis Lister, Spring Byington, Movita, Mamo, Ian Wolfe, Ivan Simpson, DeWitt Jennings, Stanley Fields, Wallace Clark, Vernon Downing, Dick Winslow.

SYNOPSIS: In 1787, *H.M.S. Bounty* sets sail for Tahiti on a scientific expedition. Captain Bligh (*Charles Laughton*), a competent seaman but a cruel master, is in charge of the ship which is to bring breadfruit trees back from the South Seas. Young Roger Byam (*Franchot Tone*) sails on the *Bounty* for his first cruise as a midshipman. From the first, he is disillusioned about sea life when he witnesses Bligh's cruelty. But he becomes a firm friend of the master's mate, Fletcher Christian (*Clark Gable*), who is respected by the entire crew. Bligh resents this, and continually goads Christian.

The voyage is long and arduous and Captain Bligh keeps the men on half rations to make a little money for himself. Christian is forced to sign the order book, although he denounces Bligh for a cheat. When Tahiti is sighted, Christian is informed that he may not go ashore. Hitihiti, the chieftain of the island, takes a liking to young Byam and takes him to his home. His time on the island is happily spent with Tehani (*Movita*), a pretty Tahitian. Hitihiti fixes it so that Christian can come ashore for one day. He meets Hitihiti's granddaughter, Miamiti (*Mamo*), and they fall in love.

Vith Vernon Downing and Donald Crisp

With Movita

When the time comes to leave, Christian promises to return. Five members of the crew attempt to desert and are flogged. Bligh commands that everyone, even the deathly ill surgeon, witness the punishment. When the old doctor reaches the deck, he is overcome and dies. The crew turns against Bligh, and charging him with murder, set him adrift on the open sea. Christian takes the *Bounty* back to Tahiti, where they live happily for many months. Christian marries Maimiti and Byam marries Tehani. But one night a British frigate, the *Pandora,* is sighted and Christian and his men and their wives leave Tahiti hurriedly on the *Bounty.*

Byam and five others who had no part in the mutiny, remain behind, overjoyed at the prospect of returning to England. Bligh and his men have been picked up by the *Pandora,* and he is determined to find Christian. He charges Byam and the others with mutiny and claps them in irons. He then begins to search for the *Bounty,* but wrecks the *Pandora* on a reef. He and the men who survive the wreck set out in an open boat. Among the survivors are Byam and three others charged with mutiny. Bligh brings them to the island of Timor, from whence they are taken to England.

Meanwhile, Christian has taken his men to Pitcairn's Island. There they must build new lives, and the *Bounty* is burned so that they can never leave.

Five years after sailing from Portsmouth, Byam is returned to face court martial. He is found guilty of

With Dudley Digges and Franchot Tone

mutiny, but before sentence is pronounced, he denounces Captain Bligh and exposes his cruelties. When the King reads this report, he pardons Byam, who is then recalled to service in the Navy.

REVIEWS:

John Gammie, London Film Weekly: Gable's Fletcher Christian is a brilliant characterization; and it is the more worthy of praise because the man could so easily have been merely a violent crusader against the captain's sadism. But Gable presents first and foremost a naval man, who, until the final outrage, strives hard to maintain discipline and tradition in spite of his feelings; and who, even when he has taken the fateful step, can still regret that he has been forced to break the ideals of the Service. A fine, natural performance, full of those small touches that make a character live.

Don Herold, Life: Mutiny on the Bounty is the cinema at its best, and it does a job which the legitimate stage, lacking sweep and scope and sky and sea, could never hope to achieve. The only reservation I wish to make is that those two Tahitian sweethearts seemed snatched right out of the Vassar daisy chain.

John Mosher, The New Yorker: Those who were thrilled by the book will find that the film meets all expectations. It is a story of brutality, fierce courage, unquenchable hope, powerful drama, against a wide sweep of sea and sky. Charles Laughton achieves a superb characterization as Captain Bligh. Gable and Tone give vivid performances, while the

As Fletcher Christian

members of the crew are individuals not types; we learn to know them well. If the picture leaves any regret, it concerns the scenes on Tahiti which are so sensuous and languid that they mar the tone and retard the tempo of the film. On the whole, the direction is outstanding.

New Republic: A film that must be labeled for adults only because of its violence. Yet it adds a chapter to the history of the abolishment of injustice toward the defenseless weak. Laughton and Gable are superb.

Richard Watts, Jr., New York Herald Tribune: Seemingly destined to be one of the most important in the industry's history, this production commands attention. Long in the making, a fact that bespeaks the care and effort exerted to assure authenticity in every detail, MGM's purse strings were pulled wide open.

Photoplay: From the bare historical truths of a saga of the sea, the greatest maritime film since *The Sea Hawk* surges with virile force across the screen. Some of you, however, may miss the customary love interest and a justice-triumphant ending. For the story of the *Bounty's* mutiny—faithfully culled from the Nordhoff-Hall book, is a brutal, sweat-and-blood tale of man's inhumanity to man, and its tragic consequences. It is not a pretty film, but it is grand and real, and so are its characters. . . . A superb sweep of reality distinguishes the entire film, which is finely mounted. Laughton, Gable, Tone etch unforgettable characters seconded by Eddie Quillan, Dudley Digges, and Donald Crisp. A brief capitulation to tenderness shows Gable and Tone with their South Seas wives. Herbert Mundin supplies a grim pinch of humor.

1935 ACADEMY AWARDS
BEST PICTURE: *Mutiny on the Bounty.*

With Charles Laughton

With Movita

WIFE VERSUS SECRETARY

1936. Metro-Goldwyn-Mayer.

With Hobart Cavanaugh and Gilbert Emery

Produced by Hunt Stromberg. Directed by Clarence Brown. Screenplay by Norman Krasna, Alice Duer Miller and John Lee Mahin, based on the novel by Faith Baldwin. Photography by Ray June. Music by Herbert Stothart and Edward Ward. Edited by Frank E. Hull. Release date: February 28, 1936. Running time: 88 minutes.

CAST: Clark Gable, Jean Harlow, Myrna Loy, May Robson, George Barbier, James Stewart, Hobart Cavanaugh, Gilbert Emery, Margaret Irving, William Newell, Marjorie Gateson, Gloria Holden, Tom Dugan.

SYNOPSIS: Dan Sanford (*Clark Gable*), prosperous young publisher, and his beautiful wife, Linda (*Myrna Loy*), have been happily married for three years. As such, she would never dream of being jealous of his attractive secretary, Whitey Wilson (*Jean Harlow*), who is semi-engaged to a young man named Tom (*Billy Newell*) anyway. But finally, insinuations of other people spark a faint jealousy in her and she wonders why Dan didn't promote Whitey to a different position in the firm when he could have.

Working on a scheme to consolidate one of his magazines with a lower-priced weekly, Dan flies to Havana to make an offer to the owner. So that other publishing houses

won't outbid him, everything is kept strictly confidential.

After Dan has left, Whitey, who is the only one who knows of the pending deal, learns something that Dan must know immediately. She calls him and he tells her to come to Havana at once, that they must try to close the deal right away. So Whitey takes the next plane and joins him in Havana. They work all night and the next day Dan is prepared to present his proposition to the owner of the weekly. He succeeds in getting control of the weekly at a fair price and is so elated that he and Whitey celebrate that night. He has been too busy to call Linda, as he promised, and so she calls him. Whitey answers the telephone. Linda, now sure that Dan has been untrue to her, leaves him, and won't even speak to him.

Linda takes passage on a ship

bound for Europe. Whitey goes to the ship and tells Linda that she is a fool. She tells her that Dan loves her, and that if she goes to Europe she will lose him forever. For Dan has asked Whitey to accompany him to Bermuda. Whitey leaves the boat and returns to to the office. Dan tells her to buy some new clothes to take to Bermuda. Just then Linda comes in, and Dan takes her in his arms. Whitey goes out and finds Tom waiting for her.

REVIEWS:

The New Yorker: The traditional home-office love triangle is handled with a certain degree of incredibility and enthusiasm that makes this picture more than a chronicle of everyday human relationships. . . . For lead man Gable, the part is nearly as cliché-conceived as the plot, and is rescued, perhaps, only by the feeling he projects that he is not just any businessman who has come up against these odds, but reacts like he could be.

Photoplay: It isn't as exciting as it might be, because you will be guessing ahead in the typical course of screen clichés. Nevertheless, Clark Gable is effective and affectionate enough for his most romantic admirer. Jean Harlow underplays pleasantly the other woman and Myrna Loy eats her heart out with dignity, as a lady should, until the very last. Expert direction and pretentious production bring it well out of the ordinary groove. May Robson and James Stewart bolster with small effective parts.

London Film Weekly: Here is one of the best films seen for a long time in which next to nothing happens. . . . Gable works hard, but is more convincing as a high-spirited husband than as the bustling man of Big Deals. . . . Jean Harlow is obvious in her methods and has one excellent scene in which she forces a show-down with the distraught wife. . . . Myrna Loy almost makes you believe in the wife whose give-and-take theories collapse when suspicion assails them. . . . See this picture if you enjoy the spectacle of three clever stars shining for all they are worth.

With Myrna Loy and Jean Harlow

With Myrna Loy and Jean Harlow

SAN FRANCISCO

1936. Metro-Goldwyn-Mayer.

A W. S. Van Dyke Production. Producers: John Emerson and Bernard H. Hyman. Directed by W. S. Van Dyke. Screenplay by Anita Loos, based on a story by Robert Hopkins. Photographed by Oliver T. Marsh. Edited by Tom Held. Montage sequences by John Hoffman. Musical Director: Herbert Stothart. Musical score by Edward Ward. Song, "San Francisco," by Gus Kahn, B. Kaper and W. Jurmann. Song, "Would You," by Nacio Brown and Arthur Freed. Art Director: Cedric Gibbons. Gowns by Adrian. Dances staged by Val Raset. Operatic sequences staged by William von Wymetal. Release date: June 26, 1936. Running time: 115 minutes.

CAST: Clark Gable, Jeanette MacDonald, Spencer Tracy, Jack Holt, Jessie Ralph, Ted Healy, Shirley Ross, Margaret Irving, Harold Huber, Al Shean, William Ricciardi. With Kenneth Harlan, Roger Imhof, Charles Judells, Russell Simpson, Bert Roach, Warren B. Hymer, Edgar Kennedy.

As Blackie Norton

SYNOPSIS: During the New Year's celebration of 1905 in San Francisco, a fire in a Barbary Coast Hotel drives singer Mary Blake (*Jeanette MacDonald*) into the street where she meets Blackie Norton (*Clark Gable*), ruthless proprietor of the infamous Paradise Café. Fascinated by her beauty and learning that she is a singer, he hires her on the spot.

Blackie is running for City

With Jack Holt, Spencer Tracy, and Jeanette MacDonald

Supervisor. Backed by local colleagues, he tries to get a fire ordinance through to abolish the Coast's fire-trap buildings. But John Burley (*Jack Holt*), a major Coast landlord, polished aristocrat who lives off the so-called scum, bucks him tooth and nail. When Burley dines at the Paradise and sees Mary on the stage, he becomes enchanted with her and his companion, Baldini (*William*

As Blackie Norton

Ricciardi) of the Tivoli Opera House, says her golden voice should be for the "immortal music." The men meet Mary and offer her an audition but Blackie refuses to release her from her contract. Though strongly drawn to him, she runs away upon the advice of Blackie's best friend, Father Tim Mullin (*Spencer Tracy*).

Burley arranges her debut at the Tivoli Opera House. Blackie arrives threatening an injunction but he is so charmed by her singing in "this different world" that he relents and asks her to marry him to prove his love. He also insists she return to the Paradise. Father Tim's indignation rises against his boyhood chum, Blackie, and he persuades Mary her voice is not for this burlesque world but for the inspirational. Ashamed and heartsick, Mary resumes her operatic career and becomes engaged to Burley.

When Mary learns that Burley is out to destroy Blackie she tries to warn him but he rebukes her and tells her he never wants to see her again. Then the great earthquake of

With Spencer Tracy

With Jeanette MacDonald

1906 strikes and fire spreads through the city. For two days Blackie searches for Mary. Burley is killed. When he finds Mary she is singing a hymn to frightened refugees and he too finds belief in God as word comes that the fire has been checked.

REVIEWS:

New York Sun: With those earthquake scenes, with Miss MacDonald's golden voice and beauty, with the dimpled Mr. Gable in a he-man role, and with Mr. Tracy quietly humorous, quietly powerful as the understanding priest, *San Francisco* does not have to worry much about length or anything else.

Howard Barnes, New York Herald Tribune: It is a cunningly screened pattern of cinematic hokum. While the narrative is not to be recommended for its dramatic or emotional integrity, W. S. Van Dyke has shot the works in his direction and the performers have given the material the over-emphasis necessary to make it a showy entertainment. . . . Mr. Gable, as Blackie, is the most successful member of the company. . . .

Spencer Tracy is not so fortunate in the part of the holy father, but the role is not one that lends itself to the actor's particular talents. . . . As for Jeanette MacDonald, she is almost entirely nonplussed by the proceedings. When she is chanting ragtime ditties in a Barbary Coast cabaret she is engaging and believable, but there is not much to be said for her rendition of operatic fragments when she has been taken up by the dudes, and she scarcely ever achieves any power in her straight acting.

Newsweek: San Francisco is one of

With Jeanette MacDonald, Jack Holt, and William Ricciardi

the strangest conglomerations ever welded into a film. It has a lusty story of Barbary Coast days, a love triangle, cabaret dancing, opera, comedy, religion, and a moral, politics, and the 1906 earthquake. Despite these seeming incongruities, the picture holds together well—and the quake scenes are amazing. . . . To bring to a conclusion all these diverse stories, overlong in spots, director W. S. Van Dyke, uses the earthquake as a grand climax. Without the rest of the picture, this portion alone would be worth a steep admission price.

Frank S. Nugent, The New York Times: Out of the gutsy, brawling, catastrophic history of the Barbary Coast in the early century, Metro-Goldwyn-Mayer has fashioned a prodigally generous and completely satisfying screenplay. *San Francisco* is less a single motion picture than an anthology.

. . . Seeking symbolism in the cinema is probably a thankless pursuit, yet one might present a defensible argument that Miss MacDonald's alternate indulgence in operatic arias and cabaret chantey was no less typical of the groping, immature spirit of wayward, flamboyant, young San Francisco than was Clark Gable's arrogant godlessness as the picture's Blackie Norton.

. . . But one cannot reduce Mr. Gable, Miss MacDonald, Spencer Tracy, Jack Holt and others in the cast to mere abstractions. *San Francisco* tells their story too, and in a wealth of dramatic details that cannot be imprisoned in any brief synopsis.

. . . The earthquake is a shattering spectacle, one of the truly great cinematic illusions; a monstrous, hideous, thrilling debacle with great fissures opening in the earth, buildings, crumbling, men and women apparently being buried beneath showers of stone and plaster, gargoyles lurching from rooftops, watermains bursting, live wires flaring, flame, panic, terror.

. . . For so impressive and entertaining a picture, only a round robin of appreciation would do justice to the many who shared in its making.

With Jeanette MacDonald

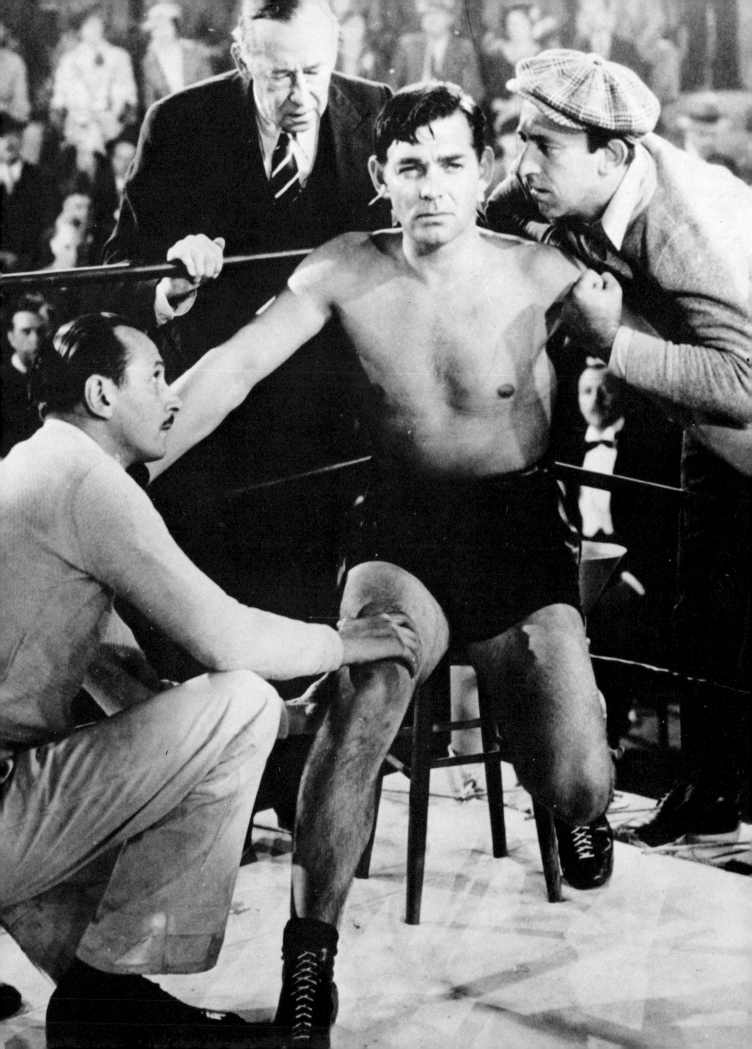

CAIN AND MABEL

1936. Warner Brothers.

A Cosmopolitan Production supervised by Sam Bischoff. Directed by Lloyd Bacon. Screenplay by Laird Doyle, based on a short story by H. C. Witwer. Photography by George Barnes. Edited by William Holmes. Release date: October 19, 1936. Running time: 90 minutes.

CAST: Marion Davies, Clark Gable, Allen Jenkins, Roscoe Karns, Walter Catlett, David Carlyle, Hobart Cavanaugh, Ruth Donnelly, Pert Kelton, William Collier, Sr., Sammy White, E. E. Clive, Allen Pomeroy, Robert Middlemass, Joseph Crehan, Eily Malyon.

SYNOPSIS: For publicity purposes, a musical comedy star, Mabel O'Dare (*Marion Davies*), is prodded to agree to a wild romance with a prize fighter, Larry Cain (*Clark Gable*), that will be headlined in all the papers. Both the fighter and the singer-comedienne are against it at first; but in hopes that the publicity will aid their careers, they agree.

Unfortunately, Mabel's show does not catch on. And Cain, although a champion, does not cash in either. To this point, their objective in teaming up has been money, not

With Marion Davies

With Marion Davies

matrimony. And love between them is spread very thin. In fact, they begin by hating each other.

Their constantly being pushed together by the papers and their agents leads to a series of escapades that bring them into an intimate association. Finally when they fall in love and plan a secret elopement,

they have to be separated, temporarily, for more publicity.

REVIEWS:

Film Daily: Like the fistic champ that Clark Gable portrays in it, this Cosmopolitan feature matches punches with the very top-flight current films. Not only does Miss Davies give a vibrant and exquisite performance—certainly her best in recent years—but the surrounding cast is flawless, production lavish and the swiftly

With Marion Davies

paced screenplay copiously packs romance, tuneful melody, pathos and humor, providing audiences with 90 minutes of flittering entertainment.

Newsweek: The studio's cycle of musical spectacles, begun with the successful *42nd Street* reaches a new low. Clark Gable and Marion Davies fit in this picture like a fat hand squeezed into a small glove. Too much talent for such a skimpy, thinly woven plot that unravels in a trite series of moments rather than a well constructed tale.

The New York Times: Miss Davies's comedy scenes are, traditionally, her best, despite the studio's notion to the contrary. Mr. Gable's roles are becoming routine matters. He needs another *Mutiny on the Bounty*.

Time: These two glorious people go off to a little rose-covered cottage-garage in Jersey, and that's the end. It's the end of some very fine feelings about Mr. Gable and Miss Davies and musical comedy, too. You see it at your own risk.

As Larry Cain

With Marion Davies

LOVE ON THE RUN

1936. Metro-Goldwyn-Mayer.

With Joan Crawford

Produced by Joseph L. Mankiewicz. Directed by W. S. Van Dyke. Screenplay by John Lee Mahin, Manual Seff and Gladys Hurlbut. From the story by Alan Green and Julian Brodie. Cameraman: Oliver T. Marsh. Costumes by Adrian. Editor: Frank Sullivan. Release date: November 17, 1936. Running time: 81 minutes.

CAST: Joan Crawford, Clark Gable, Franchot Tone, Reginald Owen, Mona Barrie, Ivan Lebedeff, Charles Judels, William Demarest.

SYNOPSIS: Sally Parker (*Joan Crawford*), a beautiful American heiress living abroad, leaves her bridegroom-elect, Prince Igor (*Ivan Lebedeff*) of Taluska, at the altar and takes refuge in her hotel suite. Michael Anthony (*Clark Gable*), a newspaper correspondent, who has been sent to cover the wedding, promises to get her out of the hotel unnoticed .

Barney Pells (*Franchot Tone*), writer for a rival paper, is interviewing Baron Spandermann (*Reginald Owen*), who with the Baroness (*Mona Barrie*) is to embark on a stratosphere flying excursion. They are stopping in the same hotel. Michael steals their flying suits, and he and Sally put them on and leave the hotel. They are escorted to the flying field, by a crowd under the impression that they are the distinguished flying pair. Just before take-off, a man thrusts a bouquet of flowers at them. Sally discovers a plan of British

fortifications in the bouquet and they realize that the Baron is a dangerous spy.

They make a rather poor landing in the French countryside, and realizing that the spies will soon be after them, they disguise themselves as peasants and go into Paris. Michael cables their story to his paper without Sally's knowledge. That night they hide out in an old palace and confess their mutual love. But the next morning, upon seeing a newspaper, Sally realizes that Michael is capitalizing on their adventures. They quarrel bitterly, and when Barney arrives on the scene she leaves with him, deciding to get even with Michael by letting Barney in on the story too. They start for Nice on the train and are followed by the Baron and Baroness who throw Barney off and capture Sally.

Barney makes his way back to Paris and finds Michael and tells him that Sally is in danger. Michael locates the Baron and Sally in Nice only to become the Baron's prisoner. They are taken to a farmhouse where a plane

is being warmed up for a getaway.

Barney sneaks in and finds Michael bound to a chair. Michael persuades him to take his place and reluctantly Barney agrees. Then Michael outwits the spies and binds them securely. He and Sally leave in the plane, while poor Barney remains still tied to the chair.

REVIEWS:

Hollywood Spectator: Such a finished trio as Joan Crawford, Clark Gable and Franchot Tone can make us believe the unbelievable and entertain us with it. . . . *Love on the Run* is screen entertainment easy to take. Its strength lies in the weakness of its appeal to the intelligence of the audience. It is content with asking us only to have a good time with it.

John Mosher, The New Yorker: The plot is a bit improbable, but these three impetuous people have caught the spirit of the story and their rogueries are all depicted with a comic touch. Clever direction, sophisticated dialogue, novel settings and ludicrous situations combined with excellent casting spell "reel" entertainment. Very good.

Box Office: Another fast, suave, sophisticated comedy about an heiress and a star reporter. We like best the sequence where the worn-out runaway girl and the tired reporter break into Fountainebleau Palace to hide and seek a night's frolic—it touches a high point in comedy this year. There a mad, fantastic old caretaker mistakes them for the shades of Louis XIV and Mme. de Maintenon is as harebrained a comedy sequence as has yet been celluloided. Joan Crawford is amusing as Sally Parker, the spoiled darling of the rich; and Clark Gable, as Michael Anthony, contributes his best comedy role since *It Happened One Night*.

The New York Times: A slightly daffy cinematic item of absolutely no importance . . . with Joan Crawford, Clark Gable and Franchot Tone in roles that by now are a bit stale. In all good conscience, the film ought to bow to several distinguished antecedents, for it has borrowed liberally here and there of tried and true screen devices and situations.

With Franchot Tone and Joan Crawford

With Joan Crawford

With Montagu Love and Alan Marshall

As Charles Parnell

PARNELL

1937. Metro-Goldwyn-Mayer.

Directed by John M. Stahl.
Screenplay by John Van Druten and
S. N. Berhman, based on the play by
Elsie T. Schauffler.
Photography by Karl Freund.
Art direction by Cedric Gibbons.
Musical score by William Axt.
Edited by Frederick Y. Smith.
Release date: June 4, 1937.
Running time: 96 minutes.

CAST: Clark Gable, Myrna Loy, Edna
May Oliver, Edmund Gwenn, Alan
Marshal, Donald Crisp, Billie Burke,
Berton Churchill, Donald Meek,
Montagu Love, Byron Russell, Brandon
Tynan, Phyllis Coghlan, Neil
Fitzgerald, George Zucco.

SYNOPSIS: Charles Parnell (*Clark
Gable*) spends two months in
America raising money to relieve the
sufferings of the poor in Ireland.
When he returns home, he realizes
that he will have to double his efforts
to obtain Home Rule for Ireland. The
whole country is behind him to such
a degree that he is referred to as
"The Uncrowned King of Ireland."

Katie O'Shea (*Myrna Loy*) is the
estranged wife of William O'Shea
(*Alan Marshal*), an unscrupulous and
ambitious man. She makes her home

With John Qualen and Myrna Loy

with her wealthy Aunt Bea (*Edna
May Oliver*), who gives O'Shea
money in order to keep him away.
Katie longs to be free, but her
husband won't allow her a divorce.
He plans to stand for Parliament, and
for this end, asks Katie to entertain
Parnell at dinner.

She calls upon Parnell at his office.
He tells her that he saw her at the
opera one night and knew that they

With Edmund Gwenn

were destined to meet. He accepts her
dinner invitation. He is called away
by urgent business before the dinner
is over. Katie follows him to the door,
and he tells her that he loves her.

At last it looks as though his long
struggle will meet with success. But
at this point, William O'Shea
reappears. He demands that Parnell
appoint him Chief Secretary when a
Parliament has been established.
Parnell refuses. O'Shea then threatens
to sue Katie for divorce, naming
Parnell as co-respondent.

That evening Gladstone (*Montagu
Love*) announces at a reception that
he is to introduce Parnell's bill for
Home Rule in Parliament. It is the
highest peak of Parnell's career.
Aunt Bea and Katie accompany him
to the reception. But on the way,
they hear newsboys calling out that
Parnell has been named in O'Shea's
divorce suit. Katie and Aunt Bea
return home and Parnell goes to his
office. He notifies Gladstone that he
will await word from him there.

The bill is not introduced and the
Irish Party feels that Parnell has
betrayed his country for a woman.
His friends all desert him. Katie is
willing to sacrifice her good name and
defend the suit, saying that she and
her husband invited Parnell to their
home in order to betray him. But
Parnell won't let her do this, and the
suit goes uncontested. Parnell tries
vainly to hold the party together,
but when it turns against him, the
party separates. At a last meeting, he
is stricken with a heart attack. He is
taken to Katie's home in time to again
tell her of his love for her, and he
dies in her arms.

REVIEWS:
Bob Wagner, Script: Parnell? . . . No!

Clark Gable, in his worst miscasting.
. . . Nor is Myrna Loy any help to
him, for she is equally stodgy and
unbending. Too bad, because the story
is good, the direction fine, and the
production all we have learned to
expect from M-G-M. It is the
secondary characters who give the
picture what little life it has. . . .
Indeed the whole show is splendid.
Except for the unfortunate casting
of the principals.

F. S. Nugent, The New York Times:
For all the dignity of its production,
the imposing cast at its command . . .
Parnell struck me as being a
singularly pallid, tedious and
unconvincing drama. . . . With its
customary generosity, the studio has
has not stinted on the physical
accoutrements. The sets are rich and
solid, the costuming is splended. [It]
lacks vitality, it completely misses the
emotional surge that swept the play
out across the footlights into the
hearts of its audiences when it was
put on last season.

John Mosher, The New Yorker:
Among the notable invertebrates, I
would list *Parnell*. Trudging as I do
to the movies year in and year out, I
seem always capable of amazement
at the amount of boredom they can
arouse. Especially do I feel so in a
case of this sort, where money has
been spent to give the whole thing a
rich setting, where persons of
recognized talent have been employed
in the making. I must say that the two
leading players, expert though they
may be in their way, give not the
slightest indication of trying to
understand anything.

With Myrna Loy

SARATOGA

1937. Metro-Goldwyn-Mayer.

Produced by Bernard H. Hyman.
Directed by Jack Conway.
Original screenplay by Anita Loos
and Robert Hopkins.
Photography by Ray June.
Music by Edward Ward.
Edited by Elmo Vernon.
Release date: July 23, 1937.
Running time: 102 minutes.

CAST: Clark Gable, Jean Harlow,
Lionel Barrymore, Frank Morgan,
Walter Pidgeon, Una Merkel, Cliff
Edwards, George Zucco, Jonathan
Hale, Hattie McDaniels, Frankie
Darro, Henry Stone.

SYNOPSIS: The finest breeding farm
in Saratoga, Brookvale, has suffered
financially. And Frank Clayton
(*Jonathan Hale*), the owner hoping
to recoup his losses, has been betting
on the races through Duke Bradley
(*Clark Gable*), a bookmaker and close
personal friend, but dies of a heart
attack before he can restore Brookvale.
Frank's daughter Carol (*Jean Harlow*)
has become engaged to Hartley Madison
(*Walter Pidgeon*), a wealthy New
York stockbroker. Duke lost a huge
sum of money to Madison at Belmont,
and hopes to win it back. But Carol
won't let her fiancé bet on the horses
anymore, much to Duke's disgust.

Duke has incurred the enmity of
the husband, Jesse (*Frank Morgan*),
of his old friend Fritzi Kiffmeyer
(*Una Merkel*). Fritzi has talked her
husband into buying Dubonnet, a
race horse, for her. Kiffmeyer thinks
that Duke is in love with his wife,
and is jealous because Duke helps

With Lionel Barrymore

With Jean Harlow

her to get Dixie Gordon (*Frankie
Darro*), a top jockey, to ride Dubonnet
in the big Saratoga race. Duke hopes
to win some real money from Madison
on this race, for Madison's horse,
Moon Ray, is entered.

Carol realizes that she has fallen in
love with Duke. She is writing a letter
to Madison breaking their engagement,
when Duke stops in to see her. He
loves her, but realizes that her father
wanted her to have a secure life, away
from race tracks. So he pretends that
he cares nothing about her. She gets
angry, tears up the letter, and makes
up her mind that Madison shall not
lose to Duke.

Knowing that Kiffmeyer hates
Duke, she calls on him and gets him to
sell Dixie Gordon's contract to her.
She tells him that this will break
Duke. Without letting Duke know
what she has done, she gets him to
her house and lets him bet a fortune
with Madison. Fritzi finds out about
the contract too late to warn Duke
but she finds another jockey to ride
Dubonnet, who wins the race. Carol
realizes that the life Duke leads is
for her and together they set out for
the next race.

REVIEWS:

Motion Picture Herald: Jean Harlow
takes her final curtain call as the least
boisterous and most attractive heroine
of her career in a comedy of the race
track which is well staged and directed
and has an excellent cast. There is
a good deal of spontaneous fun on
the part of Clark Gable, Una Merkel
and Frank Morgan.

Variety: Saratoga is a sparklingly

produced race track picture. It has
much to do with horses and racing,
which precipitates plenty of exciting
action, but it has more to do with
the individuals who follow the horses.
It is comedy romance, somewhat
tinged with light melodrama.
Dialogue, situations, action and
characterizations blend effectively and,
although the film is rather long,
there is no dragging. Interesting
persons are constantly saying and
doing interesting and most amusing
things in interesting places.

*Marguerite Tazelaar, New York
Herald Tribune:* Jean Harlow's last
picture, which opened yesterday at
the Capitol, made this particular
individual feel sad. Partly because of
a still fresh memory of the gifted
young actress's untimely death, but
also almost a premonition of disaster.
Looking ill much of the time and
striving gallantly to inject into her
performance characteristic vigor and
vibrancy, the result, in face of
subsequent events, is grievous. Her
few brief glimpses of natural brilliance
as a comedienne, such as when
Mr. Gable hides her under the bed
while he entertains her fiancé, only
seem to intensify the shadow hovering
over her spirit and subduing it.
Saratoga is, in a way, an obituary
of a lovely person and a talented
actress. The picture is entirely Miss

With Frank Morgan and Una Merkel

Harlow's, tragic as it has proved to be. And
she is surrounded by a fine, loyal cast.

Time: Glib, forthright, knowing and
adroit, released last week to
coincide with the opening of the
1937 season at New York's old spa,
it investigates the lighter side of the
serious sport of horse racing with as
much good sense as good humor.

With Jean Harlow

TEST PILOT

1938. Metro-Goldwyn-Mayer.

Produced by Louis D. Lighton. Directed by Victor Fleming. Screenplay by Vincent Lawrence and Waldemar Young, based on a story by Lt. Comdr. Frank Wead. Photography by Ray June. Edited by Tom Held. Montage: Slavko Vorkapich. Musical score by Franz Waxman. Art direction: Cedric Gibbons.

Release date: April 22, 1938.
Running time: 118 minutes.

CAST: Clark Gable, Myrna Loy, Spencer Tracy, Lionel Barrymore, Samuel S. Hinds, Marjorie Main. With Ted Pearson, Gloria Holden, Louis J. Heydt, Virginia Grey, Priscilla Lawson, Claudia Coleman, Arthur Aylesworth.

SYNOPSIS: Famous test pilot Jim Lane (*Clark Gable*) has established many new records for the Drake Airplane Company. His life is a series of great risks, enlivened by periodic binges. Gunner (*Spencer Tracy*), his mechanic, idolizes him and watches his every move.

Jim is to test the new Drake Bullet on a coast-to-coast flight. Over Kansas, he has motor trouble and makes a forced landing on the Barton farm. After meeting Ann Barton (*Myrna Loy*), they fall madly in love. And when the ship is repaired he takes her East with him. They are married in Pittsburgh. Then Jim breaks the news to Drake (*Lionel Barrymore*) and asks for a week off. They quarrel, and Drake fires him. Jim goes on a bender that lasts for five days. During this time Ann decides to leave him. But when Gunner brings him back to her, broke, she realizes that she loves him too much to ever give him up. Drake, too, relents and rehires him.

General Ross (*Samuel S. Hinds*) longs to get Jim back in the army. He kicked Jim out once for indulging in too much night-life, but now wishes he had him back. Jim is ordered to test a gignatic army bomber. Gunner is to go up with him. The ship is loaded with sandbags to equal the weight of bombs and crew. Jim hopes to be able to reach an altitude of thirty thousand feet. He almost makes it, and then the ship goes into a dive.

With Myrna Loy

With Spencer Tracy

The sandbags burst from the rear compartment, and Gunner is pinned under them. Jim tries to release him, but Gunner, wanting to save his friend, kicks him out of the ship. Jim's parachute opens, and he lands safely, but the ship crashes and Gunner is killed.

So deeply is Jim affected by the loss of his friend that Drake realizes that he won't be any good as a test pilot any longer. With the aid of General Ross and Ann, he maneuvers Jim back into the service before he realizes what is happening. In two years as an instructor, he has found happiness with Ann and their newly-born son.

REVIEWS:

Cue: As the trio, Clark Gable, Spencer Tracy and Myrna Loy turn in probably the best performances of their careers, and help enormously to

With Myrna Loy and Spencer Tracy

make this picture a leading contender for the Ten Best List of 1938.

Boxoffice: This one looks as if it's heading for "wow" grosses. In star value, it has Clark Gable, Myrna Loy, and Spencer Tracy and their performances rank well with anything they have so far done. In the case of Gable and Loy, probably their best here. In story value, the routine prevails and film often sags between its smashing air climaxes, then to buildup with a crashing and amounting excitement that makes amends.

John Mosher, New Yorker: It can be said that *Test Pilot* isn't exactly unusual, but it is not the commonplace sketch of the professional and domestic lives of fliers that its first moments seem to indicate. All flying films have fine flying scenes in them, of course, just as all boat pictures have fine sea scenes. Those in *Test Pilot*, though, are superior to the average.

Time: Credit for blending this grounded mental conflict with the melodrama of wings in the air, screaming struts and whining motors goes to Director Victor Fleming. Not the least of his accomplishments was to exact performances that verge on reality from pert, actressy Myrna Loy and loud, slam-bang Clark Gable. From amenable, sandy Spencer Tracy, currently cinema's No. 1 actors' actor, Director Fleming got what he wanted without coaxing.

TOO HOT TO HANDLE

1938. Metro-Goldwyn-Mayer.

Produced by Lawrence Weingarten.
Directed by Jack Conway.
Screenplay by Laurence Stallings and
John Lee Mahin, based on a story by
Len Hammond. Photography by
Harold Rosson. Editor: Frank Sullivan.
Release date: September 16, 1938.
Running time: 105 minutes.

CAST: Clark Gable, Myrna Loy, Walter
Connolly, Walter Pidgeon, Leo
Carrillo, Johnny Hines, Virginia
Weidner, Betsy Ross Clarke, Henry
Kolker, Marjorie Main, Gregory Gaye,
Al Shean, Willie Fung. Lillie Mui,
Patsy O'Connor.

SYNOPSIS: Chris Hunter (*Clark Gable*),
ace cameraman for Union Newsreels,
and his rival, Bill Dennis (*Walter
Pidgeon*), are entreated by pretty
Alma Harding (*Myrna Loy*), an
intrepid aviatrix. She needs their help
to finance a search party to South
America to find her brother Harry
(*Johnny Hines*), who was lost on a
flight over Brazil a year before.
Smelling a story, they agree and are
soon on their way.

In the small town of Pinto, on
the Amazon, they encounter a native
who has Harry Harding's watch. Chris'
assistant (*Leo Carrillo*), who is a
Spaniard, talks with the native, and
learns that he is a member of a
voodoo tribe. Undoubtedly they have
been practicing their secret rites on
Harry, and now want a white woman
for their rituals.

To forestall Alma, Chris and his
assistant take the native down to the
river in a canoe. Approaching the
voodoo village, they knock their

With Myrna Loy

With Leo Carillo

companion out and tie him up.
Then they cautiously make their way
toward the village, where a ceremony
is taking place. An emaciated white
man, undoubtedly Harry, is carried
out, appearing nearly dead. Chris
decides to act at once. Using the
smooth face of a cliff as a screen,
he starts projecting a series of
newsreels, in which he appears. Then
he appears in the flesh before the
astounded natives, who believe he is
a god.

That night, Chris tries to revive
Harry Harding. In the morning Alma
and Bill arrive in her amphibian.
Dressed as a native, Chris indicates
that they are to put Harry in the ship.
Meanwhile, he secretly takes pictures
of the whole thing. But the native
who led them here has been released
by another. Now he comes into the
village and exposes Chris to his
tribesmen. Alma and Bill, with Harry
in the plane, have started down the
river. Chris and his assistant jump into
a punt and hanging onto the tail of
the ship, are pulled to safety. But Bill,
not realizing who the weirdly dressed
occupants of the punt are, fires at
them, forcing them to let go.

Back in New York, Alma and
Harry are given a royal welcome. But
Bill Dennis learns, to his dismay, that
Chris has scooped him. Newsreels of
the rescue of Harry Harding are
showing all over the country. Chris is
off now, shooting a gangster gun
battle. Eager to see him, Alma, with
no regard for the danger involved,
joins him.

REVIEWS:

F. S. Nugent, The New York Times:
Too Hot to Handle is any one of a
dozen fairly entertaining melodramas
you might have seen in the last five
years. . . . Mr. Gable plays the
annoying Chris Hunter with his
customary blend of bluster and blubber.
Miss Loy's lady-flier is not only
incredible of herself, but has the
disadvantage of a completely insincere
performance.

Time: Again teaming Clark Gable
and Myrna Loy, this feature should
prove as torrid at the turnstiles as its
title, for it adroitly blends into a
strikingly superior whole every proven
entertainment element: and at the
same time proves that new ideas can
be successfully utilized in the
manufacture of films.

*Howard Barnes, New York
Herald Tribune:* It does not fall into
the class with *Test Pilot*, in which
Clark Gable and Myrna Loy recently
appeared, but interest never lags. It's
like an old-fashioned serial, chapter

*With Leo Carillo, Walter Pidgeon, and
Myrna Loy*

after chapter, each more exciting
than the last. . . . Film technique is
used to perfection, giving us our
money's worth of vicarious adventure,
and no one can call it dull.

*John Mosher, The New Yorker: Too
Hot to Handle* by sheer force bullies
us into a kind of acceptance of its
various preposterous details and even
of all its endless jargon. . . . The
first half-hour of the picture may
make you bolt. Newsreel cameramen,
like reporters, are just big, grown-up
boys, the movies tell us, but I wish
the movies wouldn't always present
them as a gang of cut-ups.

With Myrna Loy

IDIOT'S DELIGHT

1939. Metro-Goldwyn-Mayer.

Produced by Hunt Stromberg.
Directed by Clarence Brown.
Screenplay by Robert Sherwood,
based on his own play.
Cameraman: William Daniels.
Editor: Robert J. Kern.
Release date: January 27, 1939.
Running time: 105 minutes.

CAST: Norma Shearer, Clark Gable,
Edward Arnold, Charles Coburn,
Joseph Schildkraut, Burgess Meredith,
Laura Hope Crews, Skeets Gallagher,
Peter Willes, Pat Patterson, William
Edmunds, Fritz Feld.

SYNOPSIS: Following World War I,
Harry Van (*Clark Gable*), all-round
entertainer, meets Irene (*Norma
Shearer*) when a drinking mind-reader
with whom he is working fails to read
minds. Hitting it off immediately,
they spend the night together. Both
phonies in their profession, they part
with the sad feeling that somewhere in
another time they might have made a
go of it. They go their separate ways.

Harry, with a troupe of six girls,

With Norma Shearer and Fritz Feld

tours Europe, but is detained on the
Swiss border when rumors of war
spread. They put up in a swanky
hotel awaiting further news with
excited anticipation. Ammunition
Baron Achille Weber (*Edward
Arnold*), arrives with Irene and Harry
wonders if she is *the* Irene. When he
confronts her she denies it with a
thick Russsian accent that sounds
phony.

That night Harry stages
entertainment for the hotel guests.
The war, promoted by Weber, begins
with bombs falling. Irene derides
Weber for his doings and Weber
abandons her, saying if he hadn't
done it someone else would have. In
the lobby of the hotel Irene and
Harry resume the friendship they left
off years before. After he sees that his
girls are off to safety he sits at the
piano and plays "Onward Christian
Soldiers" as the bombs fall closer.
He and Irene join in singing together.

REVIEWS:

Film Daily: Novelty of characters and
plot, with an unhackneyed romance,
good cast and direction, and a
vigorous, lightly handled part
outstandingly played by Clark Gable.
This film version of Robert
Sherwood's play suffers a little in the
translation, but the fun and

With Norma Shearer

excitement are still there, however
filtered it may be.

Hollywood Reporter: Surefire boxoffice
in a big way and certainly one of the
most potential grossers of the year,
Idiot's Delight is an exceptional
comedy carrying wide audience appeal.
Gable and Shearer give their brightest
performance to date.

Time: The spectacle of Clark Gable
embracing Norma Shearer for the first
time since *Strange Interlude* (1932).
. . . The most profound problems
proposed for cinemaddicts are just
how the Hays Office chanced to
approve the character impersonated by
Miss Shearer, and just how inexpertly
Gable dances. . . . The fact that
Idiot's Delight has nothing very
important to tell its audiences by no
means indicates that it is bad
entertainment. It is first rate.

*With Virginia Grey, Joan Marsh,
Bernadene Hayes, and Lorraine Krueger*

GONE WITH THE WIND

1939. Metro-Goldwyn-Mayer.

A Selznick International Pictures Production. Produced by David O. Selznick. Directed by Victor Fleming. Screenplay by Sidney Howard, based on the novel by Margaret Mitchell. Photography by Ernest Haller. Art direction by Lyle Wheeler. Musical score by Max Steiner. Dance Directors: Frank Floyd and Eddie Prinz. Special Effects by Jack Cosgrove and Lee Zavitz. Edited by Hal C. Kern and James E. Newcom.
Release date: December 13, 1939.
Running time: 225 minutes.

CAST: Clark Gable, Leslie Howard, Olivia de Havilland, Vivien Leigh, George Reeves, Fred Crane, Hattie McDaniel, Everett Brown, Thomas Mitchell, Oscar Polk, Barbara O'Neill, Victor Jory, Evelyn Keyes, Ann Rutherford, Butterfly McQueen, Howard Hickman, Alicia Rhett, Rand Brooks, Carroll Nye, Marcella Martin, Laura Hope Crews, Harry Davenport, Leona Roberts, Jane Darwell, Albert Morin, Mary Anderson, Terry Shero, William McClain, Eddie Anderson, Jackie Moran, Cliff Edwards, Ona

With Vivien Leigh

Munson, Ed Chandler, George Hackathorne, Roscoe Ates, Eric Linden, John Arledge, Tom Tyler, William Bakewell, Lee Phelps, Paul Hurst, Ernest Whitman, William Stelling, Louis Jean Heydt, Isabel Jewell, Robert Elliott, George Meeker, Wallis Clark, Irving Bacon, Adrian

Morris, J. M. Kerrigan, Olin Howard, Yakima Canutt, Blue Washington, Ward Bond, Cammie King, Mickey Kuhn, Lillian Kemble Cooper, Donna Hyatt, Zack Williams.

SYNOPSIS: Gerald O'Hara (*Thomas Mitchell*), an Irish immigrant, settles in North Georgia and becomes a prosperous plantation owner. By great luck he marries young Ellen Robillard (*Barbara O'Neill*) of Savannah, the daughter of one of the noblest Georgian families and becomes accepted by his aristocratic neighbors. They are blessed with three daughters, Scarlett (*Vivien Leigh*), Suellen (*Evelyn Keyes*), and Carreen (*Ann Rutherford*).

Scarlett, the eldest, worships her mother. Yet, under her beauty and Southern coquetry, she is as practical and acquisitive as her father, without his softer qualities. She is a vain and ruthless flirt. She believes she is in love with Ashley Wilkes (*Leslie Howard*), a blond and delicate neighbor youth. But Ashley loves his cousin, Melanie Hamilton (*Olivia de Havilland*), a delicate aristocrat like himself. He is frightened by Scarlett's vitality and hungriness. And although he thinks he loves her, he is afraid to marry her and decides to take Melanie for his bride.

When Scarlett loses Ashley she is more certain than ever that she must have him. On their wedding day, she meets Rhett Butler (*Clark Gable*), the black sheep of an old Charleston family. Rhett, a gambler, murderer, cynic, is attracted by Scarlett's beauty and realizes that they are equally ruthless and conscienceless. And although Scarlett is interested, she realizes nothing.

At the outbreak of the war between the states, Scarlett snares and marries Melanie Hamilton's shy and colorless brother, Charles (*Rand Brooks*), to stop gossip about her and Ashley. Her frail husband dies within two months in training camp. Scarlett bears his child, Wade.

Bored with life at home, Scarlett goes to Atlanta, to live with Ashley's wife, Melanie and Melanie's Aunt

With Olivia de Havilland and Vivien Leigh

With Rand Brooks and Leslie Howard

Pittypat Hamilton (*Laura Hope Crews*). In Atlanta she sees Rhett Butler again. He has become a blockade runner and war profiteer and is making piles of money. Scarlett cares no more about war and patriotism than Rhett Butler, and again she is attracted to him. And when Atlanta is sacked and burned by the northern troops, Rhett aids her, Melanie and their children in escaping the city. Then, in the midst of confusion and danger, Scarlett drives through the woods to the O'Hara plantation, Tara.

She finds her mother dead from typhoid, her father out of his mind, all the field slaves gone, the house looted and the cotton crop burned. On her shoulders falls the terrible task of saving the plantation. Ashley comes home, a tired and spiritless wreck from the war. She makes a home for him, too. The carpet-baggers try to get

her farm by unfair taxes.

Scarlett adjusts herself quickly to the black days of Reconstruction in Atlanta. She buys sawmills, consorts with Yankee officers and scalawags, employs convict labor. All she wants is to make money, never to be hungry again; and to hold onto Ashley, to keep him in her power, even if it breaks his spirit.

Soon after her second husband, Frank Kennedy, is killed, she marries Rhett Butler, who's become rich in

With Vivien Leigh

the war. But while attracted to Rhett and glad to have the use of his money, it is Ashley, the unattainable, that she wants. And this obsession for Ashley eventually shatters her marriage to Rhett even though they have a child and he deeply loves her.

It is only after Rhett loses his love for her through her indifference and cruelty, and after the gentle Melanie dies, that Scarlett comes to earth. She finally realizes that Ashley loved Melanie, and that she had only been clinging to a girlish dream. It is Rhett she loves, but it is too late. He will have no more to do with her and leaves her. But Scarlett is not the type who can admit defeat. With her two children she returns to Tara, to get near the soil again, to soak up its strength and prepare for a stubborn, but vain, effort to win Rhett back again.

REVIEWS:

McCue, Film Daily: Mightiest achievement in the history of the motion picture. Superb entertainment which will hold the close attention of audiences for every minute of its long running time. Study groups and schools must prepare for the showing of this supreme screen masterpiece. . . . I wish I had time to write a book about it. . . . Have never seen

With Vivien Leigh

With Hattie McDaniel

finer acting. Clark Gable and Vivien Leigh are certain for this year's top awards.

Photoplay: The picture you've talked about and cast and fought over since 1937 is here ready for your inspection. These are the important things about GWTW: first, it is epic entertainment; second, it is as if the characters of Margaret Mitchell's book had come to life speaking the dialogue Miss Mitchell wrote. Certainly no one can complain of infidelity to the original story. Scarlett, played, of course, by Vivien Leigh, is the same vital, stupid, selfish, pathetic girl whose valiant fight to survive the death of the Old South you followed so breathlessly in the book. She gives a truly

Thomas Mitchell and Vivien Leigh

With Vivien Leigh

magnificent performance. Clark Gable has only to be himself, so perfectly cast he is as Rhett Butler. These two carry the burden of essential emotion from the time of their meeting at Twelve Oaks, through the fall of the Confederacy, to the denouncement after the cruel Reconstruction. Olivia de Havilland has done the finest job of her carer, as the sweet, gentle Melanie. Leslie Howard as Ashley fulfills expectations.

McCarthy, Hollywood Reporter: The

With Vivien Leigh

picture is an event, the greatest ever to date, in motion picture production. One could speak of it endlessly and still not pay it the tribute which is its due. . . . No actor and a role were ever so perfectly wed as Clark Gable and Rhett Butler.

Richard Watts, Jr., New York Herald Tribune: It is a monumental picture! Standing alone in its class, GWTW defies a reviewer to put into print its fabulous achievement.

The New York Times: Is it the greatest picture ever made? Probably not, although it is the greatest motion mural we have seen and the most ambitious film-making venture in Hollywood's spectacular history.

Newsweek: This is far too much picture to review adequately in less than several pages, with the brilliant cast itself too large to discuss in this

space. Expect to find your favorite novel brought to colorful, indeed overwhelming life in some of the finest Technicolor ever to tint the screen. Every spectacle, every emotional climax is faithfully reproduced. The characters come and go, leaving you somewhat fatigued by the most fabulous cinema pageant Hollywood has produced in its time. It was a titanic effort and a successful one.

Allen Bishop, Theatre Arts Magazine: "GWTW" is well cast and extremely well acted. Vivien Leigh seems a good, though not a sensational choice for Scarlett; Clark Gable is obviously right for Rhett Butler, and Olivia de Havilland is an almost perfect Melanie. The costuming is above reproach; the interior sets are first rate; much of the Technicolor photography is beautiful; it has some magnificent and a few highly dramatic scenes, especially in the first, and much the best, half of the film.

Time: Whatever it is not, "GWTW" is a first-rate piece of Americana, and Americans in the mass knew what they wanted before the critics had got through telling them they should not want it. . . . Better than almost anybody, producer David Selznick sensed that the first rule in retelling a legend is exactly the same as retelling a fairy tale to children— no essential part of the story must ever be changed. In the film, none is. . . . For almost four hours the drama keeps audiences on the edge of their seats with few let-downs. There are unforgettable climaxes. . . . The best of Gable's career without a doubt.

Variety: In some ways the most herculean film task ever undertaken, *Gone With the Wind* appears finally as one of the screen's major achievements, meriting highest respect and plaudits, and poised for grosses which may be second to none in the history of the business. . . . The result

With Laura Hope Crews, Leslie Howard, and Vivien Leigh

amply justifies the vast patience, the confidence, the showman's faith and courage, the time consumed and even the soaring expense. . . . The cast, headed by Gable and Leigh, is one of the best ever assembled. Gable gives the performance of the year. And Vivien Leigh is not far behind.

1939 ACADEMY AWARDS
BEST PICTURE: *Gone with the Wind*
BEST ACTRESS: Vivien Leigh
BEST SUPPORTING ACTRESS: Hattie McDaniel
BEST DIRECTOR: Victor Fleming
BEST WRITTEN SCREENPLAY: Sidney Howard
BEST COLOR CINEMATOGRAPHY: Ernest Haller and Ray Rennahan
BEST ART DIRECTION: Lyle Wheeler
BEST FILM EDITING: Hal C. Kern and James E. Newcom
SPECIAL OSCAR: William Cameron Menzies, for outstanding achievement in the use of color for the enhancement of dramatic mood
SCIENTIFIC AND TECHNICAL OSCAR: Don Musgrave and Selznick International Pictures, Inc., for pioneering in the use of coordinated equipment
IRVING G. THALBERG MEMORIAL AWARD: David O. Selznick

With Vivien Leigh

As Rhett Butler, breaking into Scarlet's bedroom

STRANGE CARGO
1940. Metro-Goldwyn-Mayer.

Produced by Joseph L. Mankiewicz.
Directed by Frank Borzage.
Screenplay by Lawrence Hazard, based
on the book, *Not Too Narrow,
Not Too Deep,* by Richard Sale.
Adapted by Anita Loos.
Photography by Robert Planck.
Art Director: Cedric Gibbons.
Musical score by Franz Waxman.
Edited by Robert J. Kern.
Release date: March 1, 1940.
Running time: 105 minutes.

CAST: Clark Gable, Joan Crawford,
Ian Hunter, Peter Lorre, Paul Lukas,
Albert Dekker, J. Edward Bromberg,
Eduardo Ciannelli, John Arledge,
Frederic Worlock, Bernard Nedell,
Victor Varconi.

SYNOPSIS: After long preparation,
eight criminals escape from a New
Guinea penal colony and strike
through the jungle to the seacoast
where a sloop awaits them. They are
picked up by Verne (*Clark Gable*),
another escaped fugitive, and his girl
friend, Julie (*Joan Crawford*).
Verne overcomes Moll (*Albert
Dekker*), the leader of the group,
and takes over their command.

They are then each influenced by
a convict called Cambreau (*Ian
Hunter*), a wild mystical Christ-like

With Joan Crawford

figure with a Bible. As Cambreau's
powers become evident, the fugitives
sense that he is not one of them and
commence to hate him because he
stands before each like a guilty
conscience.

In due time, though, his influence
draws each one to God and a splendid
repentant death before the trip is
ended. Even M'sieu Pig (*Peter Lorre*)
who has sided with Moll and held out
to the last has his justice in a cruel
death. In surrendering to Cambreau,
Verne abandons his plan of escape,
goes to Julie and declares his
willingness to serve out the few years
of imprisonment remaining to him
if she will wait for him. They return
to the penal colony.

REVIEWS:

Variety: Clark Gable plays the toughest
of the convicts; Joan Crawford, a
brothel gal. Their performances are

complemented by the mystical Ian
Hunter. Their three qualities mix and
mingle as the ingredients in a fine
drink: it leaves you in a mild but
pleasant stupor; there is no hangover,
however, other than a sense of
appreciation and admiration for a
great show.

Time: Part of its strange power
Strange Cargo derives from the tact,
restraint and experience of director
Frank Borzage (*A Farewell to Arms*).
Part of it derives from the fact that all
the actors, including Clark Gable, are
perfectly typed; as Joan Crawford,
who, under one guise or another, has
been playing Sadie Thompson so long
that the part is almost second nature.
. . . This perfect Hollywood formula
is turned into a highly unusual
picture by the surprising performance
of Ian Hunter as the Christ-like
convict, who is compassionate without
becoming mawkish.

With Joan Crawford

Film Daily: Here is a good, raw, stark
melodrama which holds suspense from
the start. Frank Borzage has given it
expert directorial attention. With
Joseph L. Mankiewicz filling the
duties of the producer. Clark Gable
fits his role admirably, while Ian
Hunter has never done better work.
The acting is high-grade with Joan
Crawford giving her best performance
to date. Peter Lorre is M. Pig, and
most expressive about it.

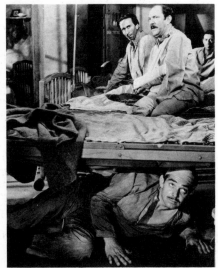

As Verne Andre

With Joan Crawford and Peter Lorre

With Joan Crawford and Ian Hunt

With Spencer Tracy, Claudette Colbert, and Frank Morgan

With Marion Martin, Spencer Tracy

BOOM TOWN

1940. Metro-Goldwyn-Mayer.

Produced by Sam Zimbalist. Directed by Jack Conway. Screenplay by John Lee Mahin, based on a short story by James Edward Grant. Photoplay by Harold Rosson. Edited by Blanche Sewell. Special Effects by Arnold Gillespie. Montage: John Hoffman. Musical score: Franz Waxman. Art Director: Cedric Gibbons. Costumes by Adrian and Giles Steele. Release date: August 30, 1940. Running time: 116 minutes.

CAST: Clark Gable, Spencer Tracy, Claudette Colbert, Hedy Lamarr, Frank Morgan, Lionel Atwill, Chill Wills, Marion Martin. With Minna Gombell, Joe Yule, Horace Murphy, Roy Gordon, Richard Lane, Casey Johnson, Baby Quintanilla, George Lessey, Sara Haden, Frank Orth, Frank McGlynn, Sr., Curt Bois.

SYNOPSIS: Oil field wildcatters "Big John" McMasters (*Clark Gable*) and "Square John" Sand (*Spencer Tracy*) meet in a developing oil town where they've come to make their fortunes. Becoming partners, they go after a well together. Square John is engaged to a girl back home, Betsy Bartlett (*Claudette Colbert*). If the well comes in, he intends to bring her to Texas and marry her. However, Betsy comes out to surprise Square John and accidentally meets Big John. It is love at first sight, and they marry on the eve of the day the well comes in.

With Spencer Tracy

With Georgia Simmons, Frank McGlynn, and Claudette Colbert

Square John accepts his loss without resentment, but when, a year later, he thinks Big John is unfaithful to Betsy, he is enraged. Big John is hurt and angered by this lack of trust. He and Square John gamble for the oil field, and Big John loses. Betsy feels that she must stand by Big John now that he's lost everything.

The following years bring many changes. Square John loses a fortune in oil and regains it. Big John enters the refining and distributing end of the business and becomes a huge success. He becomes involved with another woman, and Betsy is heartbroken. Square John attempts to bring Big John to his senses. Although losing practically all his money in the effort, he is successful in returning Big John to Betsy.

Big John is indicted under the Sherman Anti-Trust Law. It is Square John's testimony in his behalf that frees him. However, Big John's business has been ruined. Once again the two enter partnership and start from scratch in an undeveloped California field.

REVIEWS:

Bosley Crowther, The New York Times: In the manner of the wildcat driller indifferent to the laws of conservation, the Culver City producers have really shot the works . . . there hasn't been a picture in a long time to compare with Metro's roaring *Boom Town.* . . . Director Jack Conway has had some difficulty controlling the flow of the film. Like a gusher, it comes in with a blast, backed by the volcanic energy of

Mr. Gable and Mr. Tracy. . . . There is a magnificent shot of their first payhole blowing in with a mighty roar, splintering the head of the rig, and hurtling a black geyser into the sky.

With four stars in the picture, the desperate compulsions under which the director and screenwriter must have worked are obvious. Naturally Mr. Gable and Mr. Tracy have the most to do and are the best. The former looks and acts like an oil man— brassy, direct and tough. The latter flows deep and sure. Miss Colbert is a bit on the colorless side as a loyal wife and Miss Lamarr is a stunning but routine charmer.

The New York Herald Tribune: A good picture; a great cast. Spencer and Gable come across tough and alive in their kind of movie. Miss Colbert and Miss Lamarr complement

With Spencer Tracy and Frank Morgan

them with their every turn. Miss Lamarr's breathtaking beauty highlights every scene in which she appears. There is not a moment when the picture steps beyond the bounds of good taste and excellent entertainment.

Variety: The Gable-Tracy combination that gave us *San Francisco* and *Test Pilot* looks for bigger and tougher worlds to conquer. Although there is a lot of woman power in the picture with Claudette Colbert and Hedy Lamarr, the masculine sparks are the ones that light up the script about the virile, crude world of oil drilling.

COMRADE X

1940. Metro-Goldwyn-Mayer.

With Hedy Lamarr and Natasha Lytees

Produced by Gottfried Reinhardt. Directed by King Vidor. Screenplay by Ben Hecht and Charles Lederer, based on a story by Walter Reisch. Photography by Joseph Ruttenberg. Editor: Harold F. Kress. Release date: December 13, 1940. Running time: 90 minutes.

CAST: Clark Gable, Hedy Lamarr, Oscar Homolka, Felix Bressart, Eve Arden, Sig Rumann, Natasha Lytees, Vladimir Sokoloff, Edgard Barrier, George Renavent, Mikhail Rasummy.

SYNOPSIS: Comrade X, alias McKinley B. Thompson (*Clark Gable*), who had been smuggling embarrassing stories about the government out of Russia, is discovered by a porter, Vanya (*Felix Bressart*), at his hotel. Vanya blackmails McKinley into agreeing to smuggle his daughter, Theodore (*Hedy Lamarr*), out of the country because the secret police have been investigating her since she is a true Communist.

The only way McKinley can persuade Theodore to come with him to America is to assure her that he is a Communist to the core, and that he needs her to help him spread the noble doctrine in the United States. Theodore talks it over with her idol, Siminoff (*Sig Rumann*), who is the leader of a counter-revolutionary group, and finally consents to McKinley's request. But first they must be married. It is the only way she can secure a passport. This is more than McKinley had expected, but Theodore is a fine figure of a girl and it might be interesting.

Unfortunately, the secret police apprehend them before they can leave the country. They are brought before Chief of Police Gregoriev (*Vladimir Sokoloff*), who has also had Vanya arrested. Vanya does his best to shield them but to no avail. Gregoriev knows McKinley is Comrade X. All three of them are sentenced to death, and they are joined in the cell by a large group of Siminoff's followers. It seems that Siminoff has taken over Gregoriev's post and, to show his good faith, has sacrificed a hundred or so of his former comrades.

In return for their freedom, McKinley offers Siminoff the negative of a photograph that displays Siminoff in an incriminating position. Siminoff agrees, and although he tries to trick them, McKinley, Vanya, and Theodore make good their escape from the country. Embittered by the duplicity of her idol, Theodore resigns herself to a life in a capitalistic country. It may not be so bad with McKinley there.

REVIEWS:

Film Daily: The surprise of the picture is Hedy Lamarr. This gal has found herself or, better, MGM has found her, for she simply knocks over her role of Theodore, looks ravishing and is the top ingredient of the show. This Lamarr performance, however, takes nothing away from Clark Gable, who is perfection in his part, with Felix Bressart giving another of his great characterizations.

Newsweek: Performances are excellent. Gable handles his role splendidly. Miss Lamarr is neatly effective as well as decorative in the comic requirements as a street car motorman, a loftily patronizing daughter, a zealous worker for her party, a horrified then complacent bride as she realizes she has been tricked into marriage by a crass bourgeois who takes her to Brooklyn to root for the Dodgers.

The New York Times: How the wits of the lovers are pitted against the succession of menacing commissars shapes up into a tense and suspense-ridden melodrama, culminating in an escape by armored tank which carries a walloping series of thrills. Situations in the tale vary from the legitimate to the fantastic, but always maintain a high degree of entertainment and comedy which runs from innuendo and satirical wit to slapstick.

Liberty Magazine: Here's a lively, raucous farce about Russia, with Clark Gable as a rowdy American newspaperman and Hedy Lamarr as a Soviet motorman. The film is fast and funny and notable from at least one angle: it is the first time Hollywood has gone ahead with utter disregard for what some foreign government might think. Another point of public interest: Hedy Lamarr in a Soviet nightgown.

With Peter Lorre and Rosalind Russell

With Rosalind Russell

THEY MET IN BOMBAY

1941. Metro-Goldwyn-Mayer.

Produced by Hunt Stromberg.
Directed by Clarence Brown.
Screenplay by Edwin Justus Mayer, Anito Loos and Leon Gordon, based on the story by John Kafka.
Photographed by William Daniels.
Art Director: Cedric Gibbons.
Musical score by Herbert Stothart.
Special effects by Warren Newcombe.
Edited by Blanche Sewell.
Release date: June 27, 1941.
Running time: 86 minutes.

CAST: Clark Gable, Rosalind Russell, Peter Lorre, Jessie Ralph, Reginald Owen, Matthew Boulton, Edward Ciannelli, Luis Alberni, Rosina Galli, Jay Novello.

SYNOPSIS: Gerald Meldrick (*Clark Gable*), a suave jewel thief, encounters Anya Von Duren (*Rosalind Russell*), an equally smooth lady crook, in India. Both are after the same loot, a fabulous diamond pendant owned by the champagne-thirsty Duchess of Beltravers (*Jessie Ralph*). He poses as a detective from Lloyds, she as a member of nobility. She makes the heist, but is tricked out of it by Meldrick.

They become partners fleeing the police, and, posing as an eloping couple, take refuge on a tramp freighter but are discovered. The freighter skipper, Captain Chang (*Peter Lorre*), exposes them to the pursuing police inspector (*Matthew Boulton*), but they escape again.

Running short of funds in their hide-out, Meldrick conceives a scheme for collecting a bankroll by donning the uniform of a British captain. Before he can shed his disguise, he is picked up by army headquarters and sent into the interior in command of a military evacuation detachment. In a fierce fight with Japanese troops, the false officer distinguishes himself and is decorated with the Victoria Cross before he goes off to serve a prison sentence for his crimes. Anya promises to wait for him.

REVIEWS:

Film Daily: The teaming of Gable and Miss Russell, the first time since their appearance in *China Seas*, is

With Rosalind Russell and Peter Lorre

most advantageous. Their styles, light, breezy and sure, form a perfect complement as they demonstrate with their delightful assurance the personality and ability that has placed them up among the top box office names.

Time: Gable is grand as the jewel thief who is also a master in posing. Miss Russell, too, is superb. Their particular talents are exquisitely exploited in this adventure farce that proves to be high entertainment fare.

Hollywood Reporter: Preposterous is

As Gerald Meldrick, a jewel thief impersonating an officer

hardly a strong enough word for the fictional conveniences of *They Met in Bombay*, however much in a comedy vein the events are presented by the

With Reginald Owen

three writers of the screenplay. The dialogue affords a measure of smart banter, made smarter by the delivery of Gable and Miss Russell, but whichever one of the writing trio was responsible for those flights of poetic verbiage that are meant to be romantic utterances missed the values a believable love theme might have added to surrounding absurdities.

HONKY TONK
1941. Metro-Goldwyn-Mayer.

Produced by Pandro S. Berman. Directed by Jack Conway. Screenplay by Marguerite Roberts and John Sanford. Photography by Harold Rosson. Art Direction by Cedric Gibbons. Musical score by Franz Waxman. Editor: Blanche Sewell. Release date: October 1, 1941. Running time: 105 minutes.

CAST: Clark Gable, Lana Turner, Frank Morgan, Claire Trevor, Marjorie Main, Albert Dekker, Henry O'Neill, Chill Wills, Veda Ann Borg, Douglas Wood, Betty Blythe, Harry Worth, Lew Harvey.

SYNOPSIS: Candy Johnson (*Clark Gable*) and a pal, the Sniper (*Chill Wills*), are a pair of frontier sharpers about to be tarred and feathered by a mob. Candy's smooth talk and swift reach for the other fellow's gun when he's off guard get them out of trouble. They catch a passing train.

On the train, they meet Lucy Cotton (*Lana Turner*), a beautiful Bostonite, and her father, Judge Cotton (*Frank Morgan*), who is also a con-man. She takes a slight fancy to him. He

With Albert Dekker

wins her completely when they get to the new town by donating a lot of money to build a church. He takes the money from Brazos Hearn (*Albert Dekker*), the head of the town's gambling hall, in a sharp and violent ruse.

The lusty old widow (*Marjorie Main*) of a preacher puts up the church and Candy builds his own

With Albert Dekker

dancehall and palace of chance, setting out to organize the town. Soon he controls the whole town, including Hearn's place. Lucy's dad is also in on the deal. She, however, knows nothing about it. But when Candy leaves his dancehall girl (*Claire Trevor*) and marries Lucy, her dad, shocked and too weak to resist him, hits the bottle heavily and plots revenge.

He finally exposes Candy's plans to take over the town, but Candy won't harm the old man. Instead, Brazos who considers him a threat, silences him with a bullet. The shock of the murder causes Lucy to lose their expected child. Candy shoots Brazos and runs the rest of the gang out of town with the help from his old pal. Although they grow enormously rich from their grafting, they plan to go straight. He and the Sniper take it on the lam while Lucy is still deathly ill, leaving a secret fortune behind for her. When she recovers, she follows him.

With Frank Morgan and Lana Turner

REVIEWS:

Variety: Gable is in top form in the picture. He gives out with enough masculine charm to make the femme fans flutter plenty. Miss Turner, who is graced by a tremendous sex appeal, proves that she also can act as well as turn the boys on. They click together in a lively, lusty Western that makes to wish you had been there.

Film Daily: Despite a certain lack of speed, Metro's *Honky Tonk* is a good strong contender for boxoffice honors. It is sexy and lusty like the pioneers of the old west before the turn of the century. Besides, it has Clark Gable and Lana Turner in the top roles. Jack Conway's direction is without fault, and Pandro Berman rates posies for the production.

With Chill Wills

Photoplay: *Honky Tonk* rambles and it rambles, and it gets nowhere, but in its circling, it does manage to gather up Lana Turner and Clark Gable and give them a twirl on the usual sexy old merry-go-round.

Newsweek: Candy Johnson was a great role for Clark Gable, even though the story inconsistencies at times made him look a greater sucker than the mobs he trims. Claire Trevor, fighting to win the call over Lana Turner in the affections of Gable, had a tough role, but made it attractive. Miss Turner never falters in her presentation of Lucy Cotton.

With Lana Turne

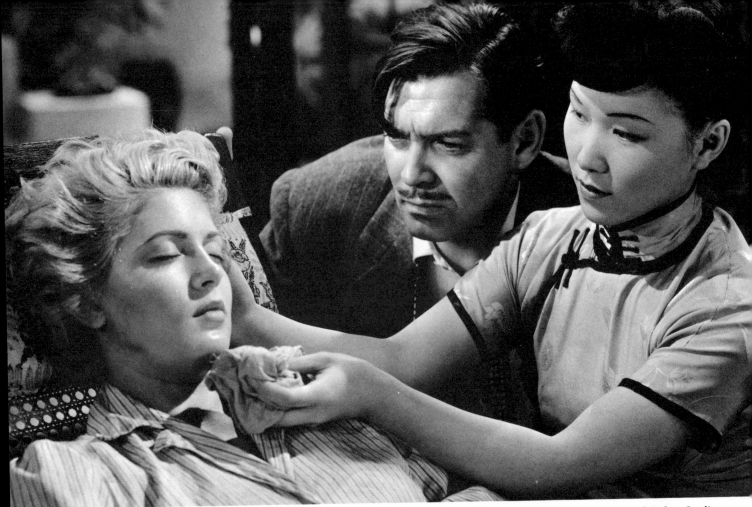

With Lana Turner

With Lana Turner and Robert Sterling

SOMEWHERE I'LL FIND YOU

1942. Metro-Goldwyn-Mayer.

Produced by Pandro S. Berman. Directed by Wesley Ruggles. Screenplay by Marguerite Roberts, based on a story by Charles Hoffman. Adapted by Walter Reisch. Photography by Harold Rosson. Art Direction by Cedric Gibbons. Musical Score by Bronislau Kaper. Release Date: August 8, 1942. Running time: 108 minutes.

CAST: Clark Gable, Lana Turner, Robert Sterling, Patricia Dane, Reginald Owen, Lee Patrick, Charles Dingle, "Rags" Ragland, William Henry.

SYNOPSIS: Johnny (*Clark Gable*) and Kirk Davis (*Robert Sterling*) are brothers with reputations as American war correspondents in numerous fields. They are ordered home by their conservative New York managing editor, who insists upon disregarding the indications of impending war in their dispatches.

While home, Johnny walks into the room of a girl boarder, Paula Lane (*Lana Turner*), in the home of old friends, introduces himself swiftly and in the bathroom doorway, kisses her violently and reciprocally. He later discovers that she is a former cub reporter who has had a crush on him for years, but is now practically engaged to his younger brother, Kirk.

With Charles Dingle and Robert Sterling

Johnny then sets out to demonstrate to his kid brother how fickle and vacillating she is. Anger blazes between them. Paula calls it off with Kirk, confident that Johnny wants to marry her. But when she is assigned to cover the Japanese encroachments in Indo-China, Johnny doesn't try

With Lana Turner

to stop her—a disillusioning shock.

Later, the brothers, broke, are sent to the Far East to revive their by-lines for their old newspaper editor. They find Paula Lane on the war frontier smuggling Chinese babies to safety. From there the three-cornered battle moves to the shores of Bataan, where Kirk is killed in action and his older brother writes a hero's story. Paula, now a Red Cross nurse, remains with Johnny.

REVIEWS:

Photoplay: The first picture made by Clark Gable since his tragic bereavement comes out a honey with Mr. Gable proving himself a true hero in his adherence to duty; a duty that must have caused him suffering, what with the pertinent lines and situations all reminiscent of his sorrow. As the

With Robert Sterling

older of a brother team of foreign correspondents, Gable is human, believable and right up there at the peak in his acting. Robert Sterling as the younger brother takes three steps at a time up the old career ladder. Lana Turner, the beautiful corner of the triangle, looks too beautiful and continues to amaze with her seasoned performance.

Newsweek: Gable plays his part with deep sincerity and utter consistency to salt it down as one of his better enactments. Miss Turner stamps hers with passionate intensity and that unsmiling conviction which set her love scenes and dramatic high levels apart from those of any other screen actress. Robert Sterling contrasts his junior brother characterization against the cynical, growling Gable role with nice discretion, to get over a more romantic and less sophisticated nature.

With Frank Faylen

John Mosher, The New Yorker: The dialogue between Gable and Miss Turner is full of meaning beyond the mere words. Their love-story is hard and realistic rather than romantic. Thus it contrasts against the idyllic adoration of the younger brother. But the sensuous tug and talk between Gable and Miss Turner, powerfully dramatic, is counterbalanced with serious things, with life-and-death matters, with eventual tragedy at Bataan, which will preclude audience smirking. It develops no cheap bawdiness of comedy—it is in no sense a comedy even at its lightest, even though its suspense is a rather deliberate script-tease.

ADVENTURE

1945. Metro-Goldwyn-Mayer.

With Greer Garson and Joan Blondell

Produced by Sam Zimbalist.
Directed by Victor Fleming.
Screenplay by Frederick Hazlitt
Brennan and Vincent Lawrence, based
on the novel by Clyde Brion Davis.
Adapted for the screen by Anthony
Veiller and William H. Wright.
Photography by Joseph Ruttenberg.
Art Directors: Cedric Gibbons and
Urie McCleary. Musical score by
Herbert Stothart. Special effects by
Warren Newcombe.
Editor: Frank Sullivan.
Release date: December 28, 1945.
Running time: 125 minutes.

CAST: Clark Gable, Greer Garson,
Joan Blondell, Thomas Mitchell, Tom
Tully, John Qualen, Richard Haydn,
Lina Romay, Philip Merivale, Harry
Davenport, Tito Renaldo.

SYNOPSIS: Adrift on a life raft after
his ship is torpedoed by the Japs,
Mudgin (*Thomas Mitchell*), a lovable
and eccentric old sailor, promises God
he will reform if He will save him
and his shipmates. Shortly afterward
Mudgin and his companions, including
Harry Patterson (*Clark Gable*), a
hard-boiled bos'n whose one tenderness
is his affection for the old Irish sailor,
are rescued and taken to San Francisco.

Within a few short hours Mudgin
has broken all his promises to God.
To his horror his soul drifts off into
the fog. Reluctantly, Harry agrees to
help his heartbroken friend search

for his soul and in the process makes
the acquaintance of Emily (*Greer
Garson*), a librarian. In spite of
Harry's arrogance, Emily is attracted
by his charm and to the amazement
of her roommate, Helen (*Joan
Blondell*), and the bewildered
Mudgin, runs off to Reno with him
where they are married.

It isn't long before Emily realizes
that for Harry it is all simply a lark.
To him, she is just another dame and
he is now ready to return to sea,
confident that she will be waiting
when he returns. Bitterly disillusioned,
Emily sues for divorce.

At sea, Harry and Mudgin quarrel
bitterly because Mudgin believes his
friend is giving up the finest thing
that ever happened to him, Emily's
love. Heartbroken when he learns
Harry intends to quit the ship, Mudgin
deliberately suffers a serious injury,
which brings Harry back. Then
Mudgin dies and Harry returns to
Emily to discover she is having his
baby. The child is apparently born
dead but Harry prays for the first time
in his life and his son breathes. In
Emily and his child he has finally
found the reason for living.

REVIEWS:

Time: Adventure was clearly
carpentered to fit the old Gable
formula; and ex-aerial-gunner-
photographer Gable himself fits the
formula as smoothly and as agreeably
as ever. If he is a little chubbier
around the jowls, he is still able to

sling his weight around—and in his
bright eye is the same old wicked fire.

Motion Picture Herald: The role of
the virile, lusty, swashbuckling
adventurer is one that Gable plays to
the hilt and that his fans will
thoroughly enjoy. While others in the
cast are a number of standout
performances . . . Greer Garson is not
suited to her assignment but delivers
with the high professional standard
that is her trademark. Joan Blondell
as the slightly giddy blonde who goes
for sailors, particularly Gable, is a
sheer delight.

Photoplay: What use for us to cite
the flaws and bemoan the story, for
it's Gable's first postwar picture and
movie fans, if for no other reason
than that, will send its rating sky high.
What we can't understand, however,
is the vociferous and he-mannish Mr.
Gable consenting to mouth the
innocuous and at times, whimsical
dialogue that means just nothing.
Words, words, words. Nevertheless,
it rates a best because it brings back
Gable to the screen, it will please
Miss Garson's fans to have her
young and gay for a change; and
because both Joan Blondell as Garson's
friend and Tom Mitchell, soul or no
soul, give fine performances.

The New York Times: By all the laws
of Hollywood, some sort of nuclear
fission should have occurred when
Metro brought Greer Garson and
Clark Gable together in a film. For
those two names joined on a marquee
have the potential, in a box office way,
of the atom splitting equation used
by the scientists at Oak Ridge. But
something went wrong in Metro's
handling of these two cosmic elements
and their *Adventure,* which should
have been a bombshell, is about
as explosive as a slightly ancient egg
. . . maybe he (Gable) tries a bit too
hard, what with this being his first
film after three years of Army routine
. . . only this time he talks too loudly,
shouts "Ha!" contemptuously too
many times, and persists in keeping
his hat on to an irritating extreme.

With Greer Garson

With Thomas Mitchell

THE HUCKSTERS

1947. *Metro-Goldwyn-Mayer.*

Produced by Arthur Hornblow, Jr.
Directed by Jack Conway.
Screenplay by Luther Davis, based on the novel by Frederic Wakeman. Adapted by Edward Chodorov and George Wells. Photography by Harold Rosson. Art Direction by Cedric Gibbons and Urie McCleary. Musical score by Lennie Hayton. Editor: Frank Sullivan.
Release date: August 27, 1947.
Running time: 115 minutes.

CAST: Clark Gable, Deborah Kerr, Sydney Greenstreet, Adolphe Menjou, Ava Gardner, Keenan Wynn, Edward Arnold, Aubrey Mather, Richard Gaines, Frank Albertson, Douglas Fowley. With Clinton Sundberg, Gloria Holden, Connie Gilchrist, Kathryn Card, Lillian Bronson, Vera Marshe, Ralph Bunker, Virginia Dale, Jimmy Conlin.

SYNOPSIS: Fresh out of the Army, former radio advertising executive Vic Norman (*Clark Gable*), takes a job with the Kimberly Tower, a swank agency. While in the office of the president, Mr. Kimberly (*Adolphe Menjou*), a phone call comes from their higgest advertiser, Evans (*Sydney Greenstreet*), the manufacturer of Beautee Soap.

With Deborah Kerr

Kimberly is quite shaken by the tongue-lashing he gets from Evans, who wants more attention brought to his soap.

Kimberly later takes Vic around the agency and they run into Jean Ogilvie (*Ava Gardner*), a nightclub singer, who warmly embraces Vic, much to the older man's envy because he has no way with women. For

With Adolphe Menjou

months he has been trying with no success to get the most important of twenty-five society women chosen to sign a testimonial for Beautee Soap and to pose for glamorous pictures.

Vic's first assignment becomes to persuade Mrs. Dorrence (*Deborah Kerr*) to cooperate. She is the daughter of an English lady who married an American General who was later killed in the war. There is a strong attraction between them and she signs. Mrs. Dorrance cools down on Vic when he tries to get her to spend a weekend with him.

Evans, still not pleased, tortures Kimberly with threats of withdrawing his account unless they come up with somehting new. Vic flies to Hollywood to sign a comic, Buddy Hare (*Keenan Wynn*), for a radio show for Evans. He hires writers and Jean Ogilvie to do a record with Buddy which turns out well.

To bait them, Evans breaks the record in front of Vic and Kimberly before telling them that he thinks it's wonderful and wants it. This infuriates Vic, who walks out on the new position offered him by Evans. It's too dirty for him he says and that he will start again "clean" with Mrs. Dorrance.

REVIEWS:

New York Herald Tribune: The Gable-Kerr team-up is ideal. Gal makes an impressive bow on the U. S. screen, and nobody is going to mind that a few liberties have been taken with the book in order to build up her role. Greenstreet is great as Evan Llewellyn Evans, who thinks of America as a blank space between

New York and Hollywood where people buy soap.

Hollywood Reporter: Clark Gable zooms back to the pre-eminent place he long held in Hollywood with this smash performance of Vic Norman, the radio advertising go-getter in *The Hucksters*. He takes with him the charming English star, Deborah Kerr, a delightful personality in her American debut. Together they manage a compelling love story that supersedes the satire of the original best-selling novel upon which this picture is based.

Photoplay: Nearly everyone read *The Hucksters* and everyone had something to say about it. Here's a good picture, quick and to the point with Clark Gable as an attractive "Huckster" and Deborah Kerr as the lady so remote from his fast and fascinating ways. Said lady comes to warmer life than she did in the book; she's handled here by that competent Britisher, Kerr. The children keep out of sight most of the time, thereby letting everyone get right on with the interesting business of producing laughs at the expense of that great American field—advertising.

Variety: Producer Arthur Hornblow, Jr., has garnered top technical talent that leaves no stone unturned to make that "Love that picture!" tag come true. Jack Conway's direction socks it all home and that goes for the ending of the Luther Davis screenplay, in which Gable gives out with the kind of denunciation of his brow-beating boss that has been standard cinematurgy for years. Script ribs everything in radio from soap operas to Forest Lawn commercials.

With Sidney Greenstreet

With Ava Gardner

211

HOMECOMING

1948. Metro-Goldwyn-Mayer.

Produced by Sidney Franklin. Associate Producer: Gottfried Reinhardt. Directed by Mervyn LeRoy. Screenplay by Paul Osborn, based on the original story by Sidney Kingsley. Adapted by Jan Lustig. Photography by Harold Rosson. Art Direction by Cedric Gibbons and Randall Duell. Musical direction by Charles Previn. Edited by John Dunning. Release date: May 28, 1948. Running time: 113 minutes.

CAST: Clark Gable, Lana Turner, Anne Baxter, John Hodiak, Ray Collins, Gladys Cooper, Cameron Mitchell, Marshall Thompson, Lurene Tuttle, Jessie Grayson, J. Louis Johnson, Eloise Hardt.

SYNOPSIS: In 1941, Ulysses Johnson (*Clark Gable*) is a tremendously successful New York society doctor. He and his wife, Penny (*Anne Baxter*), have cluttered up their lives in an effort to do the "right" things. Ulysses is so busy with social activities that he has no time to help an old schoolmate, Dr. Bob Sunday (*John Hodiak*), in a project to free a small community from disease.

When the United States goes to war, Ulysses becomes a major in the Medical Corps. His pompous, condescending manner forces Bob to call him a fourflusher and a self-centered, selfish man. On the transport

With Anne Baxter

With Lana Turner

over to Africa, Ulysses meets Lt. Jane McCall (*Lana Turner*), the nurse who is to assist him in his work. From the beginning, she resents Ulysses' assertion that a man has only to look out for himself.

For the first few months of their association, Ulysses and Lt. McCall bicker constantly. But actually, they are falling in love. There is no confession of love, however, until after circumstances force Ulysses into a realization of how little he has contributed to civilization. And this brings about a great change in him.

In Paris on his first leave in two years, Ulysses runs into Jane. They have one perfect week together, and then a new German push sends them back to their work. Months later, after Jane has died of injuries received in the Battle of the Bulge, Ulysses returns home. Now he is willing and anxious to assist Sunday in his work, and he has a new tenderness toward Penny, with whom he plans to build a better life.

REVIEWS:

Hollywood Reporter: This is what audiences have been waiting for: reteaming of the two hottest romantic figures on the screen, Clark Gable and Lana Turner. Gable scores heavily as a surgeon worried by the disturbing presence of his nurse through three years of war, and is seen in the type of characterization audiences like him best. Miss Turner's performance is on a par with the male star. She

handles the part with facile authority and makes the most of every line.

Newsweek: Homecoming respects the individual's own intelligence and common sense in reaching solutions of the mental and emotional adjustments that are present in every-day life and which are accelerated by the agitations of war. The spectator can find a sense of identification with the characters of *Homecoming* that makes for better appreciation of the pertinence of its subject matter. It is solid dramatic entertainment, brightened here and there by disarmingly human comedy, and played to perfection by a fine cast which responds intuitively to the warm and sensitive direction of Mervyn LeRoy.

Time: The basic substance of *Homecoming,* like the base of a perfume, has a terrible smell; but to many movie goers, the end product will seem quite pleasant. It is superskillfully custom-blended to please the vast public of Gable & Turner. World War II, reduced for long stretches to a faint, faraway hum, appears to have been just an old sweet song.

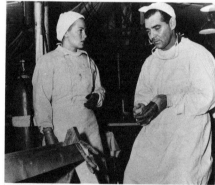

With Lana Turner

With Lana Turner

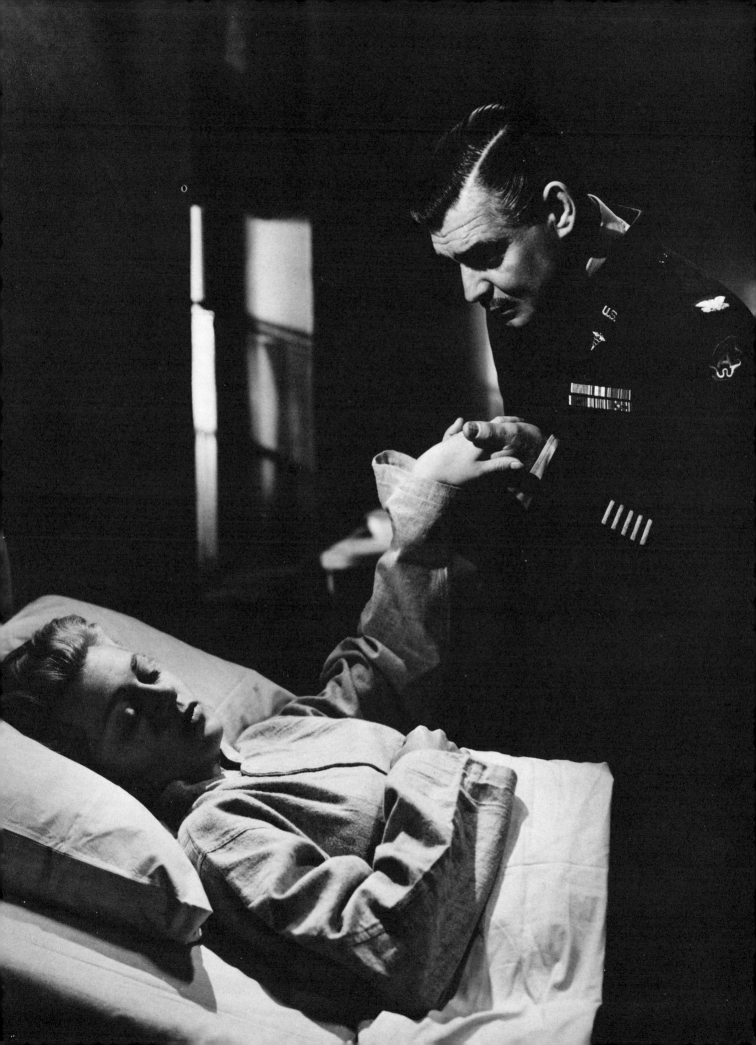

COMMAND DECISION

1948. Metro-Goldwyn-Mayer.

Produced by Sidney Franklin. Directed by Sam Wood. Screenplay by William R. Laidlaw and George Froeschel, based on the play by William Wister Haines. Photography by Harold Rosson. Art Direction by Cedric Gibbons and Urie McCleary. Musical score by Miklos Rozsa. Editor: Harold F. Kress. Release date: December 23, 1948. Running time: 112 minutes.

CAST: Clark Gable, Walter Pidgeon, Van Johnson, Brian Donlevy, Charles Bickford, John Hodiak, Edward Arnold, Marshall Thompson, Richard Quine, Cameron Mitchell, Clinton Sundberg, Ray Collins, Warner Anderson, John McIntire. With Moroni Olsen, John Ridgely, Michael Steele, Edward Earle, Mack Williams, James Millican.

SYNOPSIS: When an American bombing mission, flying deep into Germany, returns with the loss of forty-eight Flying Fortresses, the entire Allied world is shocked. Known to but a few, this is the beginning of Operation Stitch, a mission designed to destroy German production of a new, superior jet fighter. General Dennis (*Clark Gable*) has ordered the operation because of a four-day break in the weather. His superior, General Kane (*Walter Pidgeon*), is dismayed.

Certainly, such prohibitive losses may well cause the Combined Chiefs to abandon daylight, precision bombing. While Kane argues that they must not sacrifice the future of daylight bombing, Dennis points out that there will be no future unless this German fighter is kept out of the sky.

As the controversy rages, the second mission returns from Schweinhafen. The argument that the job is two-thirds done is very good until the mission leader, Colonel Ted Martin (*John Hodiak*), reveals that the bombers missed Schweinhafen and blasted a town that looked just like it. After much debate, Kane finally lets the planes return to Schweinhafen. In this raid, Martin is killed and over fifty ships are lost, but the right target is hit.

With John McIntire (far left) and Warner Anderson (second from right)

When the Congressional Committee puts the pressure on Kane, he is forced to replace Dennis with General Garnet (*Brian Donlevy*). But Garnet is swayed by Dennis' example and realizes that if the men must die, the least he can do is make them count. He orders the third phase of Operation Stitch.

REVIEWS:

The New Yorker: Command Decision deviates very little from the stage play—so little, in fact, that it seems to be simply a photographic record of the original, with some new facts substituted for the old. It is frequently exciting, even when talk takes precedence over action. . . . As a badgered Air Force general, willing to balance tremendous losses against the destruction of plane factories in Germany, Mr. Gable is properly severe and glum.

Theatre Arts: Done almost exactly as on Broadway, *Command Decision* emerges an intelligent, gripping film. The only disappointment is Clark Gable who in every way fails to match the stage performance. . . . In only one scene does Gable come to life,

and this is the one new scene that has been written into the movie. As a commanding general talking down a plane in which only the bombardier survives, he achieves a power which indicates what many still maintain—that Gable can act.

Variety: Even though the film is grounded, with limited air sequences, it communicates the splendor and excitement of the air war, and Clark Gable, as Dennis, is convincingly authoritative. The entire cast is superb, giving brittle and brilliant performances, sometimes in the most minute moments. Somehow the whole thing seems to stay in focus, probably because of the strength and vitality of the idea.

Time: Gable has one strong scene in which he "talks down" a navigator who is trying to land a pilotless bomber. Significantly, this is the movie's one big outdoor sequence. Back inside headquarters, where drama depends on the reading of lines, Cinemactor Gable cannot always hold the center of the stage.

With Walter Pidgeon

215

ANY NUMBER CAN PLAY

1949. Metro-Goldwyn-Mayer.

Produced by Arthur Freed. Directed by Mervyn LeRoy. Screenplay by Richard Brooks, based on the book by Edward Harris Heth. Photography by Harold Rosson. Art Direction by Cedric Gibbons and Urie McCleary. Musical Score by Lennie Hayton. Editor: Ralph E. Winters. Release date: July 2, 1949. Running time: 112 minutes.

CAST: Clark Gable, Alexis Smith, Wendell Corey, Audrey Totter, Frank Morgan, Mary Astor, Lewis Stone, Barry Sullivan, Marjorie Rambeau, Edgar Buchanan, Leon Ames, Mickey Knox, Richard Rober, William Conrad, Darryl Hickman, Caleb Peterson, Dorothy Comingore, Art Baker.

SYNOPSIS: Charley King (*Clark Gable*), at forty, prides himself on his successful career as an honest gambler and cannot understand why his wife, Lon (*Alexis Smith*), and his seventeen-year-old son, Paul (*Darryl Hickman*), disapprove of his profession.

On the way to his casino, Charley runs into Ben Sneller (*Lewis Stone*), once a big shot gambler, now broke. He stakes him to five hundred dollars when Ben tells him that he feels lucky. Ben enters his gambling casino with him and sits down at the poker table.

Meanwhile, Charley's worthless brother-in-law, Robbie (*Wendell Corey*), has been blackmailed into letting two crooks, Angie and Sisti (*Edgar Buchanan*), take a hand in a crap game with loaded dice. Charley becomes suspicious of the two but

With Darryl Hickman

With William Conrad, Wendell Corey, and Richard Rober

With Audrey Totter, and Alexis Smith

before he can investigate, he learns that Ben Sneller, having lost the five hundred, is attempting suicide. He takes his gun from him in the nick of time. At that moment news comes that Charley's son, Paul, has been arrested as a result of a brawl. Charley rushes off to get him out of jail, but Paul refuses to leave with him. Lon comes to Charley's aid and prevails upon Paul to go with her to the gambling house and see the place for themselves.

By this time Sisti and Angie have stopped playing craps. The loaded dice have been withdrawn. An honest game is in progress with Jim Kersten (*Leon Ames*), a rich client of Charley's playing in spectacular luck. Charley, although seeing ruin staring him in the face, refuses to stop the game. Instead he pits his own luck against Kersten's and wins back all the money lost. When Angie and Sisti try to hold up the place they are stopped by Charley. At last Paul realizes his father's worth. Touched by his son's show of affection, Charley plays a fixed hand against his employees, deliberately losing the casino to them and starts out with his wife and the boy to begin a new life.

REVIEWS:

Film Daily: This saga of gambling will need all the name value at its command to overcome the handicap of a loose, rambling, disorganized, frankly confusing script. The story starts off well enough and even looks like one of the elegant old-time underworld Gable melodramas. But in its progression, it tackles a number of story threads, and none of them comes off convincingly.

Box Office: Clark Gable and good exploitation values will give *Any Number Can Play* sturdy initial interest at the box-office. Gable walks comfortably through his assignment. . . . Alexis Smith gives just an adequate reading to her role of Gable's wife, and Audrey Totter has little to do as a sister-in-law. The part is a natural for Clark Gable and he plays it with all the debonair authority that has kept him at the top of the ladder.

Hollywood Reporter: Arthur Freed's production endows the show with interesting atmosphere and he certainly casts it from the best pages of the directory. Mervyn LeRoy's direction has punch, as it inevitably would, when the script allows him some room for imaginative action. But neither of these two highly reputable film men

With Frank Morgan, Barry Sullivan, and Edgar Buchanan

are the matches of a story whose vigor is dissipated before the end of the first reel and whose contrived situations lack conviction and credibility.

Time: Any Number Can Play sets out to prove that gambling is a true test of character. If it is, the hero (Clark Gable) is pure gold. . . . Above all, he is a "nut for human dignity" (as one of his employees puts it) and always has a kind word and a fistful of dollars for the men he has ruined. . . . Director LeRoy has tried half-heartedly to keep the suds from showing, but soap opera, like murder, will out.

KEY TO THE CITY

1950. Metro-Goldwyn-Mayer.

With Loretta Young

Produced by Z. Wayne Griffin.
Directed by George Sidney.
Screenplay by Robert Riley Crutcher,
based on the story by Albert Beich.
Photography by Harold Rosson.
Art Direction by Cedric Gibbons and
Hans Peters. Musical score by Bronislau
Kaper. Editor: James E. Newcom.
Release date: February 1, 1950.
Running time: 99 minutes.

CAST: Clark Gable, Loretta Young,
Frank Morgan, James Gleason,
Marilyn Maxwell, Raymond Burr,
Lewis Stone, Raymond Walburn,
Pamela Britton, Zamah Cunningham,
Clinton Sundberg, Marion Martin,
Bert Freed, Emory Parnell, Clara
Blandick.

SYNOPSIS: Against a background of
a convention of mayors in San
Francisco, Clarissa Standish (*Loretta
Young*), a serious-minded, prissy
woman mayor of Wenorah, Maine,
meets Steve Fisk (*Clark Gable*), an
ex-longshoreman turned mayor whose
ready smile and fists have made him
the top man of a California city.

Their innocent escapades get them
into some not-too-innocent-looking
situations, as a result of which both
of them get nearly bounced from
office. They become involved in a
nightclub fight and spend the greater
part of the conference on the verge
of being sent to jail. Running the risk
of a scandal, she returns with Steve
to his home town where he defeats
his crooked political opponents and
ends up throwing his opposition, Les
Taggart (*Raymond Burr*) into a fishpond.

Eventually, they set off to get
married, lugging with them a vast
key to the city, which had started
the day covered with flowers but has
been reduced by their adventures to a
wire skeleton. In the future, there is
to be only one politician in the family
and she happily concedes.

REVIEWS:

Variety: A comedy made to measure
for Gable and Miss Young, who,
helped by a strong team of small part
players, rise above the shortcomings
of the script. This, after some pleasant
satire at the expense of the mayoral
conference, concerns itself with
wringing every possible laugh from a
number of stock situations; the result
is on the whole amusing, but
occasionally labored.

With Loretta Young

Film Daily: Key to the City puts the
mighty Gable right back where he
belongs—on the top of the heap with
a story geared particularly to his
virile talents and the preference of his
fans. *Key to the City* is not
especially sound in plot, but what it
misses in sound dramatic construction,
it more than compensates for in the
hilarious gags, the rollicking situations,
and the exceedingly clever
characterizations. The show is an
unashamed rough and tumble comedy
in which slapstick comedy, frothy
boudoir material and all the trimmings
are blended imaginatively and
effectively.

Hollywood Reporter: The part is
tailor-made Gable, and to it he brings
the full impact of his personality,
his glib way with a comedy line and
unique capacity for making a gal
feel desirable. Loretta Young, his
co-star, comes through with a
performance which deftly accomplishes
the transition from conservative New
Englander to that of a girl willing
to put up a battle for the man she
loves; Marilyn Maxwell is terrific

With Loretta Young

as the other woman; and the late
Frank Morgan gives a characteristically
fine portrayal of Gable's sidekick. The
screen will miss his infectious laugh
and charming addle-headedness.

London Film Weekly: Slight comedy
hardly worthy of the talents of
Loretta Young and Clark Gable. It
packs a fair quota of laughs and
slapstick fooling, enough to help the
thin tale along. . . . Clark Gable
does his he-man stuff pretty well
and Loretta Young makes the most of
the part of the mayoress.

As Steve Fisk, a longshoreman
who turns mayor

TO PLEASE A LADY

1950. Metro-Goldwyn-Mayer.

Produced and Directed by Clarence Brown. Original screenplay by Barre Lyndon and Marge Decker. Photography by Harold Rosson. Art Directors: Cedric Gibbons and James Basevi. Musical score by Bronislau Kaper. Special effects by A. Arnold Gillespie and Warren Newcombe. Editor: Robert J. Kern. Release date: October 13, 1950. Running time: 91 minutes.

CAST: Clark Gable, Barbara Stanwyck, Adolphe Menjou, Will Greer, Roland Winters, William C. McGraw, Lela Bliss, Emory Parnell, Frank Jenks, Helen Spring, Bill Hickman, Lew Smith, Ted Husing.

SYNOPSIS: Mike Brannon (*Clark Gable*) is a hard-driving midget car racer whose apparently ruthless racing tactics have made him the favorite booing object of the fans. Columnist Regina Ford (*Barbara Stanwyck*) decides to interview him. She knows that a driver had previously been killed in a race with Mike and that

With Barbara Stanwyck

As Mike Brannon, a midget car racer

the latter had been blamed for the fatal crash, but is determined to give Mike an even break. She gets a fast brush-off, watches the races and is horrified when another driver gets into a mix-up with Mike and crashes into the wall to his death while Mike goes on to win. She writes a furious column which results in his being barred from every midget track.

He goes into a sideshow, performing all sorts of death-defying stunts so that he can earn enough to buy a full-sized racer and enter the regular races. He and Regina meet again and they fall in love, only to be held apart by her fear that he will kill another driver and his resentment of her attitude and her lack of understanding that the crack-ups happen only because of the other drivers' inefficiency.

At the Memorial Day Race at the classic Indianapolis Speedway, when an accident on the track allows room for only one more racer to pass, Mike waves for his rival to go through while he runs out on the rough, in hopes that he will be able to hold the wheel and get back on the track. Instead, he cracks up, but when he pulls through at the hospital, Regina is by his side.

REVIEWS:

Film Daily: Clark Gable in the rugged, hard-boiled type of role that originally brought him his immense popularity, and the news should be happy tidings for his tremendous following. Producer-director Clarence Brown has packed his auto racing picture with

thrilling race scenes, spectacular, hair-raising driving stunts, humor and rousing excitement. While the story has familiar ingredients, it does offer several novel twists and Brown has given the picture such fine production values, and set such a speedy directorial pace as to make the film a thriller from the beginning to the end.

Motion Picture Exhibitor: Gable at his charming best! Miss Stanwyck in a flip characterization which counts. In their first love scene, Gable slaps her face, and she comes back for more. Romance is tempestuous, but unbelievable, and gets over to audience in fashion which leaves no doubt that Gable still is the romantic figure of old.

Variety: Picture has excitement, thrills, with some of the greatest racing footage ever put on celluloid—plus torrid scenes between Gable and his co-star, Barbara Stanwyck, which will have distaff spectators in a tizzy. It firmly returns Gable to the rugged lover, rugged character status.

Photoplay: Clark Gable, tough and dirtied up, and Barbara Stanwyck, crisp and high-heeled, are the stars of this rather tiresome story which has the automobile racetracks of the country as its background. The romantic scenes are on the dull side; the dirt-track racing is the undoubtedly exciting point to those who like dirt-track racing. Disappointing.

With John Gallaudet and Hal K. Dawson

With Barbara Stanwyck

221

ACROSS THE WIDE MISSOURI

1951. Metro-Goldwyn-Mayer.

With John Hodiak and Alan Napier

After one start is forestalled by an Indian attack, his wife guides the expedition over a longer but safer route. The aged chief decrees peace for the trappers, who build a stockade for the winter and go to work.

Flint falls in love with his bride, originally taken for convenience, and a baby is born just before they're ready to return outside. This makes Flint decide that after he leads the trappers out, he will return to live with his wife's tribe.

The chief is killed by a vengeful trapper and that starts a running fight as the expedition returns to the home base. Kamiah is killed in the final attack, but Flint survives and with his infant son returns to the Indian village to live out the rest of their lives in the mountains.

With Ricardo Montalban

Produced by Robert Sisk. Directed by William Wellman. Screenplay by Talbot Jennings, based on a story by Talbot Jennings and Frank Cavett. Photography by William Mellor. Art Directors: Cedric Gibbons and James Basevi. Music by David Racksin. Editor: John Dunn. Release date: October 1, 1951. Running time: 78 minutes.

CAST: Clark Gable, Ricardo Montalban, John Hodiak, Adolphe Menjou, Maria Elena Marques, J. Carrol Naish, Jack Holt, Alan Napier, George Chandler, Douglas Fowley, Henri Letondal, Richard Anderson.

SYNOPSIS: Flint Mitchell (*Clark Gable*), a trapper from Kentucky, assembles an expedition for a trip into virgin beaver territory guarded by a militant Blackfoot tribe. He marries an Indian maid, Kamiah (*Maria Elena Marques*), in the belief she can assist in appeasing the tribe, which is presided over by her aged grandfather, Bear Ghost (*Jack Holt*).

As Flint Mitchell, a trapper from Kentucky

With Jack Holt

With Adolpe Menjou

REVIEWS:

Hollywood Reporter: Clark Gable does a first-class job as the two-fisted trapper. Ricardo Montalban looks handsome and plays an Indian with conviction and authority. John Hodiak is fine as another Indian. Adolphe Menjou does elegantly as a footloose Frenchman. Maria Elena Marques is a beautiful and talented newcomer.
J. Carrol Naish's conception of an Indian overlord is delightfully different.

Boxoffice: Wide Missouri carrying a powerhouse cast headed by Clark Gable and displaying outstanding Technicolor photography throughout, has an off-beat story presentation which will likely be only moderately acceptable to the action lovers.

Los Angeles Times: The absence of a strong story line in the screenplay mitigates the overall effect of *Across the Wide Missouri,* but as filmed against a breathtaking Technicolor panorama, the Robert Sisk production warrants attention for its qualities of vivid action and the interesting authenticity with which life in pioneer times is depicted among the Indians

and white settlers. These sequences abound in effective atmosphere and are enhanced substantially by Sisk's splendid choice of players to surround head man Clark Gable. The use of narrative, as it is bound to, intrudes on the fluidity of the continuity and entirely too much of the dialogue is spoken in Indian, then laboriously translated into English.

Newsweek: Essentially *Across the Wide Missouri* is an episode, and this is the approach taken by Sisk and his director, William Wellman. The latter reads many amusing comedy values into the proceedings. The sight of Indian chieftain J. Carrol Naish cavorting across the plains in a suit of armor is a howl. With Gable and color on deck to supply marquee draw, *Across the Wide Missouri* should get along in the action runs. It is, however, a long way from top Gable.

Photoplay: Clark Gable goes Western all the way in this—becoming a "squaw man" and a devoted one. Like a single chapter from a book, with so much past and future left untold, the story stands out as a little gem of Technicolor beauty and drama.

With Maria Elena Marques

CALLAWAY WENT THATAWAY

1951. Metro-Goldwyn-Mayer.

Produced, directed and written for the screen by Norman Panama and Melvin Frank. Photographed by Ray June. Art Direction by Cedric Gibbons and Eddie Imazu. Music by Marlin Skiles. Editor: Cotton Warburton. Release date: November 15, 1951. Running time: 81 minutes.

CAST: Fred MacMurray, Dorothy McGuire, Howard Keel, Jesse White, Fay Roope, Natalie Schafer, Douglas Kennedy, Elizabeth Fraser, Stan Freburg, Don Haggerty, and guest stars Clark Gable, Elizabeth Taylor, Esther Williams.

SYNOPSIS: Mike Frye (*Fred MacMurray*) and Deborah Patterson (*Dorothy McGuire*), a pair of advertising geniuses, who have dropped all their savings into acquiring the TV rights to the old pictures of one "Smoky" Callaway. The flickers are hugely successful and "Smoky" becomes an overnight sensation. But before Mike and Deborah can really get on the commercial gravy train, they have to come up with "Smoky" himself.

It seems the sagebrush star has disappeared from his Hollywood haunts to indulge in his fondness for dames and drink elsewhere. They ask an old time agent (*Jessie White*) to find him. In the meantime, they come up with a perfect counterpart, "Stretch" Barnes (*Howard Keel*), a real cowboy who at first demurs at the idea of impersonating Callaway but changes his mind at the mention of $2,000 a week.

With Dorothy McGuire and Howard Keel

Everything appears to be going according to plan when the real Smoky Callaway (*Keel*) returns to Hollywood still drunk and wants in on the gold. However, upon learning that his impersonator has signed an agreement to turn over all earnings to a boys' home, he decides to go back to South America. "Stretch" and Deborah, who in the midst of all the dealing became enamored of each other, appear ready for the preacher.

REVIEWS:

Hollywood Reporter: Fred MacMurray, an adroit farceur, plays the promoter role with no stops, garnering chuckles in nearly every scene. Dorothy McGuire is delightful as his sidekick who is smitten by the naivete of her charge. In the dual role of "Smoky" and "Stretch," Howard Keel does himself proud—playing both with conviction

and authority. Jesse White is grand as the agent. Fay Roope, Natalie Schafer, Douglas Kennedy, and Elizabeth Fraser, stand out in the supporting cast. Surprise appearances of Esther Williams, Clark Gable and other Metro headliners lend zip to the nitery sequences and implement the Hollywood atmosphere.

Film Daily: Callaway Went Thataway, but the journey shapes up as rather slow. Film has its share of genuinely funny laugh lines to enhance a neat screen idea, but overall result is hampered by slow pacing and the fact that film forecasts its conclusion at about the mid-way mark and then goes into formula proceedings.

LONE STAR
1952. Metro-Goldwyn-Mayer.

Produced by Z. Wayne Griffin. Directed by Vincent Sherman. Screenplay by Bordon Chase and Howard Estabrook, based on the magazine story by Borden Chase. Photography by Harold Rosson. Musical score by David Buttolph. Art Directors: Cedric Gibbons and Hans Peters. Editor: Ferris Webster. Release date: February 8, 1958. Running time: 94 minutes.

CAST: Clark Gable, Ava Gardner, Broderick Crawford, Lionel Barrymore, Beulah Bondi, Ed Begley, James Burke, William Farnum, Lowell Gilmore, Moroni Olsen, Russell Simpson, Ralph Reed, Jonathan Cott, William Conrad, Lucius Cook, Ric Roman, Victor Sutherland, Charles Cane, Harry Woods, Dudley Sadler, Emmett Lynn.

SYNOPSIS: Sam Houston (*Moroni Olsen*), a hero of the Texas war of independence, has gone on record as favoring an agreement with Mexico; ex-president Andrew Jackson (*Lionel Barrymore*) employs a Texas adventurer and cattle-owner, Burke (*Clark Gable*), to seek out Houston, who is in the Comanche Indian country and make him change his mind. Burke's reward will be a contract to supply beef to the army, in the almost certain event that a war with Mexico will follow annexation.

On his way to see Houston, Burke discovers that Tom Craden (*Broderick Crawford*), in the Texas Senate, favors a treaty with Mexico for reasons of personal ambition, and has the backing of influential people as well as the British ambassador.

Various intrigues follow, diplomatic and amorous Burke favoring a treaty with Craden's girl Martha Ronda (*Ava Gardner*), editor of the local Austin newspaper. Burke gets through to Houston, despite an ambush by Craden; Houston gives him a letter to take back to the Senate in Austin asking them to delay the debate on annexation until he returns. Craden's only answer to this can be force. He masses an army to prevent the Senate from meeting, greatly outnumbering the volunteers mustered by Burke and a few loyal senators.

His attack on the Senate House is

With Moroni Olsen and Broderick Crawford

stopped by the arrival of Sam Houston, who proclaims the cause of annexation. This is carried through. Even Craden is converted after a fight with Burke, to whom he cedes his girl, and all march out behind Houston to meet the expected Mexican attack.

REVIEWS:

Film Daily: A second Western in a row appears to agree with Clark Gable, who shines rough and brutal as a Texas cattle baron who straddles a not-too-neutral fence. He brings the role to life on the screen as though there were nothing more to it than walking heavily, speaking firmly with adequate facial grimacing, and smiling

With Ava Gardner

smoothly to charm the ladies, Ava Gardner in this instance. This is Gable at his virile best.

The New York Times: As the undaunted hero of the piece, Mr. Gable admittedly is a man who has been "riding and fighting for money for ten years." He looks it as he sits his black charger and as he fights it out with Bowie knives and fists. . . . Luckily for *Lone Star* the principals don't take much time out for either romance or tears.

Canadian Film Bulletin: Lone Star is not in itself a remarkable film; it is capably though not distinctively executed, and its characterization is conventional (in the romantic element, rather tired), but its material, and the presentation of it, has some interest. To begin with, there are considerable inaccuracies in its dramatization of history. Its climactic event—the stand of a handful of Texans against Craden's army—is in fact "adapted" from an event that occurred ten years earlier, when 200 Texans defended the San Antonio (not Austin) Senate House against three thousand Mexican troops, led by a Mexican revolutionary. The outcome of this was not absorption into the United States, but independence from it.

With Broderick Crawford

NEVER LET ME GO

1953. Metro-Goldwyn-Mayer.

Produced by Clarence Brown.
Directed by Delmer Daves.
Screenplay by Roland Millar and
George Froeschel, based on the novel,
"Came the Dawn," by Roger Bax.
Cinematography by Robert Krasker.
Art Director: Alfred Junge.
Editor: Frank Clarke.
Release date: May 1, 1953.
Running time: 69 minutes.

CAST: Clark Gable, Gene Tierney,
Richard Haydn, Bernard Miles, Belita,
Kenneth More, Karel Stepanek,
Theodore Bikel, Anna Valentina,
Frederick Valk, Peter Illing, Robert
Henderson, Stanley Maxted, Meinhart
Maur, Alexis Chesnakov.

SYNOPSIS: A foreign correspondent,
Philip Sutherland (*Clark Gable*)
stationed in Moscow in 1945, falls in
love with Marya Lamarkina (*Gene
Tierney*), a ballet dancer, and they
are married by the American
ambassador. On their honeymoon,
they meet Valentina Alexandrova
(*Belita*) and her English husband,
Christopher St. John Denny (*Richard
Haydn*). Soon after, Denny is suddenly
deported from Russia and forced to
leave his wife behind. The same
thing happens to Sutherland.

With Richard Haydn and Bernard Miles

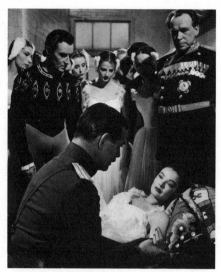

With Gene Tierney

When all efforts to get their wives
out through diplomatic channels fail,
Denny and Sutherland buy a small
sailing ship and set out with Joe
Brooks (*Bernard Miles*), a sailor, to
a pre-arranged rendezvous off the
coast in the Baltic Sea. Through the
help of coded messages from Steve
Quillan (*Kenneth More*), a radiocaster
in Moscow, the girls are notified to
swim out to sea where the boat can
pick them up. But only Belita shows
up.

Marya had been detained for a
sudden ballet performance in honor of
a Russian general. Sutherland swims
ashore, steals an officer's uniform and
smuggles her from the theatre. But
they are recognized and flee in a car.
After a wild chase they manage to
make it to safety.

REVIEWS:

The New York Times: A little older,
a little fatter, a little shrewder, and
more cynical, perhaps, he [Clark
Gable] is nonetheless pervious to
feminine beauty.

John McCarten, The New Yorker:
On a screen as expansive as the
celestial concave and with his dimples
looking like the craters of the moon,
Clark Gable in *Never Let Me Go* rips
through the Iron Curtain with all the
breeziness of a demonstrator showing
off the very latest can opener in
Gimbel's basement. Mr. Gable, at this
point in his career, is grizzled, not
withered. And there can be little

doubt that as long as he is able to
get around, he will represent all that
is wholesome, brave, kind and
regular in the American male.

Film Daily: Never Let Me Go is not
a particularly strong title for this
drama of how love outwits the
Communists. Neither is the picture a
strong starring vehicle for Clark Gable
or Gene Tierney, although their names
give it importance and booking
opportunities. . . . Love scenes between
the two stars are good, with Miss
Tierney getting a warm, tender feeling
into them.

Hollywood Reporter: An interesting,
often suspenseful yarn of the struggle
of an American newspaperman to get
his Russian bride out of the Soviet
Union. The still magic name of Clark
Gable to head the cast. . . . This
Clarence Brown production is a rather
talky screenplay which is slow in
developing action. Brown has chosen

With Gene Tierney

his cast flawlessly, all performances
being good, and embellishes the story
with captivating ballet scenes,
handsome backgrounds and excellent
photography. Brown also skillfully
utilizes newsreel insertions to add
authenticity to the film.

With Gene Tierney

MOGAMBO

1953. Metro-Goldwyn-Mayer.

Produced by Sam Zimbalist.
Directed by John Ford.
Screenplay by John Lee Mahin, based on the play by Wilson Collison.
Cinematography by Robert Surtees and F. A. Young. Art Director: Alfred Junge. Editor: Frank Clarke.
Release date: October 9, 1953.
Running time: 115 minutes.

CAST: Clark Gable, Ava Gardner, Grace Kelly, Donald Sinden, Philip Stainton, Eric Pohnmann, Laurence Naismith, Dennis O'Dea.

SYNOPSIS: Vic Marswell (*Clark Gable*) celebrated white hunter and safari-leader, is none too pleased when his headquarters in the uplands of Kenya is invaded by Eloise "Honey Bear" Kelly (*Ava Gardner*), a vivacious American show girl trying to forget. Honey Bear's attractions, however, overcome Marswell's initial hesitation, and the couple are soon in each other's arms.

This understanding is interrupted by the arrival of Donald Nordley (*Donald Sinden*), a British anthropologist, with his beautiful wife Linda (*Grace Kelly*), whom

As Vic Marswell, celebrated white hunter

Marswell has been engaged to escort into the gorilla country. Nordley does not observe the immediate attraction felt by his wife for Marswell; nor indeed the fickle, aging but still irresistible hunter's equal penchant for the young Englishwoman. Honey Bear is less slow to appreciate the situation, and it is greatly to Marswell's annoyance that a series of accidents prevents her departure and necessitates her presence on the safari.

The affair between Marswell and Linda becomes more serious as the journey proceeds, to the accompaniment

With Lawrence Naismith, Eric Pohlman, Ava Gardner, and Philip Stainton

of a ceaseless rattle of malicious wisecracks from Honey Bear, and at last Marswell decides to admit the truth to Nordley. But the naive trust of the young Britisher touches the hard-boiled American unexpectedly, and he finds he cannot bring himself to shatter his illusions. He even saves his life when he is charged by a maddened gorilla.

Returning to camp, Marswell sends Linda back to her husband by pretending that the affair was never anything to him but a diversion; and finally, after some proud shilly-shallying on the girl's part, ends up with the faithful Honey Bear in his arms again.

REVIEWS:

Time: Gable plays his he-man part with the bemused ease to be expected

With Grace Kelly and Ava Gardner

of a man who has done the same thing many times before; Grace Kelly's blonde beauty remains intact despite the remarkable silly lines she is made to say; and Ava romps delightfully with baby elephants and giraffes in the intervals between her pursuit of Gable.

Film Daily: One or two passages of direction show the master's touch, most notably some fine close-ups which could belong in a real drama; and there are some good landscape and animal shots, unfortunately curtailed by the ever-present necessity to cut back to Gable and Gardner. Most engaging, however, is the tongue-in-cheek attitude which is evident through most of the unfolding of the plot, and which makes considerable portions of the film quite acceptable light comedy.

Canadian Film Bulletin: There are two attitudes to this film. Either one may deplore the fact that one of the world's most powerful and lavish producing companies can apparently find nothing better for one of the world's greatest directors than material as commonplace and confected as *Mogambo*. Or one can regard with interest and even a certain mild enjoyment Ford's way with a typical MGM star vehicle.

With Grace Kelly

BETRAYED
1954. Metro-Goldwyn-Mayer.

As Colonel Pieter Deventer, a Dutch intellingence officer

Directed by Gottfried Reinhardt. Screenplay by Ronald Millar and George Froeschel. Cinematographer: F. A. Young. Editors: John Dunning and Raymond Poulton.
Release date: September 7, 1954.
Running time: 108 minutes.

CAST: Clark Gable, Lana Turner, Victor Mature, Louis Calhern, O. E. Hasse, Wilfrid Hyde White, Ian Carmichael, Niall MacGinnis, Nora Swinburne, Roland Culver, Leslie Weston.

SYNOPSIS: In 1943, a Dutch intelligence officer, Colonel Pieter Deventer (*Clark Gable*) is rescued from the Germans and helped on his way to England by a Resistance leader known as "The Scarf" (*Victor Mature*). The authorities in London have decided to send out a radio operator to work with "The Scarf" and Deventer selects, helps to train, and falls in love with Carla Van Oven (*Lana Turner*). She has collaborated with the Germans and is anxious to live down her reputation.

Shortly after Carla's arrival, "The Scarf's" small forces begin to suffer heavy casualties, as each raiding party finds itself met by a German ambush. Deventer arrives to investigate, suspecting Carla, who tries to convince him that the real traitor is "The Scarf" himself who has the reckless, irresponsible disposition that probably would have made him a criminal in peace time. And he is, almost pathologically, in love with his young mother (*Nora Swinburne*).

When his countrymen persecuted her, on an unjust charge of collaboration, he vowed vengeance.

Carla is trapped in Arnhem with the British forces, but Deventer, now convinced of "The Scarf's" treachery, tricks him into giving information about a secret escape route. "The Scarf" is killed, and Carla and the British troops come safely out of Arnhem.

REVIEWS:

Jack Moffit, Hollywood Reporter:
Betrayed offers the great box office names of Clark Gable, Lana Turner, and Victor Mature in an espionage puzzle drama set against the color, charm and quaintness of Holland during World War II. The Eastman color photography by F. A. Young is especially notable. The darkly tinted closeups of Gable (who is of Dutch ancestry) often look as though they'd been painted by Rembrandt. One almost wishes they'd represented him as "The Laughing Cavalier," for the humor that marked all of "The King's" great characterizations is

As Colonel Pieter Deventer

sadly lacking here. So is the element of happy-go-lucky sex. And seeing Gable without sex is a good deal like seeing *Ben Hur* without horses. An identifying scene marked all of Gable's great pictures. It was fairly simple. In it, the heroine always talked her head off, laying down the law about what she thought fitting and proper, while Gable lounged nearby with a grin and a look in his eye that said, "Baby, you're going to give in in about five minutes." The fans, particularly the women, loved it. And it is such a little thing to ask in this complicated day of atomic civilization, that one wonders why the producers of Gable pictures so persistently refuse to let the public have it. That's the biggest mystery in this puzzle drama.

Time: At 53, Gable (who was recently called by one half-crushed actress "the Pudge Heffelfinger of osculation") still has the he-manliest hug in the business.

Newsweek: It seems a little late in the day for so ingenuous a wartime adventure story to make much impact, and in fact *Betrayed,* directed, disappointingly, by Gottfried Reinhardt, proves a clumsy and over-slow pace piece of melodrama. Lana Turner and

With Victor Mature

Victor Mature go about their spying and resistance leading with no great conviction, and Clark Gable gives a rather tired, though solid, performance as the intelligence officer. The Dutch backgrounds—windmills, dykes, cobbled streets—are pleasantly enough photographed in Eastman Color; and against this picture postcard setting, the story, with its implausible "explanation" of Arnhem ("The Scarf" had tipped off the Germans), seems all the more artificial.

With Lana Turner

SOLDIER OF FORTUNE

1955. 20th Century-Fox.

Produced by Buddy Adler.
Directed by Edward Dmytryk.
Screenplay by Ernest K. Gann, based on his novel of the same title.
Cinematographer: Leo Tover.
Art direction by Lyle Wheeler and Jack Martin Smith.
Musical score by Hugo Friedhofer.
Editor: Dorothy Spencer.
Release date: June 5, 1955.
Running time: 96 minutes.

CAST: Clark Gable, Susan Hayward, Michael Rennie, Gene Barry, Alex D'Arcy, Tom Tully, Anna Sten, Russell Collins, Leo Gordon, Richard Loo, Soo Yong, Frank Tang, Jack Kruschen, Mel Welles, Jack Raine, George Wallace, Alex Finlayson, Noel Toy, Beal Wong, Robert Burton, Robert Quarry, Charles Davis, Victor Sen Yung, France Fong, Danny Chang.

SYNOPSIS: When Louis Hoyt (*Gene Barry*) disappears on a photographic trip into Red China, his wife Jane (*Susan Hayward*) comes to Hong Kong to institute a search for him. With British authorities and the U. S. Consulate, among others, being no help, she turns in despair to Hank Lee (*Clark Gable*), an American soldier of fortune who runs a profitable smuggling business on each side of the bamboo curtain.

Hank develops a personal interest in the lady, but when she repulses his advances he realizes that the only way to win her over is to rescue her husband. Aided by an incorruptible

With Michael Rennie

With Susan Hayward

English harbor policeman, Inspector Merryweather (*Michael Rennie*), he discovers that her husband is being held prisoner near Canton, where he is being brainwashed.

In an armed junk, he sails to Canton where his bold bid to rescue Louis is successful. After a running fight down the river, they escape a pursuing gun boat by getting lost in a fishing fleet.

The grateful Louis is reunited with his wife, but, sizing up the situation, he persuades Jane to remain with Hank. He decides he will always be off on some escapade and a wife is just a hindrance. But the smuggler is willing to give up his fortune-seeking for quiet happiness with the woman of his choice.

REVIEWS:

Jack Moffitt, Hollywood Reporter:
Had author Gann and director Edward Dmytryk permitted the intimate interludes to develop into really sock love scenes, this would be on a par with the great Gable pictures of the past. It's a pity that they didn't, for Miss Hayward, sultry and reluctantly fascinated, is far better than she has been in most of her recent pictures and seems potentially to be a perfect running mate for the dynamic and ruggedly handsome Gable. As it is, this Buddy Adler production is a very good adventure film but not one of the Gable smashes. It is good, however.

The New York Times: Mr. Gable is prowling in the backroom, eyes narrowed to mere slits in his face, skin leathery, and lips a bluish-purple. He's dead game for anything.

Time: Soldier of Fortune is a sizeable chunk of propaganda which, without presenting anything like a complete picture, at least does not seriously overstate its case. But while we are shown a fairly unexaggerated account of an attempt to "convert" an American photographer who tried to get in touch with "The People," we are shown nothing of the revolutionary atmosphere in which the desire to convert is natural. No doubt, though, Ernest Gann's novel emphasized the adventure rather than the propaganda; and certainly a soldier of fortune has greater entertainment quality than a vacillating Communist.

Brog., Variety: This hard-boiled adventure story by Ernest K. Gann,

With Tom Tully

the author of *The High and the Mighty,* provides an excellent tailored role for Clark Gable and a wonderfully vivid background of modern Hong Kong and adjacent territory shot by Leo Tover in CinemaScope and Deluxe color. The film gains an invaluable feeling of exotic beauty and realism from the fact that most of the exterior scenes were shot on authentic locations in Hong Kong's teeming bazaars and junk-crowded harbor.

With Gene Barry

THE TALL MEN

1955. 20th Century-Fox.

Produced by William A. Bacher and William B. Hawks. Directed by Raoul Walsh. Screenplay by Sydney Boehm and Frank Nugent, based on the novel by Clay Fisher. Cinematographer: Leo Tover. Art direction by Lyle Wheeler and Mark-Lee Kirk. Musical Director: Victor Young. Editor: Louis Loeffler. Release date: October 5, 1955. Running time: 122 minuets.

CAST: Clark Gable, Jane Russell, Robert Ryan, Cameron Mitchell, Juan Garcia, Harry Shannon, Emile Meyer, Steve Darrell, Will Wright, Robert Adler, J. Lewis Smith, Russell Simpson, Mae Marsh, Gertrude Graner, Tom Wilson, Tom Fadden, Dan White, Argentina Brunetti, Doris Kemper, Carl Harbaugh, Post Park.

SYNOPSIS: Ben (*Clark Gable*) and Clint Allison (*Cameron Mitchell*), Texans who fought for the Confederacy in the Civil War, ride north to the gold fields of Montana determined to recoup their lost fortunes. They hold up Nathan Stark (*Robert Ryan*), a businessman, for the $20,000 he is carrying. Stark, however, puts a proposition to them: he intends to drive a vast herd of cattle north from Texas to Montana, and offers Ben the Job of trail boss and a share in his profits. They accept.

On their way to Texas, Ben rescues Nella Turner (*Jane Russell*), one of a small party of settlers who have been attacked by Indians. They have to take refuge during a blizzard in a deserted shack, and they fall in love, but soon quarrel when Ben reveals that his only ambition is to settle down on a small ranch in Texas. Nella is after higher things.

With Robert Ryan and Cameron Mitchell

With Jane Russell and Argentina Brunetti

In Fort Worth, while they prepare for the journey north, Nella transfers her affections to the ruthlessly ambitious Stark, who insists that she accompany them to Montana. Antagonism between Stark and the Allison brothers increases during the cattle drive, and when they learn that the last stage of the journey is through hostile Indian country, Stark is prepared to cut his losses and to abandon the expedition.

Ben, however, insists that they go on. Clint is killed; but Ben succeeds in out-maneuvering the Indians by stampeding the herd at full speed through the narrow canyon where they have planned an ambush. Arriving in Montana, Stark endeavors to doublecross Ben but is outwitted; and on returning to his camp, Ben finds Nella there waiting for him.

REVIEWS:

Brog., Variety: The earthiness of Miss Russell's character and the masculine virility of Gable's makes for plenty of sizzle in their love scenes together. Gable can count this among one of his best in a long time, story providing him with a role that requires thespic skill as well as his particular personality to put him over. Miss Russell is a good teammate, scoring strongly. So does Ryan with his interpretation of an ambitious man, who, in a sense, carries the part of heavy in the story. Mitchell is fine as Gable's erratic young brother. It's a choice character of which he makes the most. Important to the cast and the entertainment punch is the work done by Juan Garcia, Gable's loyal Mexican friend. Other parts are small, but very well done.

Time: Come Sioux or stampede, jayhawker or dust devil, nothing bothers Clark—except, of course, the fact that he has to act. But like most of his parts, this one requires nothing much but his anxious little smirk. On the other hand, he seems comfortably conscious (as moviegoers will be awkwardly aware) that the winds which howl about his hairdo do not shake the trees in the processed background; and he arrives in Montana looking as fresh as a 54-year-old daisy can.

The New York Times: Messrs. Gable and Ryan go at it as though they were acting a deathless tragedy.

With Cameron Mitchell

Newsweek: Slowly and unobtrusively, mastery over the CinemaScope screen shape has progressed to the point where it has no equal for the treatment of certain types of story. And this is one of them. The leisurely tempo still persists, yet even that, if one has time to relax to it, may have its charm. Here the teasing question of who shall win Jane Russell (who with each film seems to grow in power and surly confidence) is a very long, drawn-out affair indeed—from Montana to Texas and back again. But in any case the actors must here take second place to the breath-taking presentation of natural settings, against which the animals appear to an unprecedented advantage. The first sequence of the herd setting out for distant Montana is superbly handled and is probably one of the most effective of its kind ever seen. Top credit is due Leo Tover for his use of the camera, and to Ray Kellog for photographic effects. . . . A big action feast and value for anyone's money.

With Jane Russell and Robert Ryan

With Jane Russell

THE KING AND FOUR QUEENS

1956. United Artists.

A Russ-Field-Gabco Production.
Executive Producer: Robert Waterfield.
Produced by David Hempstead.
Directed by Raoul Walsh.
Screenplay by Margaret Fitts and
Richard Alan Simmons from an
original screen story by Margaret Fitts.
Cinematography by Lucian Ballard.
Music by Alex North. Editor: David
Brotherton. Editorial supervision
by Louis R. Loeffker.
Release date: December 21, 1956.
Running time: 86 minutes.

CAST: Clark Gable, Eleanor Parker,
Jo Van Fleet, Jean Willes, Barbara
Nichols, Sara Shane, Roy Roberts,
Jay C. Flippen, Arthur Shields.

SYNOPSIS: A desperado, Dan Kehoe
(*Clark Gable*), seeks refuge in the
little ghost town of Wagon Mound.
The only inhabitants of the place are
the four wives and the sharp-shooting
mother (*Jo Van Fleet*) of the McDade
brothers, dangerous gunmen. Three of
the brothers are known to be dead,
but Ma believes that her fourth son
will return to claim his wife and
the gold, loot from a stagecoach
holdup, hidden somewhere on their
ranch. No one knows, however,
which of the four McDades is the
survivor.

Ma McDade suspects trouble when
Kehoe rides in, but allows him to
stay anyway. Kehoe, on the trail of
the gold, has a prospective ally in each
of the girls. Each of the young women
make a play for him, and he responds
to each in some degree, trying to
locate where the loot may be buried.

With the aid of Sabina (*Eleanor
Parker*), a cool schemer who has
merely been posing as one of the
McDade widows, Kehoe discovers the
loot and they depart together. A
sheriff's posse that had captured the
last of the McDade brothers and come
for the stashed gold prevents Kehoe
from keeping anything but $5,000 as
a reward. But the pair of connivers
ride off together, apparently to live
suspiciously of each other ever after.

REVIEWS:
Film Daily: It is a romantic Western,
but it also has mystery and comedy

With Jo Van Fleet

and it is an entertaining production.
Clark Gable shows again why he is
now and apparently ever shall be one
of the screen's few great personalities.
It is his best role in some time.
The King and Four Queens is an
amusing, fascinating, and very
interesting production that should
draw very good response.

James Powers, Hollywood Reporter:
Gable is at his most romantic and
dashing, a man in whom deviltry is
inherent and as roguish as Old Nick.
There could be no more explosive
element thrust into the midst of four
man-hungry women than Gable and

With Sara Shane and Eleanor Parker

he carries the potentially difficult role
with characteristic ease and polish.
Miss Parker is the most intelligent of
the four and the one you know Gable
will inevitably gravitate to. She is
coolly brainy without losing any
femininity.

Time: This is an amoral and rather
tawdry Western, developed as a
superficially cynical exercise in the
rival attractions of sex and money.
Clark Gable's charm as the ruffian-hero
is more realistic and resistible than
the script assumes, and in spite of a
few moderately vigorous action scenes
the story is largely played out through
dialogue exchanges which have little
pace or spirit. Jo Van Fleet, as the
embittered Ma McDade, plays with a
harshly theatrical emphasis that gives
her scenes a certain rough edge.

The New York Times: Clark Gable
may still be regarded as the "king"
of Hollywood but he won't be for
long if he continues to appear in
pictures such as *The King and Four
Queens.* It certainly represents a dreary
comedown for Hollywood royalty.

With Jean Willes

BAND OF ANGELS

1957. Warner Brothers.

With Yvonne de Carlo and Sidney Poitier

Directed by Raoul Walsh.
Screenplay by John Twist, Ivan Goff and Ben Roberts, based on the novel by Robert Penn Warren.
Cinematography by Lucien Ballard.
Art Director: Franz Bachelin.
Music by Max Steiner.
Orchestration by Murray Cutter.
Editor: Folmar Blangsted.
Release date: August 3, 1957.
Running time: 127 minutes.

CAST: Clark Gable, Yvonne de Carlo, Sidney Poitier, Efrem Zimbalist, Jr., Patric Knowles, Rex Reason, Torin Thatcher, Andrea King, Ray Teal, Russ Evans, Carole Drake, Raymond Bailey, Tommie Moore, William Forrest, Noreen Corcoran.

SYNOPSIS: A reformed slave trader, Hamish Bond (*Clark Gable*), has turned gentleman and maintains a plantation outside New Orleans. At the slave mart he sees a beautiful girl, Amantha Starr (*Yvonne de Carlo*) put up for auction. She is the daughter of a supposedly wealthy Kentucky planter. After her father's death she discovered he has left her nothing but debts. She also discovered her mother was a Negro slave and that, according to the custom of the time, she is classified as a slave and literally sold down the river to discharge her father's debts.

The girl is horrified and degraded at the treatment she—a well-bred white girl—receives when she becomes classified as a Negro. The trader buys her for $5000 apparently because of a guilt complex about being a former slaver. He has already reared a strong-willed Negro slave, Rau-Ru (*Sidney Poitier*), educated him, again to salve his conscience. Hamish doesn't relegate the proud Amantha to slave quarters but treats her as a lady in his household, where romance buds.

When the War Between the States breaks out, the young Negro, Rau-Ru, joins the North in hatred of the trader. New Orleans is finally taken and when Rau-Ru confronts his former benefactor and the girl, he plans to turn them in. But he relents, and with his help, Hamish and Amantha escape together.

REVIEWS:

James Powers, Hollywood Reporter: Warners' *Band of Angels* already has stirred up some excitement and controversy because of its love story, which concerns a white man and a part-Negro girl, and it will need a lot of controversy to help sell it. The Raoul Walsh-directed Civil War romance concerns itself very little with its title—which referred to the short life expectancy of freed Negroes who fought with Union troops during the war. It is concerned mostly with the love story between Clark Gable and Yvonne de Carlo. But unfortunately it is so static in its treatment, so ponderous in getting under way, that it only occasionally and far too seldom flickers with the kind of excitement its story and its players should have produced.

The New York Times: Mr. Gable is persistently bristling as the ex-blackbirding millionaire. . . . Gable, Miss de Carlo and Poitier are the only members of the cast who come across with any force. The rest of the characters move like shadows, never clearly defined or realized with any depth. Although the problem of racial antagonism or understanding is certainly as pertinent as anything in contemporary life, these issues in *Band of Angels* have no more impact than such a faintly similar sub-plot has in *Show Boat.* The problems of the characters and their solutions for them seem melodramatic and absurd.

Whit, Variety: Gable's characterization is reminiscent of his Rhett Butler in *Gone With the Wind,* although there is no paralleling of plot. As former slave-runner turned New Orleans gentleman with bitter memories of his earlier days, he contributes a warm, decisive portrayal that carries tremendous authority. It is too bad, however, that Gable is allowed to look so unusually and unfairly worn. It makes his romance with Miss de Carlo, convincingly presented as a young woman in her early twenties, seem somewhat incredible. Most of the other actors are allowed to play their roles as if they were giving their first readings and it is unfair to blame them for what is the director's responsibility.

The New Yorker: Mr. Gable's dimples look tired.

Newsweek: Here is a movie so bad that it must be seen to be disbelieved. Performances, including Gable's, make summer TV seem as dramatically powerful as the Old Vic.

With Yvonne de Carlo

S H O P P E R S
B A Z A A R

BILLIARDS withELEGANCE

"Our tables reflect not just their quality, but a statement of true elegance. Many wood species as well as metal finishes, from around the world, have been brought together to create an unparalleled beauty. As fourth generation craftsmen it is our commitment to create an exquisite show-piece for your home or business. We would like to take this opportunity to welcome you to our extended family of clientele."

B.V. *Wilms*

69-930 HWY.111 STE.112 • RANCHO MIRAGE • PHONE 760.770.7717

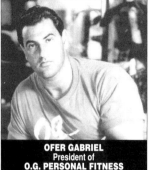

OFER GABRIEL
President of
O.G. PERSONAL FITNESS
and O.G. ENTERPRISES

O.G. PERSONAL FITNESS
ALWAYS ONE-ON-ONE TRAINING
Workout in relaxing private studios with non-intimidating atmosphere OR the privacy of your home.

FREE CONSULTATION
• WORKOUTS FOR ALL AGES
• SHAPING • STRETCHING • WEIGHT LOSS
• TONING • LIGHT & EASY FOR SENIORS

Call today for our local specials.

NOW TWO LOCATIONS TO SERVE YOU.

4751 East Palm Canyon Drive, Ste. A
PALM SPRINGS / 770-0073
72-880 Fred Waring Drive, Ste. G
PALM DESERT / 779-5532 • 779-5502

PREMIER SECURITY

EXPERTS IN CCTV CAMERAS AND ELECTRONIC SECURITY THROUGHOUT SOUTHERN CALIFORNIA

760-323-7395
1-800-320-2527

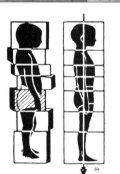

ORDER NOW FOR FALL DELIVERY

Do you need swatches — call us! Or, send us swatches to match! Plan ahead. Rely on our expertise to coordinate all your bed and bath needs.

THE LINEN MAN
A Very Special Bed and Bath Shop
73-725 El Paseo, Suite 22D
Palm Desert, CA 92260
(760) 568-6686 (800) 541-6686
Fax: (760) 773-5078
E-mail: LinenMan@worldnet.att.net

The West's Largest Family Owned Termite & Pest Control Company

Celebrating Our 75th Anniversary

• Residential, Industrial, Commercial Services
• Heat Treatment & Fumigation
• Termite Inspections & Reports
• Complete Pest Elimination for Food Handling Facilities

Palm Springs	(760) 324-9581
Palm Desert	(760) 346-2893
Indio	(760) 347-5443
High Desert	(760) 365-7006

1-800-WEST-EXT
1-800-937-8398

WESTERN
EXTERMINATOR COMPANY

Discover Rolfing®
with Bill LeGrave
Certified Rolfer

• Realignment
• Good Posture
• Faster times
• Fewer Injuries
• More Fun

For a free consultation or to make an appointment with the desert's only year-round, full-time, gentle Rolfer,
Call Bill at (760) 322-5373
Palm Springs & Los Angeles
E-mail Address: BLEGRAVE@aol.com

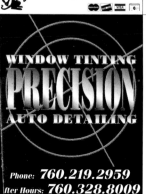

WINDOW TINTING
PRECISION
AUTO DETAILING

Phone: **760.219.2959**
After Hours: **760.328.8009**

Let Us Bring Our Courteous Professionals To Your Home or Office!

• Full-Service 100% Hand Car Wash
• Complete Interior & Exterior Detail
• Steam-Clean Engines
• High Speed Machine Compounding Available for Oxidation, Scratches, Waterspots, Tar & Overspray Removal.

We Use State-of-the-Art Methods with Only the Best Materials!

THE UNSINKABLE FLOAT
Our buoyant puncture-proof float needs no inflating, is long-lasting, soft and comfortable. Elevated headrest protects your hair, textured surface keeps you from sliding. It conforms to your body like a waterbed. Super Soft II $89.95.

LIBOTT POOLS
216 N. Indian Canyon Dr.
Palm Springs (760) 325-2143

THE SPRINGS

It's good to be The King.

Text from *The Palm Springs Villager*. Photo by Jim Frey.

Dateline: Palm Springs, June 1955: "This season, people came early, stayed longer and are still coming for health and sun and fun on the desert.

"Take **Clark Gable**, for instance. He wanted a rest and to go about undisturbed. With traditional Palm Springs courtesy he was given reasonable freedom of the village, the curious occasionally crowding a little close, but photographers, reporters and villagers giving him a wide berth.

"He checked into Sam Taylor's Tennis Club for an indefinite stay at the Bungalows. Days and weeks passed, finally totaling a full month. Kay Spreckles was a frequent companion on Thunderbird golf course, riding out from the popular Ranch Club, operated by the Noel Clarkes, and dining at the Doll House, Chi Chi and other places.

"Then the word was out that Gable would give the cameramen a day's hunting. It was almost too much. They had their victim almost to his knees. But he was a real good sport about it. He obliged them all and the total shots must have been 100. Most of the pictures were the usual run, but this taken by **Jim Frey** was different, we thought." ***PSL***

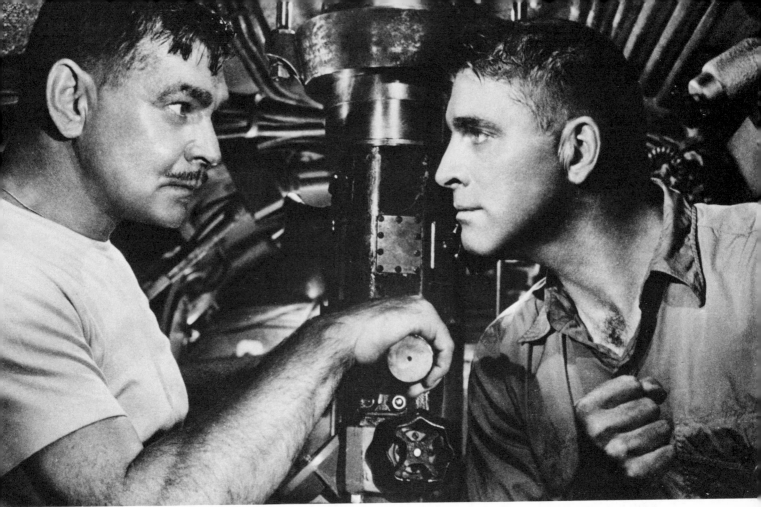
With Burt Lancaster

RUN SILENT, RUN DEEP

1958. United Artists.

A Hecht-Hill-Lancaster Production. Produced by Harold Hecht. Associate Producer: William Schorr. Directed by Robert Wise and Commander Edward L. Beach. Screenplay by John Gay. Cinematography by Russ Harlen. Art Director: Edward Carrere. Musical Score by Franz Waxman. Release date: March 24, 1958. Running time: 93 minutes.

CAST: Clark Gable, Burt Lancaster, Jack Warden, Brad Dexter, Nick Cravat, Joe Maross, Mary LaRoche, Eddie Foy III, Rudy Bond, H. M. Wynant, John Bryant, Ken Lynch, Joel Fluellen, Jimmie Bates, John Gibson.

SYNOPSIS: After his submarine is sunk by a Japanese Akikase destroyer in Japan's Bongo Straits during World War II, Commander "Rich" Richardson (*Clark Gable*) gets a new. sub, the U.S.S. *Nerka*. The crew he inherits is antagonistic, as is his new executive officer, Lt. Jim Bledsoe (*Burt Lancaster*), who had hoped for the command himself.

Richardson cannot forget the Akikase and his nightmares about it. Determined to sink it, he puts his ship and crew through many difficult training maneuvers anticipating the inevitable encounter. When he learns of the destroyer's whereabouts, he deliberately disobeys orders by seeking it out in the Bongo Straits. Upon locating the Japanese destroyer, they sink it with their well-rehearsed "down the throat shot."

Their victory celebration is cut extremely short to discover that a greater menace is a Japanese submarine lurking in the waters near the sunken Akikase. In a dangerous duel, the enemy sub is shattered by Richardson's well placed torpedoes. They surface only to find the area

With Burt Lancaster

alive with enemy planes. Richardson is killed when the planes strafe his sub before he can submerge it. Having won the respect of Bledsoe and the crew, he is given the military burial at sea as the *Nerka* heads for home.

REVIEWS:

Life: The film is good Gable—and a convincing look at the terror-filled hours submarine crews spend in battle.

Bosley Crowther, The New York Times: A better film about guys in the "silent service" has not been made. Good ones

With Burt Lancaster

there have been, including the fairly recent *The Enemy Below*. This one has much more than drama. It has the hard, cold ring of truth. It doesn't waste movement, time or words. Severely, nail-bitingly tense. Superior acting on the part of Mr. Gable. Although nothing should be detracted from Burt Lancaster's performance.

Time: Run Silent, Run Deep runs noisy, runs shallow. But it gives the movie-goer who is in the market for thrills a fairly good run for his money . . . something more interesting to think about from time to time (than the plot)—mostly good sea fights. Otherwise, it's damn the torpedoes, half-speed ahead.

William K. Zinnsser, New York Herald Tribune: It is almost like a training film—instructive, methodical, well photographed, but not dramatic. Robert Wise has directed with as much action as possible within a cramped frame, but the characters in John Gay's script have little color or depth. Lancaster is the best of the actors. Gable plays the doughty captain in his mild resolute way.

TEACHER'S PET

1958. Paramount.

Produced by William Perlberg. Directed by George Seaton. Screenplay by Fay and Michael Kanin. Cinematography by Haskell Boggs. Process photography by Farciot Edouart. Art Directors: Hal Pereira and Earl Hedrick. Musical score by Roy Webb. Editor: Alma Macrorie. Release date: April 1, 1958. Running time: 120 minutes.

CAST: Clark Gable, Doris Day, Gig Young, Mamie Van Doren, Nick Adams, Peter Baldwin, Marion Ross, Charles Lane, Jack Albertson, Florenz Ames, Harry Antrim, Vivian Nathan.

SYNOPSIS: When asked to lecture to a University evening-session journalism class, self-taught city editor Jim Gannon (*Clark Gable*) refuses in a letter full of contempt for people who "teach" journalism. His publisher, however, orders him to attend.

He arrives in time to hear Professor Erica Stone (*Doris Day*) denouncing

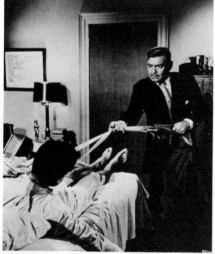

With Gig Young

him for the opinions expressed in his letter. Taken with her good looks, Jim enrolls as a student. Although he successfully eliminates his competition, Dr. Hugo Pine (*Gig Young*), Jim is less successful in keeping his identity a secret.

With Doris Day

Already angry with him, Erica is outraged when Jim demands that she criticize her father's Pulitzer Prize-winning newspaper articles as outmoded compared with his own modern ones. She tries to prove him wrong, but in all honesty can't. And when they discover that one of Jim's best reporters is a former student of Erica's, teacher and pupil are reunited.

REVIEWS:

Hollis Albert, Saturday Review: While [the film] is funny at times, it isn't at others. Perhaps this is because the stars . . . aren't good at comedy. Miss Day looks too businesslike, and Mr. Gable looks and sounds a little too much like President Eisenhower. Gig Young turns in a blessedly funny performance. . . . One of the movie's gimmicks has several of the nation's motion-picture reviewers acting as staff

With Gig Young and Doris Day

members on the paper. They are outright hams, one and all.

Variety: The Kanins have decorated the framework with some hilarious comedy lines and scenes which director George Seaton has set up with skill and delivered with gusto. Gable frankly mugs through many of his comedy scenes and it is effective low comedy. One of his best performances in years. Miss Day, who apparently can do almost any kind of role, is bright and fresh. Gig Young gives the picture its funniest moments,

With Doris Day and Gig Young

milking the scenes with the expertness of a farcical master.

Ellen Fitzpatrick, Films in Review: This pleasant programmer would not merit a review in *Films in Review* but for a sad fact: Clark Gable is feeling and showing his age (57). The masculine self-confidence he has projected for 30 years—has gone. Gable himself seems to know it has gone and he resorts in this film to mugging of so stereotyped a kind it is heart-breaking to see. . . . And film historians can perceive the beginning of the end of Gable's great career.

The New York Times: All concerned have welded romance, ribbing and reality into a cheerful and charming entertainment. . . . Gable . . . is not a caricature, nor are the other staff members. . . . Perhaps Miss Day is a mite too exotic for the role . . . but she does convey some of the dedication needed for teaching . . . and she certainly has the equipment to turn the head of . . . Mr. Gable.

With Mamie Van Doren

BUT NOT FOR ME

1959. Paramount.

Produced by William Perlberg and George Seaton. Directed by Walter Lang. Screenplay by John Michael Hayes, based on the play *Accent on Youth* by Samuel Raphaelson. Cinematographer: Robert Burks. Art Director: Earl Hedrick. Editor: Alma Macrorie. Release date: August 19, 1959. Running time: 105 minutes.

CAST: Clark Gable, Carroll Baker, Lilli Palmer, Lee J. Cobb, Barry Coe, Thomas Gomez, Tom Duggin, Charles Land, Wendell Holmes.

SYNOPSIS: Russell Ward (*Clark Gable*), a reluctantly aging Broadway producer, is having script trouble with his latest play, *A May-December Romance*. Stymied at every turn, he decides to quit Broadway, close down

With Lee J. Cobb and Carroll Baker

his office, and admit to being a has-been.

His 22-year-old secretary, Ellie Brown (*Carroll Baker*), an aspiring young actress, berates him for quitting and then passionately declares her love for him. In a flash Russ sees the solution to his script problem: let the young girl in the play pursue the older man instead of vice versa! He talks the author, a disillusioned drunk named Jeremiah MacDonald (*Lee J. Cobb*), into sobering up and doing a re-write; Ellie is given the feminine lead; the out-of-town tryout problems are solved; and the play becomes a smash hit.

Completely rejuvenated, Russ decides to marry his new young star despite the objections and interference of his ex-wife, Kathryn (*Lilli Palmer*)

*As Russell Ward,
an aging Broadway producer*

and the now teetotaling Jeremiah. To prove he is still irresistible to young women, Russ dutifully describes to Ellie all the reasons why she shouldn't marry him. But Ellie, who has decided she really loves a young actor named Gordon Reynolds, admits the marriage would be a mistake and blesses Russ for having "the wisdom that comes with age." Jolted back to reality, Russ finally decides to admit his age and start life anew by remarrying the mature, but still desirable, Kathryn.

REVIEWS:

The New York Times: The quaint but refreshing thing about Clark Gable is that he is willing to act his age. What's more, he is willing to make jokes about it and let his script writers make jokes about it, too. That's

With Lee J. Cobb

what is most refreshing about his film comedy, *But Not for Me.* . . . With a delightful pretense of uncertainty about the age of the character he plays, which ranges in the course of conversation from 44 to 56, he runs through this glib little trifle. . . . He also hauls a bevy of good actors with him, all of them laughing as they go.

Life: For more than a quarter of a century Clark Gable's persuasive charm has drawn movie-lovers by the millions. Radiating good-humored masculine appeal, he had something for everybody. For ladies he was the great lover; for men he was the hard-fighting man's man; for both he was the fun-loving comedian. Now in his 65th film, he proves that despite his 57 years he is still the indestructible all-around charmer.

Time: So frail that only the acting mastery of Lee J. Cobb and Lilli Palmer saves it. Then too there is Clark Gable. No director has ever been presumptuous enough to ask "The King" to act, but his presence alone gives any film the atmosphere of Hollywood's glorious pre-Method past. Gable's voice may croak a little, but he still has the confidence of a man who

With Lilli Palmer

knows that so long as he goes on playing the King, no one will dare play the Ace.

John McCarten, The New Yorker: Mr. Gable, Mr. Cobb, Miss Baker and Miss Palmer are mischievous as all getout, but their antics don't result in any hilarity.

With Carroll Baker

With Lee J. Cobb

IT STARTED IN NAPLES

1960. Paramount.

Produced by Jack Rose. Directed by Melville Shavelson. Screen-play by Melville Shavelson, Jack Rose and Suso Cecchi d'Amico, based on the story by Michael Pertwee and Jack Davies. Cinematographer: Robert L. Surtees. Art Directors: Hal Pereira and Roland Anderson. Musical score by Alessandro Cicognini and Carlo Savino. Release date: August 7, 1960. Running time: 100 minutes.

CAST: Clark Gable, Sophia Loren, Vittorio De Sica, Marietto, Paolo Carlini, Claudio Ermelli, Giovanni Filidoro.

SYNOPSIS: Philadelphia lawyer Michael Hamilton (*Clark Gable*) arrives in Naples to settle the estate of his

With Sophia Loren

philandering brother. He learns that his brother had taken a common-law wife who died with him in an automobile accident, leaving a ten-year-old love-child named Nando (*Marietto*). The boy has been staying with his Aunt Lucia (*Sophia Loren*), a fun-loving, wine-drinking woman who dreams of someday becoming a movie star.

Almost immediately, Mike and Lucia clash over the boy's upbringing; Lucia preferring to let the lad live as he chooses and Mike insisting he be given a proper formal and social education.

When he is beaten at every turn, Mike finally has his Italian lawyer, Mario Vitale (*Vittorio De Sica*) institute a custody suit. But Vitale, completely taken with Lucia's charm and fraudulent tears, delivers such an impassioned speech on her behalf that even the judge is moved to applause. Though Mike loses the case, he does

With Marietto, Sophia Loren, Paolo Carlini, Giovanni Filidoro, and Vittorio De Sica

make Lucia see that it is little Nando who is the real loser. In an effort to make the boy go with Mike, Lucia pretends that she is leaving with a guitar player named Renzo (*Paolo Carlini*). Heartbroken, Nando gets drunk, goes to Mike and volunteers to become an American. But Mike, realizing that Nando belongs to Lucia and Naples and would never be happy away from them, decides to leave alone.

On the train, when he hears the departing tourists making deprecating remarks about the natives, Mike finally awakens to the fact that he too now belongs to Lucia and Naples. He leaps off the train and races to join his new family.

REVIEWS:

The New York Times: The major thing to look at is Miss Loren, and all else is but background for her, strong light to put her femininity into profile. That goes for the script as well—a featherweight, obvious romance. . . . Whether Miss Loren is singing in a night club or throwing herself about in robust fashion, with her garments in becoming disarray, the lady is not for spurning. She is very much to be beheld. . . . Clark Gable, who isn't precisely an inconspicuous sort, lets himself be exposed throughout the picture as a sort of sourpuss in the shadow of the girl. He glowers, Gable-wise and makes crude noises, betokening the superior male. But the screenplay has him shaded from the outset. Miss Loren gets everything.

New York Herald Tribune: Obviously the picture was meant as simply warm and light-hearted entertainment with glimpses at whatever the Mediterranean might have to offer, but it falls considerably, short of its mark. . . . It makes a noticeable effort to set a merry pace but follows old story ruts so persistently that even the brisk charm of its principals cannot keep the film in the air. . . . One is too often struck by the suspicion that its basic theme—the contrast of American with Italian behavior—ought to have provided more inspiration than seems to have been the case. It is entirely the presence of Miss Loren, Gable and De Sica, who in combination or separately have an authority that makes even a palid line or an overly familiar situation feel like it may lead to something, that gives the picture what comic vitality it has.

Variety: Both the script and Shavelson's direction try too hard to make the film uproariously funny and risque. This will disturb a great many spectators. When the wit flows naturally, it is a delight; when it strains, it pains. One of the most memorable lines of comedy crops up when tired tourist Gable, wandering the noisy streets of Capri at 1:15 a.m., asks a waiter, "How are people supposed to sleep on this island?" "Together" is the matter-of-fact reply. Gable and Miss Loren are a surprisingly effective and compatible comedy pair.

The New Yorker: The picture gains an adventitious interest from the fact that Clark Gable often sounds exactly like President Eisenhower.

With Vittorio De Sica

With Sophia Loren

THE MISFITS

1961. United Artists.

With Montgomery Clift

A Seven Arts-John Huston Production. Produced by Frank E. Taylor. Directed by John Huston. From an original screenplay by Arthur Miller. Photography by Russell Metty. Music by Alex North. Art Directors: Stephan Grimes and William Newberry. Edited by George Tomasini. Release date: February 4, 1961. Running time: 124 minutes.

CAST: Clark Gable, Marilyn Monroe, Montgomery Clift, Thelma Ritter, Eli Wallach, James Barton, Estelle Winwood, Kevin McCarthy. With Dennis Shaw, Philip Mitchell, Walter Ramage, Peggy Barton, J. Lewis Smith, Marietta Tree, Bobby LaSalle, Ryall Bowker, Ralph Roberts.

SYNOPSIS: While staying at the Reno rooming house of Isabelle Steers (*Thelma Ritter*), newly-divorced Roslyn Tabor (*Marilyn Monroe*) meets Gay Langland (*Clark Gable*), a ruggedly independent, aging cowboy. Immediately attracted to each other, they move into a partially completed ranch house belonging to Gay's friend Guido (*Eli Wallach*), a part-time mechanic who has turned into an aimless wanderer since the death of his wife in childbirth.

The brief idyll ends when Guido comes up with a plan for going into the hills and rounding up some mustangs, wild horses often termed "misfits" because they are too small for riding. Needing a third partner, Gay and Guido take on Perce Howland (*Montgomery Clift*), a battered and disillusioned rodeo performer. When Roslyn learns the mustangs are to be sold to a dog-food manufacturer, she is revolted by this seemingly brutal destruction of life and begs Gay to call off the hunt. But he refuses and the three men, accompanied by the reluctant Roslyn, ride up to the salt flats in the Nevada foothills. Six of the horses are driven out onto the flats by Guido's flivver plane and then chased and roped from a speeding truck.

Sickened by the pathetic plight of the creatures, Roslyn appeals to the sensitive Perce, who frees the animals. Enraged by this defiance of his authority, Gay single-handedly recaptures the lead stallion and, after a battle of sheer physical endurance, succeeds in subduing it. Then, having asserted his will, he sets the animal free. More understanding and respectful of each other, Gay and Roslyn return home, while Perce and Guido go their separate ways.

With Marilyn Monroe

With Thelma Ritter and Marilyn Monroe

*With Marilyn Monroe and
Montgomery Clift*

With Marilyn Monroe

With Eli Wallach, Montgomery Clift, and Marilyn Monroe

REVIEWS:

Kate Cameron, New York Daily News: Gable has never done anything better on the screen, nor has Miss Monroe. Gable's acting is vibrant and lusty, hers true to the character as written by Miller. . . . The screen vibrates with emotion during the latter part of the film as Marilyn and Gable engage in one of those battles of the sexes that seem eternal in their constant eruption. It is the poignant conflict between a man and a woman in love with each other trying to maintain individual characteristics and preserve a fundamental way of life.

Newsweek: The artistic touch of director John Huston gives the release its special quality, an unusually lifelike character almost New-Wavish in mood and technique. But he failed to instill an even tempo and there are some unaccountably awkward passages. . . . An outstanding contribution is Alex North's score.

New York Herald Tribune: A picture that I can only call superb. After the long dought of vital American pictures one can now cheer, for *The Misfits* is so distinctly American nobody but an American could have made it. The acting throughout reflects the eager sympathy with which Gable, Monroe, Clift and Wallach live their role—and I don't mean to forget Thelma Ritter. Gable's performance is little less than great.

Saturday Review: Powerful experience. It is noteworthy as a serious attempt by a major playwright to conceive a work directly for the screen. Gable as Gay Langland finally became the actor he might have been all along, if a part had come along to test him to this degree.

Variety: The flashy, informative "mustanging" sequence is a gem of filmmaking from start to finish. And it is here that Gable really shines, meeting the brutal physical demands of the action with the masculine grace, ardor and dexterity of a young man.

Henry Hart, Films in Review: Gable's role is so illy conceived, and written, he could do little more than smile his way through it. . . . He was not good in a drunken scene in which he cried out for his children, but the scene was improperly written, shot and edited. Nor was he too good after Miller switched his character from a carefree woman-chasing cowboy to a catcher of mustangs for a butcher.

With Montgomery Clift